The Goat, the Devil and

the Freemason

Author's note:

I am grateful to many people for their help in writing this book but the opinions expressed in it remain my own. The book does not necessarily represent the opinions of the United Grand Lodge of England, the masonic Province of Essex, St Laurence Lodge No. 5511 nor any of my brethren. I would like to state quite firmly that it has no official status whatsoever.

ISBN: 978-0-9550352-8-9

Published by:
Hamilton House Publishing Ltd.

**Rochester Upon Medway,
Kent.**

Printed by:
**Graphy Cems, Navarra,
Spain.**

Distributed by:

Lewis Masonic

www.lewismasonic.com
Riverdene Business Park,
Molesey Road, Hersham,
Surrey, KT12 4RG

The Goat, the Devil and the Freemason

David West

En ce qui touche les idées, on peut, avec quelque érudition, soutenir ce qu'on veut.

André-Jean Festugière

Dedication and thanks

This book is dedicated to the memory of my father and my wife's father, both of whom were committed freemasons and decent men. I thank them both for the gift of Freemasonry - and I thank the latter more especially for the 'gift' of my wife.

It is also a statement of thanks to the brethren of my mother lodge for their fraternal affection and support, especially to my cousin and brother, Len West. I also thank Peter Currie for his unfailing good humour in bringing this book to fruition; Lawrie Morrisson for his involvement in the many projects we have undertaken together; and my wife, Jenny, for her editorial advice and unflagging attention to detail.

About the author

Dr David West gained his first degree in Philosophy from the University of Exeter and his Doctorate of and in Philosophy from the University of Leicester. He taught at universities in England and Canada for several years, publishing in the academic press. His business career included Ford and Xerox. He served on several committees on the future of work, was special adviser to a cabinet minister and later founded *The Working Manager Ltd*, creating the core content of its web based management education process. He is the author of *Employee Engagement and the failure of leadership*.

Dr West is a member of three lodges and four chapters under the English Constitution. He served as Grand Registrar of the Masonic Province of Essex and is now Past Provincial Junior Grand Warden.

David is married to Jenny, a retired Consultant Clinical Psychologist who specialised in Learning Disabilities, and they celebrate forty-five years of marriage in 2013. They have two children, one a lawyer on the side of the angels and the other a professional musician.

Dates of events in and around the text

	Egypt	Greece & Rome	Judæa	Asia	Religious events
1500	Book of the Dead		Moses perhaps	Herodotus's timing of Troy	
1000			Solomon perhaps	Zoroaster perhaps	
800		Homer perhaps			
700		Legendary birth of Rome, Hesiod	Sources of Pentateuch		
600	Psamtik II	Parthenon & Acropolis built	Exile in Babylon	Nebuchadnezzar king, 605	
500		Pindar	Zerubbabel	Croesus, Cyrus, Darius	
400		Herodotus	*Nehemiah*	Xerxes, Artaxerxes	
300	Ptolemy I, Euclid	Alexander the Great	*Ezra, Chronicles*		
200					
100	Rosetta stone	Plutarch	*Daniel*, Maccabæus, Monotheism		
50	Cleopatra	Julius Caesar	Honi, Great revolt		
0		Tiberius, Death of Pan	Jesus people		Paul
50		Destruction of the temple	Q, Gospel of Thomas		Official Gospels
100		Josephus			Marcion, Valentinius
200	Earliest date for *Sefer Yezirah*	*Corpus Hermeticum*	*Mishnah* collated		Mani
300				Constantine and the *Nicean Creed*	Eusebius
400					Augustine

	Judæa	France	Other Europe
900	Latest date for *Sefer Yezira*, Masoretes		Bogomils
1000	First Crusade		Leningrad MS, Pope Urban II
1100	Knights Templar, Saladin	Chivalric legends, Cathars flourish, *Book Bahir* appears.	Richard I, first mention of King Arthur by Geoffrey of Monmouth
1200	Final defeat of Crusaders	Albigensian Crusade, Roman de la Rose	Moses de Leon *Zohar*, Aquinas
1300		End of Templars	*Regius* Poem, Chaucer, Wycliffe's Bible
1400		Christine de Pizan, Francois Villon	Gutenberg moveable type 1439, Copernicus born 1473, Possible date of Malory and *Le Morte d'Arthur*
1500	Isaac Luria	Rabelais, *Gargantua and Pantagruel* 1532-1564	Cornelius Agrippa, Martin Luther *Ninety-five Theses* 1517, Pedro Mexia

	England & Scotland	France	USA	Elsewhere
1550 to 1600	John Dee *Monas Hieroglyphica* 1564, Elizabeth I 1533-1603		Approximate *floreat* of some Indian Nations	
1600 to 1650	James I crowned 1603, Francis Bacon *Advancement of Learning* 1605, *Novum Organum* 1620, *Chymical Wedding* 1616, John Donne 1572-1631	René Descartes, *Discours de la méthode*, 1637	Blackfoot 1200 - 1881 Apache 1500 - 1886 Sioux 1600 - 1890	Elector Palatine marries Elizabeth, *Fama* 1614, *Confessio* 1615, Papal denunciation of Galileo 1633
1650 to 1700	Elias Ashmole initiated 1646	Jean Dodal's *Tarot*	Kiowa 1600 - 1890 Comanche 1700 - 1880	
1700 to 1750	Isaac Newton *Principia Mathematica* 1713, Premier Grand Lodge 1717			Kant *Critique of Pure Reason* 1781
	American War of Independence 1775 - 1782			
1800	Union of the two Grand Lodges 1813	Alphonse Louis Constant born 1810	Albert Pike born 1809 Tecumseh died 1813	
1820			Santa Fe Trail 1822, Jedediah Smith Mojave Desert 1826	
1830	George Adam Browne wrote RA lectures c1834		Jedediah Smith killed by Comanche 1831, Pike on Santa Fe Trail 1832	
1840	Elizabeth Barrett Browning *Death of Pan* 1844	Marie-Noémi Cadiot and Constant married 1846	Wagon Trains start 1841, Oregon Trail proper 1846, Pueblos kill Charles Bent 1847, Utes kill Old Bill Williams1849	
1850	Elizabeth Barrett Browning *Aurora Leigh* 1856, 'a feminist epic'	Constant *Dogme et Rituel* 1855/6	First Kit Carson novel 1849, Bridger's Pass 1851	
1860		Constant *L'Histoire de la Magie* 1860	Civil War 1861-1865, Bosque Redondo 1866-1868, Bridger Trail 1864	
1870		Franco-Prussian War 1870/1, Constant died 1875	Kit Carson died 1868, Pike *Morals and Dogma* 1871, Battle of Little Big Horn 1876	
1880		Marie-Noémi Cadiot died 1888	Jim Bridger died 1881	*Humanum Genus* 1884, Nietzsche *Thus spake Zarathustra*, 1885
1890	Aleister Crowley at Cambridge 1895-1897, Waite's translation of *Dogme et Rituel* 1896, Waite attacks Taxil 1896	Taxil's Confession 1897	Sitting Bull died 1890, Albert Pike died 1891	
1900	Wittgenstein *Tractatus* 1921, *Philosophical Investigations* 1953, Wheatley *The Devil Rides Out* 1934	Sartre *La Nausée* 1938	Wyatt Earp died 1926 of prostate cancer, First electric bus in NY City	First Zeppelin flight, Quantum Physics, Special theory of Relativity

Contents

Prelude: What this book is about

My masonic brother Leslie is a vegetarian, a retired policeman and a counsellor. He is a very kind person and therefore I was somewhat taken aback to learn that members of his extended family consider him a devil-worshipper! A little while ago, someone I consider intelligent and rational asked me whether a live goat was really a part of masonic ceremonies. That took me aback too.[1] Where do such ideas come from?

Rational or irrational, beliefs rarely spring anew from one individual's imagination. They usually have a history with one idea leading to another, being combined with a third and then amended by a fourth and so on. So, this book is a family history of ideas, seeking the ancestry of beliefs about goats and devils and their association with freemasonry. The search has taken me into many fascinating areas and while I admit that there have been several excursions along the way, that has been part of the enjoyment. Some of the excursions I refer to as interludes and these expand the discussion of a subject introduced in the text.

My cousin and masonic brother Len described an early draft of this book as a *miscellany*, a lovely old-fashioned word. There is a richness about the history of these ideas which comes not only from denotation (what they are about) but also connotation (what they bring to mind). The history can often be surprising. Take this complaint:

> You are scrupulous in investigating charges in far less serious cases but take less care in analysing accusations against us; accusations which are so horrible that impiety is too mild a word for them. You fail to make a full inquiry about the truth of such condemnations and so it becomes obvious that we are accused not because of any sinful conduct on our part but simply because of our name.

That is Tertullian (160–225 CE) in his book *Ad Nationes* complaining of accusations made against the early Christian Church which was accused of many crimes of which it was innocent but of which it later, and frequently, accused other people. Such accusations, as we will see, form a standard list.

What this book is not about

I am not writing a book to persuade people that freemasonry has a complete absence of goat (live or not) and an equal absence of devil-worship. People who believe such nonsense do not do so on the basis of evidence, and so presenting facts to the contrary would have no effect whatsoever. I will give an example of this later. Nor am I writing about the psychology of belief. Why people believe the irrational things they do is the subject of academic research. At the University of Chicago[2] there is a project entitled *Magical Thinking and the Belief in Tempting Fate*, seeking to understand the superstitious acts many of us perform.

---

[1] A moment's thought would show that such an idea is very silly. No such animal, clearly not house-trained, would be allowed in a local hotel, masonic temple or Freemasons' Hall itself – the most beautiful example of art deco in England – if only on health and safety grounds.

[2] Eugene M. Caruso and Jane Risen, the Center for Decision Research at the Booth School of Business, University of Chicago.

Knocking on wood or crossing one's fingers does nothing to alter the future. Belief in fate is irrational but this does not stop people saluting magpies or avoiding naming *the Scottish play* in the theatre. I admit that I am myself guilty of superstition. It seems to me that in my life there is a man with a sand filled sock with which he wallops me around the ear if I get too pleased with myself. I have good authority for this. Herodotus had a profound belief in *Nemesis*, the goddess who punished excessive pride and undeserved happiness. The fates were central to his philosophy of history.

My masonry

Let me immediately set out my interest. I am an English freemason, initiated (without goat) by my father into my mother lodge in 1982.[1] My father-in-law assisted in the ceremony and in 1935 his father was a founder of the lodge. All three were Masters of the lodge as I was myself in 1992. I enjoy membership of a further two lodges and four Royal Arch Chapters.

The Royal Arch, which plays a part in this book, is an additional order considered by the United Grand Lodge of England (which stems from 1717) to be an integral part of freemasonry. I am not a member of other masonic orders. While such orders give their members a great deal of pleasure, they are not considered integral to freemasonry by the United Grand Lodge of England which in 1813,

> *... declared and pronounced that pure Antient Masonry consists of three degrees and no more, viz. those of the Entered Apprentice, the Fellow Craft, and the Master Mason, including the Supreme Order of the Holy Royal Arch.*

The position is rather different in the USA and in Grand Lodges that follow the American pattern. There, a large percentage of freemasons pass through what we refer to as the Craft and what Americans call blue lodges (those that offer the three degrees of the phrase *three degrees and no more*) and then go on to the York Rite or the Scottish Rite. The former includes the Knights Templar while the latter includes the Rose Croix and its 33 degrees. Christopher Hodapp's book, *Freemasons for Dummies*, will explain everything you may need to know about freemasonry in the USA in a very readable fashion. I recommend it highly.

It is important to understand that in no country is any masonic order in any way superior to craft (or blue) masonry and that the governance of freemasonry is always a matter for the Craft and for no other, extra or appendant body.

Names, dates and a lower case g

I use lower case *g* for the word *god*. In my view, using a capital G for the Christian or Jewish god but not for other religions shows a lack of respect to the latter and to use the capital for plural gods seems logically if not grammatically inappropriate. I use *Yahweh* as the name of the Christian or Jewish god.

I am in no way a Hebrew scholar but I am intrigued by the explanation of the sacred name in the *Catholic Encyclopædia* which suggests Samaritan as the word's likely origin:

---

[1] One's mother lodge is the lodge one was initiated in, no matter how many other lodges one later joins. My mother lodge is the St Laurence Lodge, No. 5511.

... the Samaritan pronunciation Jabe *probably approaches the real sound of the divine name closest ... Inserting the vowels of* Jabe *into the original Hebrew consonant text,[1] we obtain the form* Jahveh *(or* Yahweh*), which has been generally accepted by modern scholars as the true pronunciation.*

This Samaritan derivation would have materially annoyed a certain person known as C (*The Chronicler*), of whom more within. The word *Jehovah* appears about 1270.

Without ever thinking seriously about it, at the back of my mind when growing up was the naïve idea that we had Judaism and Roman gods up to AD and then we all switched to Christianity. After all, that seemed to be the point: BC before Christ and AD, *anno domini*, the year of the lord, after. Even a moment's reflection shows this to be very silly. There are many dating systems, some religious and others not, which have nothing at all to do with BC and AD.

The Islamic system counts from Muhammad's journey from Mecca to Medina which occurred in 622 CE; the Jewish, from the creation of the world which traditionally occurred in 3760 BCE.[2] A late Roman system counted from the founding of the city of Rome, often thought to be 753 BCE. The Mayan system starts in 3114 BCE but the mathematical workings are beyond me.

Given the many cultures, religions and ideas that this book delves into, it seems appropriate to use non-aligned dating terms, hence my use of CE (*common era*) BCE (*before the common era*). In a practical sense, BCE and CE are the same as BC and AD, so that 2000 BCE is 2000 BC and 2 CE is 2 AD.[3]

How about Stardates? When pressed for an explanation, Gene Roddenberry said:

This time system adjusts for shifts in relative time which occur due to the vessel's speed and space warp capability. It has little relationship to Earth's time.

The Stardates specified in the log entry must be computed against the speed of the vessel, the space warp and its position within our galaxy to give a meaningful reading ...

and cheerfully admitted he didn't understand a word of what he had said!

---

[1] The so-called Tetragrammaton, YHWH.

[2] The masonic *Year of Light* is based on the Jewish system but we round it up to 4,000 years. Thus 2012 CE is 6012 AL (*Anno Lucis*).

[3] There is no 0 BCE or 0 CE. We move directly from 1 BCE (or BC) to 1 CE (or AD).

Chapter one: The Goat of the Sabbath

We start the book with this jolly figure. It is perhaps the most common image in occult circles and is popularly perceived to be a depiction of the devil, although that is not how its author saw it. The search for its sources will lead us to the roots of the ideas of the goat and the devil and the image will act as an agenda, to which we will periodically return. Understanding the image requires an understanding of its creator: the man, his life and his beliefs. He saw himself as an expert on freemasonry as well as the occult. He wasn't, but even today he is often uncritically taken to be one.

We will look into his early life as a priest and his religious writings which are delightfully way out and provide an excellent introduction to his later works on the occult and magic. We take an excursion into the life of his wife. She was a significant figure in herself: a feminist, political activist, sculptor and novelist. Her rejection of her husband throws more light on him.

The creator of the image had his own (wildly incorrect) views on the origins of freemasonry and so the first interlude of the book is this subject.

Alphonse Louis Constant *aka* Éliphas Lévi

The image on the previous page, which many people refer to as the *Baphomet*, is an engraving from a book by a fascinating nineteenth century character who called himself Éliphas Lévi. You can just see this name on the globe that the creature perches on. He himself equally often called the creature *le bouc de sabbat* (the goat of

ELIPHAS LEVI
- 1862 -

the sabbath) and it forms the frontispiece of his book, *Dogme et Rituel de la Haute Magie*, the first volume of which was published in 1855, the second in 1856. The engraving is based on earlier depictions, notably the tarot card of Jean Dodal which we will come to later, but is the product of his own imagination and draughtsmanship.

His real name was Alphonse Louis Constant. Born in 1810, he had quite a life, if not always a happy one, spent in and around Paris with a couple of trips to England and a sojourn in Germany before dying in 1875.

He trained for the priesthood, first at the Séminaire Saint-Nicolas du Chardonnet near the Sorbonne and the Odéon in Paris and then, from age 20 to 26, at the Séminaire d'Issy, to the southwest of Paris just outside what is now the Périphérique.

Adèle Allenbach

There, and in the last years of his studies, he became responsible for the preparation of a group of young girls for their first communion. One day *a woman of poor but honest appearance, dressed in rags*, as he describes her, came to plead with him to allow her daughter to join the class. According to Constant, the virtually penniless woman had failed to persuade any other priest to take the child on. Constant agreed and:

> … *the girl raised her eyes to mine and stammered a few words of thanks. Only then did I notice the touching and pure quality of her features, the innocence and love in her eyes. I returned to the seminary filled with quiet emotion.*

He fell in love with the young girl, Adèle Allenbach, whom he thought of as the Virgin Mary re-embodied. The relationship raised a certain amount of gossip because, as Constant says:

> *Our relationship was so innocent that we took no care for the ordinary rules of prudence.*

As we will learn, this is a rather typical Constant event. He went to his confessor who told him to terminate the relationship immediately or leave the seminary. Even though he was about to become ordained, he decided that he could not reject what had now become a major part of his belief.

I understood that for me love was the very bedrock of my religion and my soul and that I could not, without hypocrisy, deny myself before the altars of a self-centred and unfeeling church.

In his life there seem to be many occasions when he took one view of events while others took a different one; in this case, perhaps, that engaging in a relationship with a young girl for whose spiritual tuition he was responsible was highly improper. In the event, no serious damage seems to have been done to Adèle who, to Constant's great dismay, did not wait for him to sort himself out but got on with her life. She seems to have visited Constant occasionally over the next forty years and was present at his funeral.

So aged 26, broken hearted, with no career and little else to do, he considered entering a monastery but instead did a bit of teaching at a school near Paris and then accompanied an actor friend on tour. He fell in with Flora Tristan, a socialist author and one of the founders of modern feminism, and attended soirées at the house of Mme de Girardin where he met Balzac.[1] Constant also worked with Alphonse Esquiros just about the time that the latter published *L'Évangile du Peuple (The Gospel of the People)* in which he treats Jesus as a champion of democracy, and for which he was imprisoned for eight months. Esquiros became a major left wing politician[2] and Constant himself was a man of the left. His view was that everything belongs to god and thus to everyone. (*Property is theft* perhaps.[3])

Returning to the religious life, if for no other reason than he was near starving, Constant took a position at the Abbaye Saint-Pierre de Solesmes[4] not far from Le Mans in north-west France and famed for its library. While there, he wrote his first book, *Le Rosier de Mai (The Rose of May* - literally the *Rosebush of May)* in which the Virgin Mary is depicted as dying on the cross with Jesus. Being Constant, he fell out with the Abbot and left, penniless again but not before having looked into the gnostics, the works of Cassian[5] and the Quietist, Madame Guyon,[6] all of whom saw spiritual perfection as the absorption of the soul into the divine.

---

[1] French novelist and playwright (1799-1850) whose major work was *La Comédie Humaine*.

[2] Esquiros was elected to the National Assembly in 1850 but expelled by Louis-Napoleon in the coup d'état of 1851. He was re-elected in 1869 and became a member of the Senate in 1876. He voted against the disastrous Franco-Prussian War of 1870-71. He died in 1876 and is buried in the Cimetière de Saint-Pierre, Marseilles.

[3] French anarchist, Pierre-Joseph Proudhon, writing at the same time as Constant.

[4] Early in the 20th Century, the monks were forced out of the Abbaye and found a home at Quarr Abbey near Fishbourne on the Isle of Wight between Wootton Bridge and Ryde. They later returned to France but Quarr Abbey still operates and is open to visitors.

[5] Saint John Cassian (John the Ascetic), 360-435 CE.

[6] Jeanne-Marie Bouvier de la Motte-Guyon, 1648-1717.

First spell in prison

He then found a job at the Collège de Juilly in a town just north-east of Paris. He was ill-treated in his opinion and in 1841 wrote *La Bible de la Liberté*, some say in revenge. He must have known that his views would be seen as heretical and the book was immediately condemned for *attacks against property and outrages against public and religious morals*. Its destruction was ordered by the Court of Assizes of the Département de la Seine and Constant was sentenced to eight months in prison and fined 500 francs. The publisher, Auguste-Pierre Legallois,[1] received three months with a fine of 300 francs.

La Bible de la Liberté is a rambling combination of self-justification, left wing politics, impassioned prose, eccentric religious views and what one can only describe as sexual frustration. He had transformed his longing for Adèle into a virtual religion of sex. The preface addresses the book to the love sick, those suffering from a broken heart and failing to find love in an evil world. He offers them consolation in a second coming predicted by the prophet Joel,[2] and - interjecting that as long as property is not abolished, slavery will not disappear from the earth - issues a diatribe against suicide; something that he may even have contemplated himself.

He argues that god is *being* – not *a* being but *existence itself*.[3] He says that if there is existence, there is god and god exists because things exist; that the universal archetypes of being have always existed and that the apparent variety we see is the result of different numerical combinations of these archetypes. This seems to be a version of Plato's theory of Forms.[4] He argues that creation will never cease. God is the cause of everything that exists[5] and, since the world is in a constant state of change, god can never have stopped creating. He sees god within man:

> *Why do you men look up to the heavens, looking for god outside yourselves? God is in man because man exists (and god is existence) and what is god in man is intelligence because man thinks and love because man loves.*

Views on women

Constant idolises women and, in one of his phrases in which sound probably outweighs meaning, he says that man is the love of intelligence while woman is the intelligence of love. Woman is the final purpose of god's revelation and the crown of his works. Couples in love kiss, embrace and reproduce. In their fruitful union

---

[1] Legallois had also published *L'Évangile du Peuple* for Esquiros but had escaped prison on that occasion. He was a noted author in his own right.

[2] The book of *Joel* is part of the Hebrew Bible and is a long poem about the misdeeds of the people, showing the plagues of locusts to be a result of the people forgetting their duties towards god, calling for repentance and promising all good things afterwards.

[3] This sounds like St. Thomas Aquinas in the *Summa Theologica*. *God is the very existence to subsisting things*. Aquinas referred to god as *Qui est*. He who is. It also sounds like the much later Paul Tillich: *God is called the being as being, or the ground and the power of being*.

[4] In the *Timaeus*, for example, Plato distinguishes between the physical and visible world and the eternal world which we can comprehend only by reason. The latter is the world of Forms, eternal models of perfection.

[5] This is from Philo (20 BCE–50 CE) *God never ceases from making something or other. As it is the property of fire to burn and of snow to chill, so it is the property of god to be creating*.

they sense the whole deity, for they become one soul which is nothing other than love. (That is my rather literal translation.)

One of Constant's themes is the need for man to be free from the laws of religion that have enslaved him. The price of man's obedience to these laws has been the loss of animal pleasures. He distinguishes between the slaves who submitted and perished and the children (Constant's word for those of free will) who obeyed the dictates of freedom and were thus saved by love. He reveals just how much he resented the rules that prevented him from continuing his relationship with Adèle.

Even if this had not got him into trouble, his views on Lucifer certainly would have. Part of my thesis about Constant concerns his ability with words. He has enormous word-power and it is this, perhaps as much as the content of his books, which gets him into trouble. Once translated, much of the power is lost so I will give some passages in his original French, with my translation if it helps.

> *L'ange de la liberté est né avant l'aurore, et dieu l'a appelé l'étoile du matin. Gloire à toi, O Lucifer, parce qu'étant la plus sublime des intelligences, tu as pu te croire l'égal de dieu!*

> The angel of liberty was born before the dawn and god has named him the star of the morning. Glory to you, O Lucifer. The most sublime of all intelligent beings; you have dared to see yourself the equal of god!

Constant compares Lucifer to Christ. As the latter suffered the tortures of the cross, so the former suffered the agonies of hell. It is not surprising that the authorities of the time took exception to a (partly ordained) priest writing such stuff [1] but it seems too complex to have been written for revenge.

Mère de Dieu

Leaving prison, Constant was lucky enough to get work at the church of Choisy-le-Roy, due south of Paris, where for once he apparently behaved himself and became a popular preacher. So much so that he was recommended to the Bishop of Evreux who offered him a post for as long as he changed his name to avoid scandal. This, it seems, he attempted to do. While in prison, he had written *Des Moeurs et des Doctrines du Rationalisme en France (The Customs and Doctrines of Rationalism in France)* which he published under the name Abbé Constant Symon de Latreiche, but it seems he used the name Abbé Beaucourt, the maiden name of his mother, for cover purposes at Choisy-le-Roy.

The Bishop should have known better. As part of the PR plan, the Catholic daily newspaper, *L'Univers*, announced that l'Abbé Constant had died. The plan failed as other newspapers picked up the story, identified Beaucourt as Constant and ran with his background, trial and conviction. While the Bishop was distressed and tried to help, Constant had been writing another book, *Mère de Dieu (Mother of God)*, another ecstatic vision of woman and his theme of love.

> *Mes yeux étaient fixés sur les yeux de la femme qui était assise près de moi; ma main restait doucement unie et abandonnée à la sienne; une douce chaleur d'amour venait d'elle à moi et enivrait mon âme sans troubler mes sens; un bien-*

---

[1] In today's theologies, what he says, of course, would be nothing unusual.

être paisible, une quiétude divine reposait mes membres et me faisait presque oublier; mais toutes les joies de l'amour, toutes les ivresses de la possession d'un objet aimé fondaient mon âme avec sienne. A toutes les questions de mon intelligence elle répondait en silence par une secrète parole d'amour.

My eyes were fixed on those of the woman seated beside me. My hand became softly united with hers, slowly ceasing to be mine, as the warmth of love came over me, intoxicating my soul. A peaceful and divine calm made me forget everything but the joy of love and melted my soul into hers. To my reasoning, she replied in silence with a secret word of love.

He makes a pæan to chastity which he says is true love and the perfect image of man and woman in one being. He goes on to say that his beloved loves the man-that-is-god and he loves the woman-who-is-the-divine-mother. Men and women in love are the embodiment of love itself, participating in the divine. (Again it reads better in French!) For Constant the church was failing, primarily because it did not understand or communicate his message of love.

The present generation is dying of ice in the soul because it lacks love. Without love, all belief is extinguished and without religion social order becomes impossible … The world today understands the concept of god the father and of god the son but still does not understand the secrets of the love of a mother which is where the holy spirit resides … Our father is in heaven but Christ in dying bequeathed Mary to us, saying, 'Here is your mother!'

Referring to the church as a mother, he calls for change in ringing phrases:

Ne t'afflige pas, O ma mère, des cris et des blasphèmes de ceux qui passent en branlant la tête; ne t'étonne pas du froid qui gagne tes veines épuisées de sang; ne t'épouvante pas du voile de ténèbres qui descend sur tes yeux; ne dis pas, dans le grand cri de ton agonie, que ton dieu t'a abandonnée. Quand la femme est près d'enfanter, elle se plaint, parce que son heure douloureusement est venu; mais lorsqu'elle voit son enfant, elle ne se souvient plus de son angoisse, parce qu'elle a mis un homme au monde.

O my mother, do not grieve at the cries and blasphemies of those who pass by, shaking their heads. Do not be surprised at the cold which grips your veins, emptied of blood. Do not fear the veil of darkness which descends on your eyes and do not, in a cry of agony, say that your god has abandoned you. When a woman is close to giving birth, she cries because her hour of pain has arrived, but she forgets her anguish when she sees her child, because she has brought a man into the world.

Leaving the church

Constant, perhaps unsurprisingly, then left the church and used his undoubted literary skill, combined with his talent for drawing and painting, to get by. He taught, composed songs, illustrated books (two by Alexandre Dumas[1]), and increasingly turned his attention towards the occult. From 1850, he called himself

---

[1] *Louis XIV and his Century* and *The Count of Monte Cristo.*

Éliphas Lévi[1] and his subsequent *Dogme et Rituel de la Haute Magie* was a great success. He wrote a further seven books on the occult and seems to have been able to support himself pretty well, albeit with occasional difficult periods. Another twenty or so works by him were published posthumously.

However, nothing is simple in the life of Alphonse Louis Constant. While at Choisy-le-Roy, he had met Eugénie Chenevier, a teacher at the Institute Chandeau. Among her students was the fifteen year old Marie-Noémi Cadiot and Constant was in the habit of escorting both on Sunday excursions. Eugénie became pregnant,[2] intending to marry Constant as the father of the child, but here we have another Constant moment. One theory is that he wanted to marry Eugénie but had already had a liaison with Marie-Noémi who ran away from home to be with him. Outraged, her father demanded that Constant marry his daughter, threatening him with an action for statutory rape if he did not comply. Constant thus had to abandon hopes of marrying Eugénie and married Marie-Noémi instead – on July 13 1846. Her family were so angry that they refused to give the married couple any money whatsoever and their wedding breakfast was *quelques sous de pommes de terres frites achetées sur le Pont-Neuf.*[3]

That is the explanation given by the descendants of Eugénie Chenevier but it presents some difficulties. Firstly, the age of consent in France at the time was 11. It was raised to 13 in 1862 and is now 15. So while a sexual relationship with Marie-Noémi might well have been improper, it was not illegal. Secondly, it is said that Marie-Noémi's mother had disappeared when Marie-Noémi was two, which puts doubt on the claim that the family was angry. Moreover, the same account says that her father, a somewhat bohemian sculptor, was not at all put out when his daughter failed to return one evening, remarking with a shrug, that it was inevitable.

While at this distance, we may find it difficult to judge why Constant married Marie-Noémi and not Eugénie, we have seen Constant's views on women and on young women in particular. Whatever is the case, as with Adèle Allenbach, Constant maintained reasonable relations with Eugénie until 1867 when he had a row with her over money, never seeing her or his son, eleven at the time, again. The fact that the row was over money may indicate that he had made some efforts towards the support of the child – one hopes so.

Marie-Noémi Cadiot

The new Mme Constant turned out to be a very powerful figure. Far from being a demure child bride living in the shadow of the great writer, she pushed her husband into politics, persuaded a Government Ministry to commission paintings from him, published in the magazine he edited, wrote for national journals including *Le Moniteur du Soir* and, after studies with Jean-Jaques Pradier,[4] became a successful sculptor, several of her works being acquired by the Louvre. When in

---

[1] Said to be his translation of his given names, Alphonse Louis, into Hebrew.

[2] The child, a son, Xavier Alphonse Henri Chenevier, was born September 29, 1846 and lived until 1916. His descendants come down to the present day.

[3] A penn'orth of chips bought on the Pont Neuf.

[4] Forgotten today but a major artist in his time.

1847 Constant was imprisoned for a second time,[1] his young and pregnant wife successfully petitioned for his early release and even obtained his full pardon.

Marie-Noémi was a force to be reckoned with. It is said that she had been drawn to Constant because of the bohemian life that he seemed to offer. She wanted freedom and independence and had no intention of being the passive idol that Constant thought a wife should be. Constant may have been a rebel in most matters but his views on women were conservative.

> *The children of the new Eve adore their mother in the sweet delights of love. The mother bears them in her arms, feeds them at her breast and caresses them as they fall asleep on her heart.*

Marie-Noémi was having none of this and, once delivered of her own child, hired a wet nurse. Constant was horrified and recognising that she had got him wrong, Marie-Noémi left him for the Marquis de Montferrer, who owned several of the radical journals for which her husband wrote. Constant's view of such behaviour is expressed in a later work, *L'Histoire de la Magie (History of Magic.)* On the subject of the *radical emancipation of women*, he writes:

> *If ... the woman leaves the passive and enters the active realm, she abdicates her sex and becomes a man, or rather, as such a transformation is physically impossible ... she becomes of neither sex, a sterile and androgynous monster.*

That would not have gone down well with Mme Constant! Marie-Noémi's liaison with Montferrer was short lived - but it led to a dalliance with Emperor Napoleon III who awarded her a pension from his privy purse - and in 1872 she married for the second time, this time, as David Allen Harvey writes,

> *...(to) an ambitious young lawyer fourteen years her junior, Maurice Rouvier, who would be elected to the Chamber of Deputies and would go on to a long and successful career in the governments of the Third Republic.*

She played an active role in the feminist movement of the Revolution of 1848 and served on the governing board of the *Club de la Voix des Femmes*, the principal feminist organization of the time. She was a speaker at the *Banquet régénérateur des femmes démocrates et socialistes*. Under the *nom de plume* of Claude Vignon,[2] she wrote for political journals and was French correspondent for the newspaper *Independence Belge*. She published a number of collections of short stories and five novels in which she expressed outrage at the class and sex discrimination in French society. The novels, Harvey describes as,

> *... realistic, perceptive examinations of domestic dramas and the fate of strong-willed women in the society of her time.*

---

[1] This time for writing *La Voix de la Famine* which David Allen Harvey calls *an incendiary denunciation of the indifference of the rich and powerful to the plight of the impoverished masses.*

[2] Borrowing the name of the 17th artist, one of whose paintings is entitled *Solomon and Sheba* and can be seen in the Bentlif Art Gallery in the museum at Maidstone in Kent.

He says of her work:

> *Rooting her literary work firmly in her own experiences of hope, frustration and desire, Vignon offered a feminist response to the misogyny of nineteenth-century French society, and also to the idealization and marginalization of women offered by the male romantic socialists with whom she was intimately acquainted.*

The 'ravishingly beautiful' Marie-Noémi (Claude Vignon) as imagined by Kath Walker.

An observer of her later marriage to Maurice Rouvier said:

> *I envied them greatly. They were both quite young, she was ravishingly beautiful, they were in love, they both had great talent, they were accustomed, by difficult and fruitful experience, to the struggles of life.*

Rouvier[1] became Prime Minister of France and remained loyal to Marie-Noémi throughout her life despite attacks from his political opponents. Following Marie-Noémi's death in 1888, he helped the career of her son by Constant, even making

---

[1] Rouvier was Prime Minister of France 1905-6. He died 23 years after Noémi in 1911. In Saint-Jean-Cap-Ferrat, a path along the waterside, *Promenade Maurice Rouvier,* commemorates his birth place. The promenade continued to be romantic. On it is a house once called *Lo Scoglietto,* built in 1880. Its inhabitants included Consuelo Vanderbilt, the Duchess of Marlborough; Leopold III of Belgium; Charlie Chaplin and David Niven. The square in front is called *Place David Niven* and a plaque gives his dates: 1909-1983.

him his Chef de Cabinet. The son was also named Claude Vignon. The *New York Times* of May 27, 1888, carried an account of her life, opening with:

> One of the strangest careers of the present century has been brought to a close by the death of 'Claude Vignon' in her beautiful and picturesque villa at St Jean, near Nice. Her life was a singularly remarkable one, for she was in turn the wife of a famous Roman Catholic priest, the mistress of an Emperor, a famous sculptress, a journalist of European reputation, the trenchant sarcasms of whose pen resulted in her being expelled from the Chamber of Deputies, a popular novelist, a most successful electoral agent and lastly the wife of a powerful Prime Minister.

Éliphas Lévi

Meanwhile Constant reinvented himself as Éliphas Lévi and came under the influence of Joseph Maria Hoene-Wronski (1776-1853), whom he had met through Marquis de Montferrer (so his wife's *affaire* was not all loss.) This may be the ultimate Constant moment.

Wronski was an amazing eccentric. He reached the rank of major in the Russian Army and fought in the Polish rebellion of 1794.[1] Leaving the army, he set himself the task of the complete reform of philosophy, mathematics, astronomy, technology, politics, history, economics, law, psychology and music. In 1810, he published his conclusions which, unsurprisingly, were dismissed as rubbish. He claimed to have rebuilt the foundation of mathematics, but was wrong, and to have discovered the ultimate knowledge, but no one understood his explanation. He designed a number of fantastical machines, one of which was the *prognometre*, a machine to predict the future, which later came into Constant's possession.

Wronski was interested in the occult and found in Constant a willing ear and thereafter Constant became famous in the occult world. Constant visited another devotee of the occult in London, the playwright Edward Bulwer-Lytton, and gave lessons to the Bishop of Evreux on Kabbalah, a somewhat ironical event.

In 1861, Constant was initiated into freemasonry in the Lodge *Rose du Parfait Silence*, Paris, under the constitution of the Grand Orient of France. This was not a happy event. Initiates normally give a short acceptance speech, simply thanking the brethren for welcoming them into the lodge and into freemasonry but Constant opened with:

> Je viens rapporter au milieu de vous les traditions perdues, la connaissance exacte de vos signes et de vos emblèmes, et par suite, vous montrer le but pour lequel votre association a été constituée.

> Brethren, I come to bring you your lost traditions, the exact meaning of your signs and symbols, and to show you the purpose for which your institution has been constituted.

---

[1] Having been founded in 966, Poland was invaded by Catharine the Great in 1791 and the country was partitioned. Tadeusz Kosciuszko, a Polish national who had been a successful general on the American side in the War of Independence and who then became a very successful military leader for Poland, sought to create a national uprising.

He attempted to demonstrate that masonic symbolism is derived from Kabbalah. This was not well received and nor was his reaction when, a month later, he walked out when another brother commented on a talk that he was giving. He did not attend lodge again. He later said that he left because freemasons had been excommunicated by the Pope – another Constant moment.

Magic

In his major work, *Dogme et Rituel de la Haute Magie,*[1] he sums up, in a wonderful phrase, the aims of magic as:

> *Etre toujours riche, toujours jeune, et ne jamais mourir: tel a été de tout temps le rêve des alchimistes.*[2]

He warns us not to play around with what we do not understand.

> *Comme nous avons déjà dit plusieurs fois, les opérations de la science ne sont pas sans danger.*[3]

He rarely provides actual details. He talks around them and describes the true Magus (which he is, of course) as one who bewitches without the need for mumbo-jumbo and from whose pronunciation of doom there is no escape.

> *There are no ceremonies nor invocations; he does but abstain from eating at the same table or, if forced to do so, neither accepts nor offers salt.*[4]

The wonderful throw away line about the salt is pure Constant! He is also a master of gory detail. Take the passage concerning the bewitchments of sorcerers - beings he considers beneath his dignity:

> *They get hold of hair or clothing belonging to him they seek to destroy; select an animal to symbolise him and using the hair or clothing, create a magnetic connection from the symbol to their victim. Giving the animal the victim's name, they kill it with one blow of a magic knife, cutting open the breast, tearing out the heart, enveloping the still palpitating organ in the magnetism and all day for three full days, drive into that heart nails, red hot needles and long thorns, casting spells on the bewitched victim. They are persuaded, and often rightly so, that the target of their infamous acts experiences tortures as if his own heart had been pierced. He wastes away and dies of an unknown ailment.*

It seems to me that Constant frequently writes with his tongue in his cheek:

> *To govern elemental spirits and master the occult elements, we must first undergo four ancient ordeals of initiation but, since these ancient ordeals are no longer available, we must find alternative trials: handling fire, crossing over an abyss by means of a tree trunk, climbing a vertical mountain face in a storm, swimming through a whirlpool or cataract. A man who is afraid of water will never rule the Undines; one who is afraid of fire will never govern Salamanders; those who suffer*

---

[1] Translated into English by AE Waite as *Transcendental Magic, its Doctrine and Ritual* in 1896.

[2] *To be always rich, always young, and never die: such has always been the dream of the alchemists.*

[3] *As we have already said many times, the machinations of the science are not without danger.*

[4] This translation is from A.E Waite. It cannot be bettered.

from vertigo must leave the Sylphs in peace and avoid irritating Gnomes; for lesser spirits will obey only one who has overcome them in their own element.

His talents

He makes use of an impressive range of religious and occult literature. For example, introducing his engraving of *le bouc de sabbat,* he mentions *the dragon of all the theogonies* and *the hundred headed Typhon of the Egyptians.* A *theogony* is a family history of the gods and Hesiod's *Theogony,* written about 700 BCE, tells how the world grew out of chaos. There are a couple of dragons in it, including,

> *... fierce Echidna, half nymph with glancing eyes and fair cheeks, and half huge snake with speckled skin, eating raw flesh beneath the secret places of the earth.*

and the terrible Typhon who was joined in love to her.

> *Up to his thighs he was of human shape and of such prodigious size that he towered over all mountains with his head brushing the stars. One of his hands extended to the West and the other to the East, and from them projected a hundred dragons' heads. From the thighs downward he bore huge coils of vipers, which when uncoiled hissed deafening and reached up to his very head. He set alight the very rocks, spouting great jets of fire from his mouth. When the gods saw him rushing at heaven, they made for Egypt in flight.[1]*

Perhaps in that library at Saint-Pierre de Solesmes Constant had read Hesiod and the *Bibliotheca* from which the latter description is taken.[2] He could draw but, above all, he could wield a superb *plume de ma tante.* The opening lines of the second volume of *Dogme et Rituel de la Haute Magie* were used by the English novelist Anthony Powell, himself a master of language, when the old fake Trelawney introduces the fortune-teller Myra Erdleigh to Nick Jenkins, the narrator.

> 'Connaissez-vous la vieille souveraine du monde,' he said, 'qui marche toujours, et ne se fatigue jamais? In this incarnation, she passes under the name of Mrs Erdleigh.'

The sound of his words, so wonderfully louche and other-worldly just roll along.

> *Quand elle passe, les portes s'ouvrent d'elles-mêmes; elle entre à travers les murailles, elle pénètre jusqu'à l'alcôve des rois, elle vient surprendre les spoliateurs du pauvre dans leurs plus secrète orgies, s'assied à leur table et leur verse à boire, ricane à leurs chansons avec ses dents dégarnies de gencives, et prend la place de la courtisane impure qui se cache sous leurs rideaux.*

> When she goes by, doors open themselves; she passes through the strongest walls; she penetrates into the private rooms of kings; she surprises the plunderers of the poor in their most secret orgies; sits at their table, pours their wine, grins at their songs with her toothless gums, and takes the place of the lecherous courtesan hiding behind their curtains.

---

[1] Why Egypt? As we shall see later, Egypt was seen as the original home of the gods.

[2] The *Bibliotheca* is a sort of dictionary of Greek myth, thought to date from around 200 CE.

The goat of the sabbath

Constant loves to be mysterious and to have things both ways. He chooses chapter fifteen for his explanation of *le bouc de sabbat* because it is the number of the devil card in the tarot. He starts the chapter with some typical Constant phrasing:

Recreation of Jean Dodal Tarot, 1650. Note the devilish posing pouch.

Nous voici revenues à ce terrible nombre quinze, qui, dans la clavicule du tarot, présente pour symbole un monstre debout sur un autel, portant une mitre et des cornes, ayant un sein de femme et les parties sexuelles d'un homme, une chimère, un sphinx difforme, un synthèse de monstruositiés; et, au-dessous de cette figure, nous lisons en inscription toute franche et toute naïve: LE DIABLE.

We now arrive at that terrible number fifteen which the tarot pictures as a monster perched on an altar, wearing a mitre and horns, having female breasts and male sexual organs; a chimera,[1] a misshapen sphinx, a synthesis of monstrosities; and underneath this figure we find, artlessly and openly, the title THE DEVIL.

Constant's engraving owes so much to the Dodal tarot that we might be excused for thinking his picture also to be of the devil but no; he says that it is to be taken as the god Pan and:

... the god of our modern schools of philosophy, of the Alexandrian theurgic school and of our own Neoplatonists, the god of Lamartine and Victor Cousin, the god of Spinoza and Plato.

At first sight this list is quite silly. The idea that Plato or Spinoza would have had anything to do with his goat appears quite preposterous, as indeed is the thought that Victor Cousin would approve. A contemporary of Constant, Cousin (1792-1867) insisted on a proper method of observation, analysis and induction in philosophy (not something to Constant's taste.) However, it is significant that Spinoza rejects the idea of an existent devil and any personification of evil. Put simply, Spinoza (1632-1677) thought of god as an impersonal (and no longer present) creator, and of the created world as like a machine; what happens is completely determined. Without free will, there can be no choice and thus nothing

---

[1] A monster created from parts of several different animals, typically a lioness, a snake and a goat.

that is done is either good or evil. It is just the working out of the machine's design. Constant also rejects the idea of personified evil when, with relish, he picks up St Augustine's definition of evil as the absence of good:

> *Non, tu n'es pas l'esprit du mal, généreux esprit de la révolte et du noble orgueil! Le mal, c'est le néant, c'est la privation du bien, et le bien c'est la liberté! Car la liberté est fille de l'intelligence et mère de l'amour.*

> No, you are not the spirit of evil, generous spirit of the revolution and noble daring. Evil is nothingness, the absence of good and the good is liberty. For liberty is the daughter of intelligence and the mother of love.

So, while what Constant means is rarely static in his writing, at least in what he says here, for him there is no evil supernatural being. Not that anyone has believed this.

> *'It is the Goat of Mendes, Rex!' whispered the Duke. 'My God! This is horrible!' And even as he spoke the manifestation took on a clearer shape; the hands held forward almost an attitude of prayer but turned downward, became transformed into two great cloven hoofs. Above rose the monstrous bearded head of a gigantic goat ... The two slit-eyes, slanting inwards and down, gave out a red baleful light. ... and from the bald, horrible unnatural bony skull, which was caught by the light of the candles, four enormous curved horns spread out - sideways and up.'*

Dennis Wheatley uses Constant's creation in his best seller, *The Devil Rides Out*; written in 1934, but still a gripping tale. It scared the wits out of me when I first read it, under the covers at night, aged 15.

Summary of Constant

Unique? Well read? Gothic? Intriguing? A charlatan? A bit dodgy around young girls? Something of a rogue? He is perhaps all these things but he was also a man of some charm when he wanted to be. After all, various priests, all of whom should have known better, gave him succour and the women in his life seemed to bear him no ill will, even after their affairs with him had ended.

He had an enormous breadth of reading and understood several languages including Hebrew. He had some weird ideas and loved anything mysterious, the more arcane the better but perhaps his understanding was not always the equal of his knowledge. Constant was a man who needed to be noticed. I see him as a life long *installation*, to use that word beloved of modern artists. The way he dressed, what he did and what he wrote, form an artistic if not an intellectual whole.

Having lived through the 1870 siege of Paris during the Franco-Prussian War which his friend Alphonse Esquiros had tried so hard to prevent, he died in genteel poverty in 1875. His work seemed to have died with him but there was a resurgence of interest some twenty years later. Aleister Crowley, who described himself as *the wickedest man in the world,*[1] was born in the year of Constant's death and saw himself as Éliphas Lévi reincarnated. Perhaps there is something about Constant and reincarnation. Rudolf Steiner,[2] the esotericist, pronounced Constant to be the reincarnation of a Mexican *connected with the utterly decadent, pseudo-magical mystery cults* which, while they had degenerated into superstition, were still *replete with vitality, saturated with the fruits of older civilisations.* Constant would have been delighted.

He was well-known enough at his end for his death to be reported in the national press. *Le Figaro* (Thursday 2 June, 1875) reported that L'Abbé Louis Constant, better known as Éliphas Lévi, had been long occupied in magic and chiromancy.[3] It mentions the *charmante* Marie-Noémi and her marriage to Rouvier, remarking that Constant for some time had lived quietly alone in a modest apartment surrounded by his ancient and bizarre magical objects.

In his occult phase, Constant may have actually believed what he was writing, which might give one concern for his sanity. Nevertheless, this may be one of those irregular verbs: *I am creative; you are eccentric; he is raving mad.* Maybe he just thought the occult a safer subject. It is ironic that his religious works constantly got him into trouble when his occult writings did not – at least not until after his death. Constant was initially buried in the Cimitière d'Ivry but was exhumed six years later and re-buried in a common grave. I like to think that he would have appreciated that.

Going on

Fascinating in himself, Constant is also a springboard for our search for the goat and the devil in freemasonry if only because his engraving played a major part in the family history of these ideas. Constant and his ideas have become famous among those who wish to attack freemasonry, particularly in the USA. It is strange that the writings of an obscure 19th century French occultist should have such a reputation in America. As we will see, the reputation is not really his. The reason for it rests on a tale of plagiarism on a grand scale.

---

[1] Crowley was a major figure in occultism whose motto of *Do what thou wilt* combined with his drug taking earned him notoriety. Today he might be considered eccentric rather than evil. He was initiated into irregular freemasonry in France but was more famous as an influential member of the Hermetic Order of the Golden Dawn which had masonic connections. He died in 1947.

[2] Rudolf Steiner, who died in 1925, maintains a following today. He attempted to discover a science of spiritual knowledge, words which Constant might have used with as much sense. Robert Uzzel writes that Steiner saw himself as having been sent by the spiritual world to undertake important work for humanity. He was certainly very hard working, writing some 330 books.

[3] Palm reading.

Interlude: The Origins of Freemasonry

As soon as he had been initiated, Constant decided to tell the brethren all about freemasonry and I am sure that Constant's account would have been enormously imaginative. The truth is a little less gothic although early official writings about the fraternity are just as unreliable.

In the *CONSTITUTION, History, Laws, Charges, Orders, Regulations, and Usages of the Right Worshipful FRATERNITY of Accepted Free MASONS*, published in 1723, the author James Anderson traces freemasonry all the way back to Adam who,

> ... *no doubt taught his sons Geometry, and the use of it, in the several Arts and Crafts convenient at least, for those early times.*

Even James Anderson, whose imagination frequently outruns his historical powers, does not claim that the fraternity came into being with Adam. (After all, there would not have been enough brethren at the time to open a lodge.)[1] Anderson leaves the establishment of the first lodge to the,

> ... *Israelites, (who) at their leaving Egypt, (formed) a whole Kingdom of Masons, well instructed, under the conduct of their Grand Master Moses, who often marshall'd them in to a regular and general Lodge while in the wilderness, and gave them wise charges, orders etc.*

He also says that the Royal Art[2] was brought to Egypt by Mitzraim, a son of Ham (*Genesis* 10:6) and that the flooding of the Nile caused an improvement in geometry because masonry was much in demand. This is Anderson's imagination given full rein. Obviously a knowledge of geometry and building techniques was required by the Egyptians and equally obviously they were remarkably highly skilled in both. This has absolutely nothing at all to do with freemasonry as we know it today or even as Anderson knew it in 1723.

The theories of origin

There are several theories about the origins of the Right Worshipful[3] Fraternity as Anderson terms it. The difference between them turns largely on their view of the connection, if any, between what we call *operative* and *speculative* masons. The word *operative* describes working masons, those who actually worked with stone. The trade of the working stone mason reached its zenith with the building of the castles and great cathedrals from the 12th to the 16th centuries. AJ Taylor speaks of the construction of Beaumaris Castle (in about 1290) which involved a labour force of

---

[1] A masonic joke. A decision by the Board of General Purposes of the United Grand Lodge of England is that a Lodge cannot be opened nor a degree worked with fewer than five present. Two must be members of the Lodge and one an installed Master.

[2] So called because of the numerous Princes of the Blood Royal who have been freemasons.

[3] The word *worshipful* has little to do with the word *worship* except in its derivation. It is a formal title used of people or organisations meriting respect. In the UK, most mayors are referred to as *The Worshipful*; some are referred to as *The Right Worshipful* while a few are addressed as *The Right Honourable*. Senior Judges in the UK are referred to as *My Lord / My Lady*; Circuit Judges as *Your Honour* but Magistrates as *Your Worship*. The Livery Companies of the City of London are so styled: for example, *The Worshipful Company of Farriers*.

400 masons, 2,000 minor workmen, 200 quarrymen and 30 smiths and carpenters with a supply organisation of 100 carts, 60 wagons and 30 boats.

It is said that masons working on such buildings created lodges, shelters at the building site or quarry in which to talk, exchange views and no doubt complain about the Master Mason and their pay. In the middle ages, masons went through an apprenticeship at the end of which they were considered qualified, or free. The word is still met in Livery Companies and in the title *Freeman of the City of London*. Because they worked so hard and for so long to become qualified, understandably masons did not want unqualified workers, often called *cowans*, taking their jobs.

Since few people then could read and write, certificates were of little use and, so the theory goes, the masons used modes of recognition - signs and words - to prove that they were properly qualified and these they kept secret for obvious reasons. At some point, men who were not working masons either joined existing lodges or created their own in imitation of them. This is the beginning of what we call *speculative* masonry; pondering on or speculating about the meaning of things.

The speculative mason uses the tools and practices of masonry allegorically for moral lessons. For example, the operative mason is said to use the 24-inch gauge to *measure the work*, the gavel to *knock off all superfluities* and the chisel to *further prepare the stone for the more experienced workman*. The speculative mason uses the 24-inch gauge to remind him of the 24 hours of the day, *part to be spent in serving a brother in time of need*, the gavel to remind him of the force of conscience *to keep down all unbecoming thoughts* and the chisel *to point out the advantages of education*.

So this theory is of a transition from operative to speculative masonry. Once the period of cathedral building was over, most masons would have been working in the larger conurbations, not spread out as before, and after the Great Fire of London, masons were pulled in from all over to rebuild the city. As the work became more concentrated, masons ceased to meet on building sites in favour of more comfortable surroundings and men who did not work in the trade joined in. There is a view that King James VI of Scotland (later James I of England) was accepted into a Scottish Lodge in 1601. From 1620, there is evidence of the *Acception*, part of the London Company of Masons open to people who were not operatives. This is the derivation of part of the name, Free and *Accepted* Masons.

Professor Charles Lawrence has argued that the shift happened before the time of the great fire. His view is that the dissolution of the monasteries by Henry VIII between 1536 and 1541 was the death knell of the masons' trade. It took away their major source of revenue, one which was never replaced. Not only did the masons lose the income from new religious buildings but they also lost the more important revenue from maintaining them.

The only large source of revenue for the building trade then became the rising middle classes who could not afford immense buildings of stone. Instead their self-advertisements were built in brick, made from clay which is abundant around London and other southern cities. The skills of a bricklayer can be gained in much less time than the skills of a mason. Lawrence shows that St Paul's Cathedral, often thought of as the pinnacle of the masons' trade, is really a brick building with stone cladding.

Professor David Stevenson puts forward a persuasive theory that the transition from operative to speculative freemasonry happened earlier in Scotland than in England. He shows that Scotland can claim the earliest:

> *use of the word 'lodge' in a masonic sense*
>
> *lodge minute books*
>
> *non-operatives joining lodges*
>
> *use of ethical concepts expounded by masonic symbols*
>
> *references to the mason word*
>
> *masonic catechisms (learning by Q & A)*
>
> *use of the terms 'entered apprentice' and 'fellow craft'*

Other scholars disagree with this transitional theory. They see speculative freemasonry as a quite separate creation, arising probably in the 16th century, perhaps in reaction to the religious troubles of the time. Just think of Henry VIII, Bloody Mary, Cromwell and the later Jacobite rebellions. This may have led well-meaning men to seek ways of meeting together, irrespective of creed. The fact that from its very beginning, speculative freemasonry has been open to men of all religions may be evidence for this and freemasonry still forbids all religious and political discussion in lodge.[1] The secrets of freemasonry, so this theory goes, would have been words and signs of recognition, not to protect jobs but to protect the members from spies. On this theory, the metaphor of the mason's trade was mainly *cover*. To be honest, I have always considered the *cover* theory a little too dramatic and romantic for my tastes and at present, after a period in the doldrums, the transitional theory seems to be holding sway again.

Whatever its origins, during the 17th century, we see the spread of speculative freemasonry. In 1646, Elias Ashmole, the great antiquary whose name lives on in the Ashmolean Museum in Oxford, was made a freemason in Warrington in Cheshire. In 1686, the writer Robert Plot and the celebrated diarist John Aubrey both mention and describe aspects of freemasonry. The first printed attack on freemasonry in England dates from 1698 and it must have been fairly widespread at the time to be worth attacking.[2] In 1717, four existing lodges in London got together *and resolv'd to hold an annual assembly and feast.* The first meetings were held at the *Goose and Gridiron,* alas in St Paul's Churchyard no longer, and led to the Premier Grand Lodge. Freemasonry grew from there.

---

[1] Primarily to avoid two major causes of disharmony. The Royal Society, founded officially in 1660 after a lecture by Christopher Wren, adopted a similar rule.

[2] Stevenson indicates that such attacks start earlier in Scotland.

Chapter two: The Scottish Rite and the Mountain Men

In this chapter, I want to introduce you to a figure famous in American masonry but virtually unknown elsewhere. He had an enormous effect on freemasonry in the USA, though not always the one he desired, and he is forever linked to Constant, whom he knew as Éliphas Lévi - not that they ever met.

He and Constant were born just 41 days apart. Both got into trouble over Lucifer. Both had strong and unique views. Both needed the limelight and both died in relative poverty. Both wrote and have caused to be written a very large number of books and articles.

Unlike Constant who, no doubt to his posthumous glee, was disinterred and reburied in unconsecrated ground, I will introduce you to someone who is today commemorated by a statue in Washington and in the name of a public highway. He had many talents and faults but one should never underestimate his courage and endurance. His experiences in the Old West are well worth recording to show the character of the man.

They may also excuse an excursion into the wonderful lives and times of the mountain men and fur trappers. After all, it is not everyday that the Comanche and the Blackfoot Indians, the exploration of the North American continent, wagon trains and the civil war come into the history of freemasonry.

An incongruity

So here we are in America during the Old West. It seems a strange time and place to be seeking a goat, a devil or even a freemason. Be that as it may, Albert Pike was initiated into freemasonry in the Western Star Lodge No. 2, Little Rock, Arkansas in 1850. He was founder of the Magnolia Lodge No. 60,[1] also in Little Rock, and was its Master in 1853/54. He was appointed Sovereign Grand Commander of the Scottish Rite, Southern Jurisdiction five years later, converting a dying order into a thriving one, but he is probably best known for his seven hundred page tome, *Morals and Dogma of the Ancient and Accepted Scottish Rite of Freemasonry.*[2]

We often think of events in history as independent chunks and it comes as a surprise to find just how often heterogeneous events overlap with each other. The writing of a very large book on the somewhat esoteric subject of the Ancient and Accepted Rite occurred during the life and times of Kit Carson, Cochise, Geronimo, Sitting Bull, Wyatt Earp, Belle Starr, Doc Holliday, Calamity Jane and Billy the Kid.[3] As incongruous as it might seem, Pike's major work was published in the same year that Wild Bill Hickok became Marshall of Abilene and five years before Crazy Horse led the Sioux in the battle of the Little Big Horn River.

Go west, young man

Pike's personal experience of the Old West was somewhat before the era of the cowboys, stage coaches, marshals and gunfighters. He went west in the time of the fur trappers, the mountain men, the final glory of the Indian Nations and the discovery of the routes through the Rockies.

In 1826 and living in Massachusetts, Albert Pike was offered a place to study at Harvard University but could not raise the money to pay the fees. He took a series of teaching jobs in and around Newburyport Mass. with the idea of studying on his own and saving to enter the University later but, in 1831, took off for the Western frontier. His first biographer, Fred W. Allsopp, puts this down to the restrictions and lack of opportunity in his home environment.

> He attended less and less to academic studies as time wore on, and found himself pondering more and more over tales of the new western land which he read about ... Confined in a small town, and thrown in with rigid Puritans, he longed to see the wider world, to have more action, to lead a broader and freer life.

A later biographer, Walter Lee Brown, suggests that it was his literary aspirations, combined with a love affair he was too poor to pursue, which drove him. He had published more than fifty poems in Boston magazines but his teaching commitments, for what he described as *the scanty pittance of a livelihood,* did not give him as much time to write as he wished. He had also fallen for *fair-golden-haired* Elizabeth Perkins, one of his students,[4] but with no money to marry and like many

---

[1] Both lodges continue to meet today.

[2] First published 1871. Constant's major work, *Dogme et Rituel*, was published 16 years earlier.

[3] Kit Carson (1809–1868), Cochise (1815-1874), Geronimo (1829-1909), Sitting Bull (1831-1890), Wyatt Earp (1848–1929), Belle Starr (1848–1889), Doc Holliday (1851–1887), Calamity Jane (1852–1903) and Billy the Kid (1859–1881).

[4] As we shall see, Pike and Constant have many similarities.

a young man in many a country, he went west. Mind you, it might have simply been the restlessness which many commentators use to explain the wagon trains.[1]

William F Drannan

What sort of world did Pike think he was heading for? By 1831, missionaries and fur trappers had long been journeying through the West, attracted for many reasons but especially by a love of its space, freedom and beauty. West of the Mississippi, the country was permanently inhabited solely by the Indian Nations who had been there, according to various theories, at least 7,000 years, perhaps 9,500 years or conceivably 12,500[2] years.

A curious book entitled *Thirty-One Years on the Plains and in the Mountains*, advertises itself as *an authentic record of a life time of hunting, trapping, scouting and Indian fighting in the far West as written by Captain William F Drannan*.[3] It describes the life of a man, born in 1832 on board a ship bound from France to America, orphaned almost immediately and brought up in unkindness. Escaping, at age fifteen, he sets out to walk to St Louis, meets the great Kit Carson who treats him like a son and introduces him to such famous Western figures as John Charles Frémont, James Beckwourth and Jim Bridger.[4] He becomes a deadeye shot, hunts buffalo, scouts for the great Indian fighters of the period, kills a grizzly bear weighing eight hundred and sixty pounds with one shot and even signs on with a schooner as a seal shooter in the Yukon.

Today, we might call it *faction*, the use of factual events as a background in which to set a fictional story, such as George Macdonald Fraser's glorious tales of *Flashman*. but Drannan (1832-1913) sold his book as a true story. However, while there are records of people meeting the author, according to Walter Bate there seem to be few records of him ever being where he said he was and occasionally evidence that he was somewhere else at the time. This is a pity as much of the detail in his book has a ring of truth. The boasting and casual violence is typical of other books of the era, even those with greater claim to truth such as *The life and adventures of James P. Beckwourth, mountaineer, scout and pioneer, and chief of the Crow nation of Indians*.[5]

Drannan claims to have trapped with Jim 'Beckwith' (his spelling) but it is more likely that he read Beckwourth's book, published in 1856. Drannan was by his own account for a time an hotelier and by other accounts the part-owner of a restaurant in Seattle and I suspect that he was a good listener and fascinated by the stories told by his customers, many of whom were genuine explorers and plainsmen.

---

[1] McLynn writes that only 25% of those in San Francisco in 1850 were still there in 1860.

[2] Human remains unmistakably Indian date to 7000 years ago; an earlier skeleton, *Wizards Beach Man*, is dated to 9,200 years ago and has features *within the variability of modern Indian people* although other finds from that time are more like Polynesians; finds in Chile date from 12,500 years ago. *Paleoamerican Origins*, Encyclopædia Smithsonian.

[3] He wrote a second and later volume in which he promoted himself to Colonel.

[4] Frémont (1813-1890) explorer, soldier and anti-slavery candidate for the Presidency; Beckwourth (1798-1866) mountain man, fur trader, Crow warrior and author; Bridger (1804-1881) mountain man, trapper and linguist who spoke English, French, Spanish as well as several Indian languages. The Bridger Pass shortened the Oregon Trail by 61 miles.

[5] David J Weber refers to Beckwourth as a *notorious liar.*

He seems to have developed a vicarious love of the West and the details stuck in a retentive memory.

> *In a few days we passed Fort Scott[1] and then we were entirely beyond the bounds of civilisation. From then on, until we reached our destination, the only living things we saw were jack-rabbits, prairie-dogs, antelope, deer, buffalo, sage-hens and Indians, barring, of course, insects, reptiles and the like, and the little owls that live with the prairie-dogs and sit upon the mounds of the dog villages, eyeing affairs with seeming dignity and wisdom.*

> *The high mountains with scattering pine trees on the sides; the snowy white peaks above the timber line, and the many little mountain streams and rills that paid tribute to the mainstream that coursed this beautiful valley, all combined to form a scene of magnificent grandeur. The quaking-asp, balm and various other kind of small timber that grew along the streams all helped to add to the beauty.*

Trapping was easy in this paradise.

> *Each man had his string of traps, and it was his business to go to each trap every day, take the beaver out, skin them, set the traps, carry the skins home and stretch them. Sometimes we would trap as far as seven miles from camp ... After we had trapped here about three weeks there came a light fall of snow which drove most of the game to the valley and we experienced no trouble in getting all the meat we wanted close to camp; in fact we could kill deer and antelope from our cabin door.*

The effect of such tales[2] on the active imagination of men like Pike must have been powerful. Here was the opportunity to escape poverty and Puritanism for a broader, freer and easier life.

Setting off

Accompanied by two friends, Luther Chase and Rufus Titcomb[3], Pike set off; first to Rochester on Lake Ontario, then south-west along Lake Erie to Cleveland and then in a straight line to Cincinnati and Nashville, Tennessee.

Finding no work there, the companions turned north-west to Paducah where the Tennessee River meets the Ohio and took a keelboat down to Cairo and a steamboat up the Mississippi to St Louis. We can only admire Pike's stamina and that of his friends. Much of this journey was on foot.

---

[1] In the State of Kansas, built in 1842. The animals listed are all prairie creatures.

[2] Drannan was writing later than Pike's journey but it seems typical of such literature.

[3] According to the *Newburyport Index*, there was a Rufus Titcomb born in Newburyport in 1806. There was a Chase family in Newburyport at the same time but no Luthers born at an appropriate date. The *Index* does tell us that a Luther R. Chase married a Lucy D. Follansbee on February 24, 1839. Since we know that Chase left Pike and Titcomb when they arrived in Santa Fe, returning to Newburyport, we may (romantically) assume that he did so to marry his sweetheart, Lucy.

A keelboat in 1872. These were river boats, powered by poles or occasionally oars, used for carrying freight and people. The keel was internal. The boats could be 80 foot long and 9 foot wide.

In St Louis, Pike met Charles Bent, one of the famous Bent Brothers,[1] who offered Pike and his companions jobs as guards for a wagon train, travelling from nearby Independence to Santa Fe. Bernard De Voto writes:

> *The Bents and St Vrain ... attracted more veteran mountain men than all the others put together and probably made more money. The Bents were the fairest manipulators of Indians in the history of the mountain trade and maintained an elsewhere unheard-of standard of honour in dealing with them.*

---

[1] George, Robert and William were the other brothers. William started trapping at age 15. In 1835, he married a Cheyenne lady named Owl Woman and they had four children. She died in 1847. William had two more children by other Indian wives, one being born after his death. In November 1864, around one hundred Cheyenne men, women and children were slaughtered at Sand Creek, a reservation where three of William's children were living. He himself had been arrested to prevent him giving a warning. The leader of this attack was US Army Colonel John Chivington who is reported as saying, *Damn any man who sympathizes with Indians! I have come to kill Indians, and believe it is right and honorable to use any means under god's heaven to kill Indians.* This ghastly person was also a Methodist preacher and, I am so very sad to say, a freemason. He was the first Grand Master of Colorado. Five years after this dreadful event, William Bent died.

Charles Bent had started trading for furs in 1828 on leaving the army and had led wagon trains from St Louis to Santa Fe in 1829 and in 1830. In partnership with Ceran St. Vrain, he created a major trading organisation and built two fortified trading posts on the Santa Fe Trail and another, St. Vrain's Fort, further north. The posts traded furs and buffalo hides with the Cheyenne and Arapaho.

Bent became the brother-in-law of Kit Carson, the most famous of the mountain men, and in 1846 was appointed the first Governor of New Mexico.[1] It is therefore something of a pity that Pike thought Charles Bent stupid.

The mountain men

The Bents were part of the exploration of the West, trading with the mountain men who made their living trapping beaver in the headwaters of the great river systems, particularly in the Rocky Mountains. It was these men who discovered and opened up the routes westward, including the California and Oregon trails which were later used by the pioneer wagon trains.

Unique individuals, many French in origin, they were often linked through their Indian wives to the nations and tribes that they lived among, as Frank McLynn writes. Besides the most famous characters of the Old West like Kit Carson and Jim Bridger, they included such fascinating figures as:

> *Jean Baptiste Charbonneau,* 1805-1866, who spoke French, English and Shoshone, his mother's tongue, and picked up German and Spanish while travelling for six years in Europe with Friedrich Paul Wilhelm, Herzog[2] von Württemberg.

> *Charles Larpenteur,* born in 1807 near Fountainbleau, his father was a Bonapartist who left France for America after Waterloo, hoping to be a part of an American rescue of Napoleon from St Helena. Charles spent forty years from 1833 to 1872 trading furs and wrote his life story.

> *Captain Joseph Walker,* 1798-1876. 'Uncle Joe' led a party which discovered the route across Nevada to California.

> *Jedediah Smith,* 1799-1831, who never smoked, drank alcohol or swore, but discovered the South Pass, survived three massacres and crossed the Mojave desert.

> *Pierre Lesperance,* 1791-1879, a Quebecois who lived so long in Mexico he forgot his mother tongue.

> *Thomas Fitzpatrick,* 1799-1854. Known as *Broken Hand* and born in Ireland, he ran away to sea, managed the Rocky Mountain Fur Company, survived

---

[1] Bent was killed in 1847 during a rebellion against American behaviour after the incorporation of New Mexico into the USA. William H Wroth, for the New Mexico Office of the State Historian, writes that *In spite of the peaceful occupation of the territory, many New Mexicans ... resented the invasion, the loss of sovereignty, and loss of direct contact with Mexico. Some were afraid of losing their land (and did) and the occupying American soldiers and their ethnocentric attitudes were a continual source of friction.*

[2] Duke of Württemberg.

a dozen battles with Indians, guided wagon trains, smoked a pipe of peace with the Cheyenne and spoke Sioux.

Not forgetting the Sublette Brothers:

William, 1798-1845, discovered the geysers of Yellowstone Park, built Fort Laramie, and was a founder of St Louis where he retired. Sublette County along the Green River is named after him.

Milton, 1801-1837, the *Thunderbolt of the Rockies*, died at Fort Laramie of a leg infection after several amputations.

Young *Pinckney*, 1812-1828, killed by the Blackfoot on the Pontneuf River.

Andrew, 1814-1853, died in California, lingering a while after being mauled by two grizzly bears, both of which he killed with a knife.

and *Solomon*, 1816-1857, a restless spirit, who roamed the West; trading, trapping and finally taking on a no-good farm in Missouri where he died.

Reading sign

As De Voto tells us, the mountain men had to know where to find beaver, how to recognise indications of their active presence; where to set traps; how to make the bait using the beaver's own pheromones and avoid their own scent scaring beaver away; how to skin and rough cure the pelt - but they had to know a lot more.

They worked unknown country among potentially and often actively hostile indigenous peoples, a thousand miles or more away from help. They fought when they had to but avoided trouble if they could. As a result, their craft was *as intricate a skill as any ever developed anywhere*. As Bernard de Voto writes.

> *Why do you follow ridges into or out of unfamiliar country? What do you do for a companion who has collapsed from want of water while crossing a desert? How do you get meat ... without gunpowder in a country barren of game? What tribe of Indians made this trail, how many were in the band, what errand were they on, were they going to or coming back from it, how far from home were they, were their horses laden, how many horses did they have and why, how many squaws accompanied them, what mood were they in? ... how old is the trail, where are those Indians now and what does the product of these answers require of you?*

They had an almost unconscious interpretation of events.

> *A branch floats down a stream - is this natural, or the work of animals or of Indians or of trappers? Another branch or a bush or even a pebble is out of place - why? On the limits of the plain, blurred by heat mirage, or against the gloom of distant cottonwoods, or across an angle of sky between branches or where hill and mountain meet, there is a tenth of a second of what may have been movement - did men or animals make it and, if animals, why? Buffalo are moving downwind, an elk is in an unlikely place or posture, too many magpies are hollering, a wolf's howl is off key - what does it mean?*

Based in Oregon (still known as the Beaver State), the Canadian trappers of the Hudson Bay Company worked the watershed of the Columbia River and its major tributary, the Snake, up to the Green River Valley. In the South, the Rocky

Mountain Fur Company based in Taos, New Mexico, worked the Colorado, the southward flowing Rio Grande and the headwaters of the eastward flowing Red, Arkansas and Canadian rivers. The American Fur Company centred its operations in the Green River Valley and worked the headwaters of the Missouri, Colorado, Snake, and Yellowstone rivers.

Most mountain men worked in brigades of up to 40, especially in dangerous country, but some worked in smaller groups or even alone. They gathered together at the annual *Rendezvous* to trade and find out what was going on. Their talk, as De Voto puts it, was shop: trapping, hunting, trailing, fighting Indians, escaping from Indians, the lore of animals and plants and always the lay of the land and old fields revisited and new fields to be found, water and starvation and trickery and feasts. They loved it while it lasted but it was a hard life - not suited to a greenhorn except one willing to learn very fast.

The end of the fur trappers

By the time Pike arrived in Arkansas in 1831, the best days were ending. A few years later in 1838, Jim Bridger found so little beaver sign in Crow country around the area of what is now Billings, Montana that he took his brigade eastward into Blackfoot[1] country, northeast of what is now Yellowstone National Park. All three Blackfoot tribes were capriciously dangerous but the Kainah (Bloods) were lethal.

---

[1] Tom Fitzpatrick, Jedediah Smith and trader William Henry Ashley first made contact with the Blackfoot Indians (*Niitsítapi* - the Original People) in 1829 on the Upper Missouri River. Fitzpatrick had so many encounters with Indians that his hair went white.

> *Nobody liked them, including their friends. They were the first to take offence, the first to break a truce, the first to murder.*

The Blackfoot Indians fought the Crow, the Sioux, the Shoshone, the Flathead, the Cree, the Gros Ventre and just about anyone with whom they came into contact. Going into their lands was risky even for the best of the mountain men. The painter, Alfred Jacob Miller, who knew the mountain trade well, said that the Blackfoot killed more than thirty trappers a year.

Fort Laramie, built by William Sublette. Painting by Alfred Jacob Miller.

They killed William Henry Vanderburgh[1] just before his 32nd birthday in 1832 and put an arrow into Bridger himself the same year.[2] In 1838 Bridger found few Blackfoot and virtually no beaver sign. Smallpox had accounted for the Indians and over-trapping had seen to the beaver. The world of the mountain men came to an end in 1841. Some retired to a normal life; a few carried on unable to leave the mountains they loved; a few joined the Indian bands to which their wives belonged and others - Fitzpatrick, Black Harris, Bridger, Joseph Walker and the Meek Brothers - became guides to the wagon trains then starting across the country.

The Santa Fe trail

The town of Independence had been founded two years before Pike arrived and had a couple of thousand inhabitants. At the convergence of the Kansas and

---

[1] Vanderburgh had attended West Point, the US Military Academy and was described as one of the most fearless and intelligent of the mountain men.

[2] Doc Whitman dug it out and expressed surprise that he could carry on working with a three inch barbed arrowhead in him. Bridger replied, '*In the mountains Doc, meat don't spoil.*'

Missouri Rivers, it was the furthest west that steamboats could reach and it was the jumping off point for the Santa Fe Trail[1] which had been in use from 1822 when William Becknell found a route for wagons. It was the only trail that used the huge Conestoga wagon, pulled by oxen and mules.

Despite the route being well known, it was still no afternoon stroll. Eight hundred miles of arid prairie, desert and mountain, the trail led first to and then along the Arkansas River to Fort Dodge[2] and then following the Cimarron cut-off without water until the Cimarron River, crossing more rivers[3], finally hooking round the Sangre de Cristo Mountains, over the Glorieta Pass and down into Santa Fe. Frank McLynn writes,

> ... the journey was dangerous, for it crossed the hunting grounds of the Arapaho and the Comanche, the 'Spartans of the West.' So serious did Comanche depredations of the wagon trains become that in 1829 the US Army found itself fighting a long and difficult campaign against these Indians ... (This) was the genesis of the famed US Cavalry.

Bernard de Voto agrees with McLynn's judgement:

---

[1] And later for the Oregon and California trails as well.

[2] Dodge took-off in 1876 as a railhead for the cattle business. With gunfighters, brothels, saloons and even bullfights, the city flourished for ten hard-living years until the cattle business ceased and the cowboys and the hangers-on left. It became a sleepy little town, dreaming of its past.

[3] Frank McLynn writes that *drownings were second only to accidental shootings as a cause of fatalities on the overland trails.*

> *The most terrible savages of the plains were the Comanche[1] ... They were not only professional marauders and murderers, but practising sadists as well ... They also did a profitable business in white captives - Mexican, Texan and American - whom they brought back into slavery; when they could not turn a profit on them, they enjoyed themselves. No one has ever exaggerated the Comanche tortures ... They had great skill in pain, and cruelty was their catharsis. In short, the Comanche killed and tortured more whites than any other Indians in the West ...*

Bound for Santa Fe

So in October 1831, we find Pike and his two companions as guards of a train of ten wagons under the leadership of Charles Bent and bound for Santa Fe; three greenhorns about to cross the *Comancheria*. While he does not mention Bent in his 1834 account of the journey, Pike later said that he had a poor opinion of Bent because he advised Pike to sell his warm clothes to buy a horse and rifle, assuring him that the wagon train would be in Santa Fe before the bad weather came. One doubts that Bent took that much interest but in any case a guard was no use without horse[2] and rifle and Pike had no other source of funds.

Bent's train had left Missouri late in the season. Reaching and crossing the Cimarron River, the temperature dropped and it began to snow heavily. They saw the signs of a coming storm and made camp early. The wagons were arranged in a line across the mouth of a canyon and brushwood piled on the windward side. Pike was sleeping outside, wrapped in '*two buffalo robes and two blankets*' when:

> *Two or three hours before daylight the storm commenced with terrific violence, and I never saw a wilder or more terrible sight that was presented to us when day came. The wind swept fiercely out of the cañon, driving the snow horizontally against the wagons and sweeping onward into the wide prairie, in which a sea of snow seemed to be raging.*

Five days later, the wagons had crossed the Canadian River and by the 25th November they were nearing the mountains. The wagon train had been slowed to such an extent that Bent decided to send an advance party ahead on foot, taking a short cut that wagons could not use. Pike was selected for this detail: a three day march through deep snow, using pack mules to break trail. It was made slightly more comfortable by the fact that Pike had discovered deer moccasins to be warmer than heavy shoes and socks but discomfort was not unusual for the mountain men or indeed the traders who dealt with them. Bent's decision to send a party ahead was not to get help but presumably to tell his people in Santa Fe that he would be some days later than expected.

Pike's account in *Journey in the Prairie*, contains some wonderful descriptions of the prairie, of its animals and its desolate beauty. His eye for detail is impressive although the account describes his own journey only briefly and episodically. Most of the narrative is about another and concurrent journey undertaken by Aaron B Lewis, who really did suffer from a lack of clothing such that he nearly died.

---

[1] In the late 18th century, it is thought that they numbered about 45,000.

[2] Pike's horse later bolted in a sand storm.

The way back

Pike spent a little time in Santa Fe and then, in the late summer of 1832, took off for Taos about seventy miles to the north to join a trapping party that John Harris had financed and intended to lead. According to David J Weber, who gives four pages to him in Hafen's ten volume reference of the fur trappers, Harris had been in the fur trade since 1829 with his son Robert.

Harris intended to trap in the headwaters of the Red River system, the first time that any trapping party had attempted to reach the beaver areas of Texas eastwards from New Mexico. The journey required a crossing of the *Llano Estacado*, essentially a desert and unknown to anyone except the Comanche.

The Harris party was initially accompanied by another, led by Richard Campbell. According to Pike, the two parties had set out as one but, after a difference of opinion[1] between the two leaders, had separated although journeying in the same direction. While this may be true, it seems to have been fairly common for parties bound for the same general area to travel together until their paths diverged, a system calculated to dissuade Indian attacks. Both parties contained a mixture of Americans and Mexicans.

Richard Campbell is described by Robert Glass Cleland *as one of the most important of the trapper merchants* but not a lot is known about him. Weber is of the opinion that Campbell had arrived in New Mexico in 1824. He is known to have trapped on the

---

[1] Such disagreement was not that unusual. Democracy was well established and frequently practised. Ten years later, Andrew Sublette was employed to guide the 1842 Wagon Train on the Oregon Trail. He *soon discerned the dark side of the 1842 emigration: nobody was prepared to take orders and everyone wanted to command.* Sublette quit as soon as he could. (McLynn)

Gila and Colorado rivers with such luminaries as Peg-leg Smith[1] and to have led thirty-five men to San Diego where in 1827 he sold his furs to a Russian ship in San Francisco Bay, only the second man to have led a party of trappers across the Rockies to California.

The combined Harris-Campbell party passed first through the deserted Old Village, east of the mountains exposed, as Pike says, to the Comanche.

> *The sole inhabitants of the Old Village now are rattlesnakes of which we killed some two or three dozen about the old mud houses.*

There they met a group of Mexicans on their way back from the Red River where they had been to trade with the Comanche who *took violent possession* of the Mexicans' horses and mules as well as their trade goods. Travelling onward, the Harris-Campbell party reached the Bosque Redondo[2], near today's Fort Sumner. Here they learned that the Comanche had attacked a wagon train and had threatened to kill anyone who trapped in Comanche country. Many in the Harris-Campbell party, including all the Mexican employees, refused to go on.

While Harris, Pike and others decided to continue despite the warning, Campbell returned to Taos. It was no doubt his view that the Comanche meant what they said. They had killed the great mountain man, Jedediah Smith, the previous year while he was leading a wagon train on the Santa Fe Trail, and to go on without his Mexican contingent would have meant that he was undermanned; not the thing to be in the Comancheria.

The staked plain

Pike had already shown that he was no soft-handed easterner and was to demonstrate this even more later but he has not been well-served by his first biographer, Frederick Allsopp, who, in a remarkable passage, writes:

> *Pike, although but 23 years of age, was finally chosen captain of this expedition. The selection was not accidental. He was a young man whose commanding presence, sincerity, courage and companionable disposition made him at once a leader among his fellows. Besides, he was a valuable counsellor on account of his superior intelligence and the knowledge which he had gained through his studies of the line followed by the Spanish adventurers who planted, more than 300 years before, at intervals on the plains, the bois d'arc[3] poles.*

---

[1] 1801-1866. So called because he wore a wooden leg, having been shot just above the ankle. With some help from Milton Sublette, he cut his own foot off. It did not stop him being one of the greatest horse thieves in the West. He married into the Snake tribe.

[2] A name of ill repute. In 1866, having been starved into submission, over 10,000 Navajo were force marched to the Bosque Redondo. 2,000 died between then and their release in 1868. This was thirty years after the *Trail of Tears* when the *five civilised tribes* (Cherokee, Chickasaw, Choctaw, Creek and Seminole) were removed from their homelands and moved west - repeatedly. 25% died. These tribes were called *civilised* because they had adopted the ways of the colonists; not that it did them any good.

[3] The wood of the *bois d'arc* tree is resistant to rot and termites. Fence posts made in the early 19th century still stand today. This may be the root of the legend of the staked plains. The name of the tree refers to its use by early French explorers to make bows.

Allsopp writes of explorers taking wagon loads of such poles and planting them at intervals across the plain so that they *might not lose their way on returning* but the name, *Llano Estacado*, has nothing to do with stakes. The Llano is a flat plateau, almost surrounded by an escarpment and raised about 300 feet above the surrounding country as the photograph shows. Its appearance put Franscisco Vásquez de Coronado in mind of a palisade or defensive wall, hence the name *Palisaded Plain*. There are no stakes to be found today nor were there any in Pike's time.

The problem with Allsopp's biography is that Pike is his hero. In his preface he quotes Pike's view that god,

> *... so arranges that nature and the course of events shall send men into the world, endowed with that higher mental and moral organization, in which grand truths and sublime gleams of spiritual light will spontaneously and inevitably arise.*

He sees Pike as such a man. Unfortunately, this leads him to see events in ways that support this view and he is often wrong as a result.

Separation

The remaining party set out to cross the Llano and found water and game in very short supply. Trappers were accustomed to living off the land and did not carry much in the way of provisions which weighed too much but the Llano was no place to forage and the twenty days they spent crossing it were tough. Pike, who could be an argumentative person, and who later on in life was involved in a duel,[1] fell out with Harris who seems to have had little luck with travelling companions. Earlier the same year, Harris had successfully led a party to the Snake River in Colorado when a fight broke out and one man killed another, wounding a third.

---

[1] No one was hurt.

Statue of Old Bill in the town of Williams, Arizona.

Pike decided to leave and four men went with him, one of whom was Aaron Lewis who was the subject of Pike's first *Journey into the Prairie* and who had joined the party with the great Old Bill Williams. Pike described Williams as,

... all muscle and sinew ... the most indefatigable hunter and trapper in the world.

Old Bill

Williams decided that enough was enough at the same time as Pike and with six companions, returned to Taos. His account mentions little in the way of hardships and a few hungry days would have been of little moment to him.

An ex-soldier and ex-missionary who became an Osage Indian with two Osage wives, Williams is the subject of many tales. Hunting for game, he once ran into a group of Blackfoot Indians. He killed four, hid from the rest in a side canyon for two days, then made a raft and floated down the river back to the trappers' camp. He was prematurely aged by the event, hence his nickname. Later he was surprised by a party of Apache and stripped of everything. Naked, he travelled 160 miles through mountain and desert, eventually being picked up and welcomed by the Zuni, a Pueblo people. He was killed in 1849, at the age of 62, probably by Ute Indians.[1]

Pike's friend Titcomb may have accompanied Williams or may have continued on with Harris. If so, he would have reached Fort Smith three months later. Pike and he never met again but Pike dedicated his book, *Prose Sketches and Poems*, to him; a warm, if strange, dedication:

> *Farewell:- may the world frown less upon you than it has, and may you keep a corner in your heart for the author.*

Pike then led the group (which may be the source of Allsopp's story) more or less due east, no doubt with the guidance of Lewis who had just completed the journey in the opposite direction. Even so, after six weeks, experiencing feast and famine along the way, Pike's group eventually reached a road which Lewis did not recognise or know existed.

---

[1] Hence *Utah* although Utes were also in New Mexico and Colorado.

Fort Smith

Pike had intended to go south to New Orleans but, turning the wrong way, went north to Fort Smith. It had all been a trying, if eye-opening, experience right to the end. Six days before reaching Fort Smith, Pike sold his rifle to some Choctaw Indians *for about a dozen pounds of meat.* Fort Smith was hardly a place for quiet recovery. As late as 1870, it was described as a *bustling community full of brothels, saloons and outlaws.* The remake of the film *True Grit* was set in the Fort Smith of that time.

Once back in Arkansas, Pike took up teaching again,[1] married Mary Ann Hamilton, a wealthy woman, and had ten children.[2] Pike bought the local newspaper, became a lawyer, played a major role in the development of the courts of Arkansas, learned French to assist in setting up the legal system of Louisiana and translated the Louisiana Civil Code into English. He spoke several Indian languages, won a major case for the Choctaw Indian nation against the government and fought for the Confederacy during the American Civil War. He died in 1891.

Four years later, it was discovered that he had been meeting Satan every Friday afternoon at 3 o'clock. What is more, his secretary had betrothed herself to the Demon *Asmodeus.*[3] How did he find the time?

---

[1] He taught Latin, Greek, Algebra and Higher Mathematics.

[2] Only three survived him.

[3] Ashmodeus appears in the apocryphal *Book of Tobit.* He is often referred to as the demon of lust. There is a wonderful community opera entitled *Tobias and the angel* by Jonathan Dove and David Lan. The part of Raphael for the counter tenor is exceptional.

Chapter three: The Devil and Mr Pike

Unwittingly a central figure in a masonic hoax, Pike's fame has created many problems for freemasonry, the most important being his handling of Isaiah 14:12-14. He was right but that has not stopped many people seizing on his words as proof of devil worship in freemasonry.

In this chapter, we will look at papal pronouncements, freemasonry and religion, allegories, the nature of open-mindedness and the tricky word 'belief'. That anyone was taken in by the hoax perpetrated by Léo Taxil takes some believing but some people still use it as evidence of devil-worship in freemasonry. There must be something in the background to the devil and the goat that aids such suspension of disbelief and something about Pike that enables such beliefs to stick. This something is the tale of plagiarism I spoke of earlier.

We witnessed his courage and his endurance in the previous chapter. I fear that in this chapter, we see another side to him. We need to understand more about Pike and the hostages to fortune that he has left us with.

Following the chapter is an interlude on the nature of belief which is a matter of linguistic philosophy. I have followed Ludwig Wittgenstein here, perhaps the greatest of modern philosophers. If you find it heavy going, do feel free to move on but I rather hope that you will give it a go.

M. Taxil and Pope Leo

> *In Marseille, nobody has forgotten the story of the invasion of the sharks. Letters from local fishermen described their escape from the most dire dangers. Panic spread among swimmers and beaches were deserted for weeks. A general led a hundred armed men to explore in all directions but returned empty-handed. A later inquiry showed that the letters came from fishermen who did not exist and that all the letters were written in the same hand.*[1]

> *The scientific world was thrilled by the wonderful discovery of an underwater city, glimpsed at the bottom of Lake Geneva, that must have been built during the Roman occupation. Inhabitants were astounded when tourists arrived but the local boatmen took them out on the lake and oil was spread on the water so that the city could be seen better. A Polish archaeologist reportedly recognised the remains of a town square with what might well have been part of an equestrian statue.*

Leo Taxil, the pen name of Gabriel Jogand-Pages born Marseilles 1854, was proud of his hoaxes. To top these two, he decided to dupe the Roman Catholic Church. We have the story from William Giddings Sibley's book, *The Story of Freemasonry*, written a few years after the event, and from Taxil himself.

In 1884, Pope Leo XIII issued *Humanum Genus*, the first of four encyclicals he wrote attacking freemasonry:

> *At this time, the partisans of evil are vehemently coming together, led on by that well organized and widespread association called the freemasons. No longer making a secret of their purposes, they are now rising up against God himself. They are publicly and openly planning the destruction of the Holy Church with the set purpose of despoiling the blessings obtained for us through Jesus Christ our saviour.*

Most germane to Taxil's hoax, the encyclical ends:

> *In this insane and wicked endeavour we may almost see the implacable hatred and spirit of revenge with which Satan himself is inflamed against Jesus Christ.*

The encyclical is a very strange work but it may sound just a little less strange in France than in England. In 1877, the Grand Orient of France decided not to have the *Volume of the Sacred Law* (usually the Bible) open in lodge and to admit atheists.[2] This led to the view that French freemasonry was anti-church. A useful 1952 pamphlet, written by Humphrey Johnson for the Catholic Truth Society, presents the Catholic point of view.

Leading up to *Humanum Genus*

Humanum Genus did not represent a new and sudden departure by Pope Leo XIII. It was one in a series of such pronouncements. The first such was made by Pope

---

[1] A curious story, especially given that there are said to be 47 species of shark in the Med. At the time of Taxil's hoax, hammerheads would have been sighted regularly even though the population is thought to have been in decline for two hundred years. None have been seen in coastal waters since 1963.

[2] As we have seen, the United Grand Lodge of England ceased recognition of the Grand Orient in 1878.

Clement XII as early as 1738, only 21 years after the formation of the Premier Grand Lodge. In the encyclical, *In Eminenti*, he commented that freemasonry was *spreading far and wide and daily growing in strength* and attacked it for being open to men of all religions and for its secrecy:

> *Common gossip has made clear that ... men of any religion or sect ... are joined together ... by a strict and unbreakable bond which obliges them, both by an oath upon the holy Bible and by a host of grievous punishment, to an inviolable silence about all that they do in secret together ... (and) if they were not doing evil they would not have so great a hatred of the light.*

It is a pity that the Pope relied on *common gossip* for such an important document. A little research would have clarified matters and avoided much later embarrassment. In 1751, *Providas Romanorum* did little more than reinforce *In Eminenti* but in 1821, *Ecclesiam a Jesu Christo*, while making the same accusation of religious openness, confused freemasons with the *Carbonari*,[1] taking the latter to task for their belief that it was legitimate for the people to rebel against unjust rulers. This is perhaps not the most revolutionary statement ever made but one, oddly enough, which a freemason would probably not support. After all, the first degree charge contains the injunction:

> *As a citizen of the world, I enjoin you to be exemplary in the discharge of your civil duties; by never proposing or at all countenancing any act which may have a tendency to subvert the peace and good order of society.*

In 1826, *Quo Graviora* used the accusation of secrecy to ban freemasonry for Catholics but the papal statements of 1829, 1832 and 1846 seem to represent a change in tone, as if the church had become defensive. These three statements were not directed explicitly at freemasonry but at anyone who accepted freedom of religious affiliation. Thus in 1829 *Traditi Humilitati* attacked the,

> *... sophists of this age who do not admit any difference among the different professions of faith and who think that the portal of eternal salvation opens for all from any religion.*

It also attacked new versions of the Bible:

> *We must also be wary of those who publish the Bible with new interpretations contrary to the church's laws. They skilfully distort the meaning by their own interpretation ... rarely without perverse little inserts to insure that the reader imbibes their lethal poison instead of the saving water of salvation.*

In 1832, *Mirari Vos* bemoaned the fact that people no longer accepted the statements of the church without question and attacked *indifferentism*:

> *(A) perverse opinion ... spread on all sides by the fraud of the wicked who claim*

---

[1] A loose political and anti-clerical association in Italy, France and Portugal which sought a constitution of benefit to the common people. While they adopted the slogan of *freedom and independence*, there was no real agreement as to what form of government they sought. The Carbonari were prepared to use direct action and took up arms several times between 1820 and 1830. Their most famous member was Lafayette who had served under Washington in the American Revolution. The Carbonari had surface similarities to freemasonry but then so did many other bodies.

that it is possible to obtain the eternal salvation of the soul by the profession of any kind of religion, as long as morality is maintained.

In 1846 *Qui Pluribus* is aimed likewise at those who,

... boldly venture to explain and interpret the words of god by their own judgement, misusing their reason and holding the opinion that these words are like a human work.

Thus, by the 1890s, there was a tradition, almost an autonomic response, of attacks on anyone who did not immediately accept the Catholic Church's exclusive right to determine the nature of belief.

Devil worship

Taxil had been initiated into freemasonry in 1881. He had gone no further but, using the encyclical as a springboard, created an imaginary set of masonic rites, representing them as *a hideous form of Devil-Worship*. Sibley gets a bit carried away himself:

One entire volume he devoted to Female Masons, on which impossible foundation[1] he constructed a shameful edifice of fiction, full of shockingly scandalous and beastly fabrications that were received with delight by the papal authorities, who saw in them perfect justification for the attitude of their church toward masonry.

One of the rites that Taxil invented is admittedly fairly revolting but if you are of a bloodthirsty disposition you might enjoy the fecundity of his imagination:

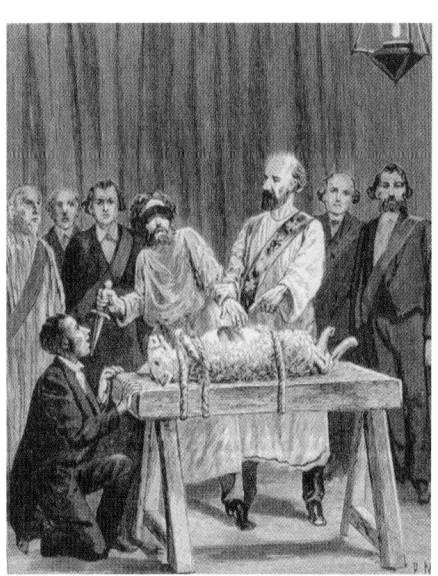

Before a man is admitted to the higher degrees he is blindfolded and led into a room with a live sheep on the floor. The animal's mouth and feet are secured and it is clean shaven so that its skin feels to the touch like that of a human being.

The candidate is told that the sheep's body is that of a Mason who has given away the secrets of the order and must therefore die according to ancient law.

He is given a knife as the executioner and, and after some ceremonial, is persuaded to 'kill the traitor' by plunging the knife repeatedly into the body of the sheep, which he imagines to be that of a human being.

Not easy to believe perhaps, unless you were already convinced. As the central character in Umberto Eco's novel, *The Prague Cemetery,*[2] says:

---

[1] Less impossible today; there are several organisations of women's freemasonry.

[2] A very funny account of the creation of conspiracy theories.

People only believe what they already know and this is the beauty of the Universal Form of Conspiracy.

Luciferan masonry

Taxil had his greatest fun in creating *Palladism* or *Luciferan Masonry*.

> *We located the centre of Palladism at Charleston in the United States, with the late General Albert Pike, Grand Master of the Scottish Rite in South Carolina, as Founder. This celebrated freemason, endowed with vast erudition, had been one of the highlights of the order. Through us, he became the first Luciferan Pope, supreme chief of all freemasons around the globe, conferring regularly each Friday at 3 pm with Lucifer in person.*

Taxil's typist, Diana Vaughn, became, as Sibley reports,

> *... the direct descendant of a man to whose embraces the lascivious Venus-Astarte submitted, and whose life had been extended thirty-three years for the propagation of demoniacal designs. As a girl she betrothed herself to the Demon Asmodeus, afterwards appeared before Satan in Charleston, and was by him consecrated as his masonic high priestess in the presence of Albert Pike. She possessed supernatural powers, with the ability to turn herself into liquid and pass through stone walls; a Very Terrible Personage indeed.*

For these and other revelations, Taxil claimed to have been congratulated by the Roman Catholic Church who, as difficult as it is to credit, seem to have accepted and believed what he wrote. It was seen as evidence for the truth of *Humanum Genus*. Johnson offers support for this:

> *Stories of the cult of Lucifer in the lodges (in France) were eagerly accepted and the writer, Léo Taxil, was enabled to practise an elaborate hoax. A notorious free-thinker, he feigned conversion to Catholicism, obtained absolution from the nuncio in Paris, Mgr. Rendi, and concocted a series of bogus revelations about Luciferan Masonry ...*

However, people started to demand evidence of his claims especially when in 1896 AE Waite published *Devil Worship in France*, saying that Taxil's story:

> *... deserves to rank among the most extraordinary literary swindles of the present, perhaps of any, century.*

In April 1897, Taxil called a meeting in the hall of the Geographical Society in Paris, ostensibly to produce Diana Vaughn, the bride of Asmodeus. Instead he confessed to the hoax. Taxil's audience did not receive his confession in quite the way he had hoped. Rather than laughter and applause, he received a police escort out of the hall. He left Paris and lived quietly thereafter, dying in 1907.

Taxil and Pike

Taxil used Pike's name because he was dead and because he had a reputation and a standing in freemasonry. Despite Taxil's confession, many people to this day still claim to believe his story about Pike and the devil. I said earlier that it is impossible to dissuade some people from even the most irrational beliefs and here is an example. Rather than accept Taxil's story as a hoax, some people prefer to believe that the meeting at which Taxil retracted his claims, never occurred. For example:

The record of the confession runs to more than 13,000 words. It is recorded in full conversational style so it is clearly not a press release. Go back in your mind to the means of writing available in 1897 and then try to imagine these 13,000+ words being recorded in their full moment by moment spontaneity. Even today this would be a serious undertaking for any journalist using sophisticated equipment. The 'confession' is a carefully crafted deception.[1]

The writer's word count is wrong and the confession amounts to nearly 25,000 words. He is also wrong about the nature of the confession. It is not in *full conversational style* but even then, the disbeliever could argue that no editor is going to devote space for 25,000 words in a daily newspaper to any one subject. After all, Parisian daily newspapers at the time only had four pages. It seems a good argument but let us look at the opening lines of the report in *Le Frondeur*.

With more or less impartiality, all newspapers reported the memorable evening at the Geographic Society on April 19, 1897. We thought the best thing to do was to reproduce the full text of M. Léo Taxil's conference.

The dailies did indeed report Taxil's event but only *Le Frondeur* gave the full text. The latter was not a newspaper but a weekly journal and it had Taxil's speech notes. After all, Taxil had once been its editor. Read the ending:

An indescribable tumult meets this conclusion. Some laugh more and more and applaud the lecturer. Catholics scream and hiss. Abbot Garnier steps on a chair and attempts to address the audience, but he is hindered by the hoot. A few listeners strike up the comic song: O Sacred Heart of Jesus!

Taxil wrote the copy himself and gave the event a very different ending. The audience is reported to be very much on his side, loving what he said. The meeting did happen, if not quite this way. Here is my translation of the report in *Le Figaro*. Its account of Taxil's reception does not accord with his own.[2]

'You seem to have no doubt yourself that you are a filthy scoundrel!' This interruption, absolutely devoid of kindness if not of truth, was the first to be made last night in the hall of the Geographical Society, during the most instructive statements made by Mr Léo Taxil. Indeed, it seemed that the interruption accurately reflected the views of the audience, save a few friends – themselves rather disgusted – from the speaker's claque.

Mr Léo Taxil seemed quite oblivious to the disgust that he aroused in an audience in which free-thinkers were as numerous as Catholics. For nearly two hours he boasted, a smile on his lips, of having acted out a comedy of conversion during twelve years under the banner of the Church and of having tricked priests, bishops, cardinals and the Pope himself. However, he may have fooled fewer people than he imagines.

Mr Léo Taxil summarised what he calls 'the most colossal hoax of modern times' … Diana Vaughan played the part of a former Luciferan converted to Catholicism, whose preposterous revelations about the mysteries of Palladism and freemasonry, astonished the religious world in recent years. These alleged revelations came, of

---

[1] From *freedom-ministries.com* among others.

[2] I have edited out a metaphor which does not translate into English.

course, from Léo Taxil. His objective, he admitted, was to make money by exploiting the credulity of Catholics.

But all comes to an end and we now learn that Diana Vaughan was a myth and Léo Taxil simply a comedian … Last night he was roundly booed. But the clergy, who all too easily opened their arms to him, would do well to be less gullible in the future. This is the only moral to be drawn from the adventure.

Pike and Lucifer

So why would anyone wish to deny that Taxil had retracted his story? The answer is Pike. If a freemason as prominent as Pike is shown to be a devil-worshipper, all freemasons can be tarred with the same brush. Can Pike be so accused? At one point in his writings, Pike comments on *Isaiah* 14:12-14 which in the King James Version reads:

How art thou fallen from heaven, O Lucifer, son of the morning! How art thou cut down to the ground, which didst weaken the nations! For thou hast said in thine heart, I will ascend into heaven. I will exalt my throne above the stars of god. I will sit also upon the mount of the congregation, in the sides of the north. I will ascend above the heights of the clouds. I will be like the most High.

This is the only appearance in the Bible of the word *lucifer* and of it Pike writes:

Lucifer, the Light-bearer! Strange and mysterious name to give to the Spirit of Darkness! Lucifer, the Son of the Morning! Is it he who bears the Light, and with its splendours intolerable, blinds feeble, sensual, or selfish souls? Doubt it not!

The word *lucifer* is derived from the Latin *lux, lucis* meaning *light* and thus can be taken to mean *light bearer* or *light maker*. The name *Lucifer* was chosen for a brand of matches invented by British chemist John Walker in 1827.[1] Pike is saying no more than that *Lucifer* is an odd name for a being usually thought of as the Prince of Darkness but his comments have been seized upon by those with more enthusiasm than comprehension as proof that freemasonry is devil-worship:

What a revelation! From the first degree, the first Initiation, the Mason is urged mightily to 'seek the Light'! Almost every person in Western Civilization will assume that this 'Light' is the revelation of the god of the Bible. Yet, here, Albert Pike is saying that Lucifer is the Light-bearer of freemasonry. Freemasonry is actually a worship of Lucifer.[2]

I was recently given a copy of the Gideon Bible, frequently found in hotels and also known as the *New International Version*. Here *Isaiah* 14:12 is set out as poetry:

How are you fallen from heaven,
O morning star, son of the dawn!

No *lucifer*. The word has disappeared. The Bible collector, Glyn Jarrett, says that apart from the 1982 New King James version, the only recent Bibles that use the word are a Welsh edition and a Spanish one of 1960. Pike was right to be puzzled

---

[1] As in: *While you've a Lucifer to light your fag, smile, boys, that's the style.* The chorus from the WWI song, *Pack up your Troubles*.

[2] From *Cutting Edge Ministries* but the identical passage occurs on many similar websites.

by the choice of the word *lucifer* as the name of the devil. It has been a misunderstanding all along and isn't a name at all. Moreover, the reference has nothing to do with a supernatural being. If we seek to find who the phrase, *morning star, son of the dawn,* refers to, we find in *Isaiah* 14:3:

> On the day the lord gives you relief from suffering and turmoil and cruel bondage, you will take this taunt against the King of Babylon:

It is a title given to the King of Babylon. If there is a devil, he is not named Lucifer.

Open-mindedness and Catholicism

Freemasonry says nothing at all about religion except that discussion of religion is forbidden in lodge. Freemasonry is open to men of all faiths. That is one of its strengths and a great source of pride. As Pike himself says:

> … masonry wisely requires no more than a belief in one great all-powerful deity, the father and preserver of the Universe.

Open-mindedness is central to freemasonry but, as we have seen, it is common for encyclicals to attack open-mindedness. Leo XIII:

> They thereby teach the great error of this age - that a regard for religion should be held as an indifferent matter and that all religions are alike.

Masonry does nothing of the kind. It says that each man should worship in his own way and that way is of no concern to other freemasons. Pope Leo sees open-mindedness as,

> … calculated to bring about the ruin of all forms of religion, and especially of the Catholic religion, which, as it is the only one that is true, cannot, without great injustice, be regarded as merely equal to other religions.

The Roman Catholic Church holds that all other religious beliefs (Christian and otherwise) are in error. In the Catholic Encyclopædia, we read about *dogmatic intolerance*:

> Nowhere is dogmatic intolerance so necessary a rule of life as in the domain of religious belief, since for each individual his eternal salvation is at stake. Just as there can be no alternative multiplication tables, so there can be but a single true religion, which, by the very fact of its existence, protests against all other religions as false … If, therefore, the Catholic Church also claims the right of dogmatic intolerance with regard to her teaching, it is unjust to reproach her for exercising this right. With the imperturbable conviction that she was founded by the God-Man Jesus Christ as the 'pillar and ground of the truth' (1 Timothy 3:15) and endowed with full power to teach, to rule, and to sanctify, she regards dogmatic intolerance not alone as her incontestable right, but also as a sacred duty.

In the words of *Humanum Genus,*

> … it is the special and exclusive duty of the Catholic Church fully to set forth in words truths divinely received, to teach, besides other divine helps to salvation, the authority of its office, and to defend the same with perfect purity.

The problem with Pike

Following Harold Netland, in his article *Inclusivism and exclusivism*, we can list five possible views of religious differences.

1. *All religions are false.*
2. *There is no way of deciding which religion is correct.*
3. *Each religion can be considered true for those who believe in it.*
4. *Each religion is partially true of the divine.*
5. *There is only one true religion.*

The first is more or less atheism[1] and the second could be called agnosticism or deism according to your choice. The third is closest to a view that freemasonry might hold, if it had one, while the fifth is the view of Catholicism (and many other religions.) Pike's stance is closest to the fourth view and might be described as *syncretism*; a combination of beliefs drawn from several religions.

That is Pike's own affair. As far as freemasonry is concerned, his choice of such a belief is a matter entirely for him. His view is not a Christian view, certainly not the Roman Catholic view and nor is it in any way a masonic view. Freemasonry has no view of religion at all. It merely says that for as long as a candidate believes in a supreme being, (being fairly vague about what this is, rather in the traditional manner of the Church of England) he is eligible to be made a mason. This counts out atheists (just about[2]) but virtually no one else.

The problem with Pike is that he sets out his own views as being truths of masonry. That, you might say, is nothing new. After all, many summonses for Lodge meetings in England quote Dr George Oliver (1782-1867) and his stricture on the number and quality of candidates. His general views on freemasonry, his *erroneous theories and fanciful speculations* as Mackey and Haywood call them, are now usually ignored. Dr Oliver is not thought of as a spokesman for the Order. Pike is.

How big is the problem?

When writing about the seventeenth degree (*Knight of the East and West*) of the Scottish Rite, Pike describes a golden age of religious tolerance and co-operation:

> *All the barriers that had formerly kept the nations apart, were thrown down; and while the People of the West readily connected their faith with those of the East, those of the Orient hastened to learn the traditions of Rome and the legends of Athens. While the Philosophers of Greece, all (except the disciples of Epicurus[3]) more or less Platonists, seized eagerly upon the beliefs and doctrines of the East; the Jews and Egyptians, before then the most exclusive of all peoples, yielded to that eclecticism which prevailed among their masters, the Greeks and Romans.*

---

[1] But not necessarily so. It is possible to have a belief in a god but not in any religion.

[2] The difference between atheism and religious belief in modern theology is not great.

[3] Epicurus was a materialist who dispensed with the Platonic theory of Forms. In his view, everything that happens is simply the result of mechanical laws. There is no reason for anything, just a cause.

Where he gets this most unlikely story from, I do not know. I have not found it in Constant,[1] and perhaps it is uniquely Pike's. He follows it with an even more amazing passage in which he lists what he says are the ideas constituted by freemasonry. He includes an account of creation which would not be recognised by any freemason:

> *The world was created, not by the supreme being, but by a secondary agent, who is but his word, and by the types which are but his ideas, aided by an intelligence or wisdom, which gives one of his attributes; in which we see the occult meaning of the necessity of recovering 'the Word' ... that the object of this terrestrial life is to disengage itself of its body or its sepulchre; that it will ascend to the heavenly regions when ever it shall be purified ...*

He speaks of angels and demons who dwell in and govern the planets and the suffering of spirits who are remote from god and imprisoned in matter and the attempt to re-enter into union with the supreme being. All this, Pike claims, is,

> *... the meaning, now almost forgotten in our Lodges, of the mode of preparation of the candidate for apprenticeship and his tests and purifications in the first degree.*[2]

He says that these ideas have been forgotten and,

> *... in the present mutilated condition of the symbolic degrees, they are disguised and overlaid with fiction and absurdity, or present themselves as casual hints that are passed by wholly unnoticed.*

Now all this gives us a very big problem. We know where he gets this stuff from, and we will deal with it when we come to discuss gnosticism and Hermes Trismegistus, but it cannot be said strongly enough that this is absolutely not the teaching of freemasonry. Pike's view is not only inaccurate but wildly inaccurate.

The Craft degrees

Pike attempts to present freemasonry as a set of specific religious beliefs, as a route to the truth. He may castigate the craft or blue degrees as being mutilated and disguised but the opposite is true. They make no attempt to present religious dogma but tell a simple story; one which really has little to do with a supreme being. It is an allegory based upon the building of King Solomon's Temple. Some of this story is taken from the Old Testament; some stems from unknown sources, perhaps to do with legends about Noah; some from stories told by the operative stonemasons, and some from creative writing in the 18th century.[3] No one pretends that the ritual's stories are true any more than the stories of Thomas Malory's *Le Morte D'Arthur*, John Bunyan's Pilgrim's *Progress*, or Dante's *Divine Comedy*. They are all allegories. Nevertheless all have important lessons to teach; those in masonry

---

[1] Which is not to say that it is not there.

[2] Among his outlandish claims is that masonry continues the teaching of the Essenes, who gathered together the truths from the Orient and the Occident. They didn't and it doesn't.

[3] The history of freemasonry and its rituals is a fascinating subject, made all the more so because so much of it is unknown and a matter of speculation. We live in hope of discovery of more old texts and references.

exemplifying virtues which we are exhorted to demonstrate in our daily lives: honesty, loyalty, citizenship, fidelity, brotherly love, charity, excellence and humility.

The genuine power of masonry is that, in being open to men (and increasingly women) of all beliefs, it brings together brethren from all over the world. Its requirement that all candidates must acknowledge a supreme being stems from the belief that, unless virtue is rewarded in heaven,[1] there will be no motivation for virtuous action. This belief may be logically and factually mistaken but that is another matter. Pike, in attempting to set out specific beliefs, does violence to what we call the *Landmarks* of the Order; the very premises and values we hold most dear.

What do we do about Pike?

Frankly there is little we can do. We can acknowledge his courage and his stamina; we can be intrigued by his experiences in the Old West; we can certainly admire his ability in languages and his work rate in the law and in politics; we can absolve him from devil worship or indeed anything to do with the devil; and we can feel sorry that his life's work was tarnished by the trickster Taxil. However, we can only regret the hostage to fortune he has left us. It might be for the best if we could disown his work but his name is so engrained in American masonry that this is impossible.

There are unfortunately other hostages he has left us. Pike was a leading lawyer and politician. Perhaps it was part of his nature and perhaps partly being self-educated that he tended to take strong and even extreme views. This led him, in the end, to support the Confederacy even though he said he believed in the Union. He took the position that each State had the right to decide its own domestic laws, particularly about property rights - and slaves were property. He was ready,

> ...to tell those Northern miscreants that we will brook no foreign meddling with our rights, our property, our lives.

His argument was doomed to failure. The North simply disagreed that men and women were property and had the political power to make this stick in Congress. The causes of the civil war were no doubt complex but their focal point was the slave question.

In 1832, the year that Pike arrived in Fort Smith, there were just over two million slaves in the USA, about fifteen percent of the total population.[2] By 1860, there were nearly four million slaves, still representing about fifteen percent of the population; but by 1860 the slave population in New England, New York, New Jersey, Pennsylvania and the Mid and Far West had effectively declined to zero. Slavery had become a Southern matter. Even within the slaving States, there were great variations. In Delaware only two percent of the population were slaves. In the District of Columbia the figure was four percent but in some states the slave population was greater than the free population. Mississippi had 436,631 slaves and 354,674 free men and women; South Carolina, 402,406 slaves and 301,302 free men and women.

---

[1] Sentimentally referred to as the *Grand Lodge above* just as golfers talk of the *Pearly Gates Links*.

[2] Always excluding Indians, which is indicative of American views about the indigenous population.

Racism

Was Pike a racist? In today's terms, yes. In the eyes of the abolitionists in those days, yes; to the black population, yes, but in the eyes of the Arkansas cotton farmers? Brown points out that the economy of the part of Arkansas where Pike earned his living depended wholly on cotton farming which itself was dependent upon slavery. Brown argues that he could not object to his clients using slaves because:

> *Fees from cotton planters composed most of his income, and anything that affected them adversely affected him likewise.*

It has been said in his defence that he argued against the reintroduction of the slave trade and he described slavery as an evil. He wrote:

> *I know it is an evil, as great cities are an evil; as the concentration of capital in a few hands, oppressing labor is an evil; as the utter annihilation of free-will and individuality in the army and navy is an evil; as in this world everything is mixed of good and evil.*

But evil in this sense is a *necessary evil*. One that cannot be prevented. Pike argued that only god is to blame for slavery:

> *Such is the rule of god's providence, and the mode by which he has chosen so to arrange the affairs of the world.*

For him slavery was a financial issue, an economic matter of investment returns. He also argued that abolishing slavery would be;

> *... not only to impoverish vast numbers of our citizens, but to release us from all obligations to provide for the sick, the feeble, the old and the disabled. Three millions of human beings would be left without protectors. We would supply ourselves with other labourers, with Lascars, Chinese, Peons from Mexico. The large body of our negroes would become drones and paupers.*

To his argument that slaves could not survive when freed, the great black orator, Frederick Douglass (1818-1895), replied:

> *It is said, what will you do with them? ... Our answer is, do nothing with them; mind your business, and let them mind theirs. Your doing with them is their greatest misfortune.*

> *They have been undone by your doings, and all they now ask, and really have need of at your hands, is just to let them alone. As coloured men, we only ask to be allowed to do with ourselves, subject only to the same great laws for the welfare of human society which apply to other men ...*

> *When you, our white fellow-countrymen, have attempted to do anything for us, it has generally been to deprive us of some right, power or privilege which you yourself would die before you would submit to have taken from you.*[1]

---

[1] Writing in 1862. Douglas, born Frederick Bailey, had escaped slavery and was a clear and living example that black people could reason, function and speak just as well as whites!

Other *distinguished coloured men* pictured

Robert Brown Elliott (1842-1884) was a South Carolina lawyer and politician, elected to the US Congress. Known for his dazzling oratorial skills, fighting for Civil Rights and against the Ku Klux Klan.

Blanche K Bruce (1841-1898) was a slave who became a successful plantation owner, and the second African American to serve in the United States Senate. He sought to protect the rights not only of African Americans but also of other minorities including Native Americans.

Henry Highland Garnet (1815 –1882) advocated militant abolitionism, urging blacks to take action to control their own future. He supported emigration of American free blacks and was appointed as the US Minister to Liberia where he died.

William Wells Brown (1815-1884), an important part of the Underground Railroad helping slaves escape to freedom, he later became the first African American to publish a novel or a play. He was an internationally known speaker and a friend of Victor Hugo. He was active in the temperance movement, women's suffrage and prison reform.

Richard T Greener (1844-1922) was Harvard's first African American graduate. He became a Professor of Philosophy at the University of South Carolina and later became Dean of the Law Department at Howard University. He was appointed US Consul, first to Bombay and then to Vladivostok. The Chinese Government decorated him with the Order of Double Dragon.

Pinckney Benton Stewart Pinchback (1837-1921) was the first African American to become a state governor (of Louisiana).

Rt Rev Richard Allen (1760–1831) founded the first American independent black church.

John Mercer Langston (1829–1897) was the first Dean of the law school at Howard University and the first president of what is now Virginia State University. He was one of the first African American people elected to public office when becoming a town clerk in Ohio.

Ebenezer D Bassett (1833–1908) was the first African-American diplomat, being the US ambassador to Haiti, then of strategic importance as a naval coaling station. He was later an advisor to President Ulysses S Grant.

Joseph Rainey (1832-1887) was the first African American Congressman, re-elected four times to the US House of Representatives.

Decline

In 1861, the civil war came. Pike was made a Brigadier-General and given the task of raising Indians troops to fight for the Confederacy. This he did on the understanding that such troops would be used only in defence of their own lands. In the fog of war, this understanding was forgotten or ignored and Indians were used, disastrously, against units of the Union Army. Pike resigned in July 1862.

After the war, his property was confiscated and he was impoverished for the rest of his life.[1] He was offered a pardon by President Johnson in August 1865 but deemed the terms unacceptable. His friends finally achieved an acceptable pardon for him a year later. Family tragedies had built one on the other. One son had drowned in 1859 and the other was killed during the Civil War. His daughter died in 1869 and his wife in 1876 with dementia. He started up a legal practice again and even edited a newspaper but it seems his heart was not in it. He became quite reclusive. In 1868, he moved to Washington DC where he lived for the rest of his life, devoting his time entirely to freemasonry from 1880 until he died in 1891.

Pike and Constant

Pike is forever associated with Constant and not only through Taxil's hoax. One's first impression of Pike's major work is that of reading Constant all over again - which turns out not to be accidental. AE Waite is most censorious of Pike,

---

[1] So much so that in 1879, the Supreme Council voted him an annuity and gave him a place to live in the Supreme Council building.

declaring his literary methods to be intolerable because he never identifies his sources and never differentiates between the words of another author and his own. More than this, Waite accuses Pike of actual plagiarism:

> *I cannot trace all its sources, nor does he offer the least assistance, but the volume swarms with citations from Éliphas Lévi ... without any acknowledgement ... and also without marks of quotation.*

He concluded that there was little original in Pike's book and that where it was not a straight translation from Constant's French, it was no more than a commentary on his ideas. The most startling plagiarism is the very phrase that gets Pike into trouble. In Constant's book, *L'Histoire de la Magie*, a book that appeared five years after his *Dogme et Rituel*, he comments on the word *lucifer*:

> *Lucifer! Le porte-lumière! quel nom étrange donné à l'esprit des ténèbres. Quoi c'est lui qui porte la lumière et qui aveugle les âmes faibles?*

I translate this to read:

> *Lucifer! The light bearer! A strange name to be given to the spirit of the shadows! Is it he who bears the light which blinds feeble souls?*

In Pike's version, it reads, as you may recall:

> *Lucifer, the Light-bearer! Strange and mysterious name to give to the Spirit of Darkness! Lucifer, the Son of the Morning! Is it he who bears the Light, and with its splendours intolerable, blinds feeble, sensual, or selfish souls?*

(Overleaf, I give a longer example of the plagiarism that Waite complains of.)

Pike's importance

When starting on this book, I had no idea that Pike and Constant were thus connected. Not knowing that Pike had plagiarised Constant, I thought that Pike was little more than the innocent victim of Taxil's hoax; and I suppose he still is.

Had Pike stuck to re-writing the ritual for the Rose Croix, his views would have mattered much less. In and of himself, he would not have been of enormous importance to masonry. Unfortunately, through his book, which was once given to every member by the Supreme Council in the USA, Constant's dodgy theories are given credibility in masonic circles, and even more so in the circles of those who wish to damage masonry.

This is all the more unfortunate because Constant's engraving of *le bouc de sabbat*, derived as it is from his own imagination, is so often taken to be a masonic picture. Without Pike, Constant would have remained an insignificant 19th century occultist and his goat faced image would have been equally insignificant.

An example

Pike *Morals and Dogma*, Page 609 in the Forgotten Books edition, *28th degree Knight of the Sun or Prince Adept*:	Constant (Éliphas Lévi) as translated by AE Waite. *Dogma and Ritual* Volume Two, Page 42/3, *The Septenary of Talismans*:
The world, the ancients believed, was governed by Seven Secondary Causes; and these were the universal forces, known to the Hebrews by the plural name ELOHIM. These forces, analogous and contrary one to the other, produce equilibrium by their contrasts, and regulate the movements of the spheres.	*In the belief of the ancients, the world is governed by seven secondary causes - secundii, as Trithemius calls them - which are the universal forces designated by Moses under the plural name of Elohim, gods. These forces, analogous and contrary to one another, produce equilibrium by their contrasts and rule the movement of the spheres.*
The Hebrews called them the Seven great Archangels, and gave them names, each of which, being a combination of another word with AL, the first Phoenician Nature-god, considered as the Principle of Light, represented them as His manifestations. Other peoples assigned to these Spirits the government of the Seven Planets then known, and gave them the names of their great divinities.	*The Hebrews termed them the seven great archangels, giving them the names of Michael, Gabriel, Raphael, Anael, Samael, Zadkiel and Oriphiel. The Christian Gnostics named the four last Uriel, Barachiel, Sealtiel and Jehudiel. Other nations attributed to these spirits the government of the seven chief planets, and assigned to them the names of their chief divinities.*

Interlude: The Trouble with *Belief*

Is there a being who opposes the deity or is the concept of a devil just a personification of temptations we feel towards what we know we should not do? In some ways, this question is about modes of thought. Just as the ancients believed that if something moved then someone must have moved it, so we may think that if we feel temptation then someone must have tempted us.[1]

Belief

In a moment, I shall introduce you to the philosopher, Ludwig Wittgenstein, but just now I want to use something he said. He spoke about the word *believe* being odd. Let us take some examples:

1. *I believe that there is a 97 bus that goes to Whitehall.*
2. *I believe that you'll find Loch Tay is in Scotland.*
3. *I believe the concert starts at 3 pm.*
4. *I believe Pete's car is a BMW.*
5. *I believe in the Devil.*

Ignoring interpersonal overtones, statements 1 to 4 are about giving information without committing fully to it. Sentence 3, for example, is hesitant, less strong than the statement, *The concert starts at 3 pm.* The message of the word *believe* in statements 1 to 4 is that the listener would be best advised to check for him or herself. Sentence 5 is the odd one out. It is not a hesitant claim. It is not a claim that can be later checked, such as the location of Loch Tay, the time of the concert or the make of Pete's car. It is a special use of the word *believe.*

Try changing the word *believe* to the word *think.*

6. *I think that there is a 97 bus that goes to Whitehall.*
7. *I think that you'll find Loch Tay is in Scotland.*
8. *I think the concert starts at 3 pm.*
9. *I think Pete's car is a BMW.*
10. *I think in the Devil.*

The sentences from 6 to 9 retain the meaning of those from 1 to 4 but 10 is very different from 5 and makes no sense at all. If we change it to a form closer to that of the other statements:

11. *I think there is a devil*

it makes sense again but now it is very different indeed from 5. To give it a context, sentence 11 may be used as an answer to a question such as, '*Are there any other characters in the school play I haven't mentioned?*' '*Oh, I think there is a devil as well,*' but the most common context of sentence 5 is not a matter of the school play but of supernatural beings and in such cases it means *know* in a very specific way – knowing without any evidence or possibility of evidence. This, Wittgenstein would have said, is odd. He advises:

---

[1] Oscar Wilde is reputed to have said, *I can resist anything except temptation.* Actually, Lord Darlington says it in Wilde's *Lady Windermere's Fan.*

Don't look at it as a matter of course, but as a most remarkable thing, that the verbs 'believe', 'wish', 'will', display all the inflexions possessed by 'cut', 'chew', 'run'.

Try these:

11. *I cut the line so the fish escaped*
12. *People used to chew tobacco.*
13. *I will run the marathon next Sunday.*
14. *I believed that there was a devil.*
15. *People used to believe in witches.*
16. *I will believe in god next Sunday.*

Sentences 11 to 13 are ordinary enough. Sentence 14 seems to tell you about the speaker's changed state of mind, not about the devil. Sentence 15 perhaps makes an implied existential claim: that witches never did really exist, but 16 is really very odd indeed. It is very difficult to imagine a context in which it could be used. Such oddity is a symptom of something going on, not in the grammar of the language, but in logic and meaning. The word *belief* in religious statements seems to obey rules different to those in its everyday use. It is almost not the same word.

Wittgenstein and meaning

In his first major work, the *Tractatus Logico-Philosophicus* Wittgenstein says:

For the totality of facts determines what is the case, and also what is not the case. The facts in logical space are the world. The world divides into facts.

This is a matter of meaning. Logical space is the totality of meaning and anything said outside such space would have no meaning; a-logical rather than illogical. Statements which cannot be referred to facts are not about the world and are not genuine statements.

Thus, to discover whether anything that is said has meaning or not, it is necessary to ascertain how it refers to logical space. An example of this occurs in Wittgenstein's later *Philosophical Investigations.*

... the proposition 'The Earth has existed for millions of years' makes clearer sense than 'The Earth has existed in the last five minutes.' For I should ask anyone who asserted the latter: 'What observations does this proposition refer to; what would count against it?' – whereas I know what ideas and observations the former proposition goes with.

The first proposition or statement, *The Earth has existed for millions of years*, is one that can obviously be referred to facts by examining the geological and fossil record. The statement, *The Earth has existed in the last five minutes*, (implying that six minutes ago it did not exist), is simply odd. What evidence could be adduced for its truth or falsity? The statement cannot be referred to facts about the world, is not in logical space and thus has no meaning. Thus, Wittgenstein said:

> *The correct method in philosophy would really be the following: to say nothing except what can be said - the propositions of natural science which have nothing to do with philosophy - and then, whenever someone else wanted to say something metaphysical, to demonstrate that he had failed to give a meaning to certain signs in his propositions.*

On such an account, the many statements which people (and philosophers in particular) puzzle over and which cannot be referred to logical space are simply meaningless. The statement, *God exists*, is rendered meaningless because there are no facts to which it can be referred. The proper answer to the question, *Does god exist?* would not be *yes* or *no* but a demonstration that the question has no meaning and so it cannot be discussed. Wittgenstein says:

> *When the answer cannot be put into words, neither can the question be put into words. The riddle does not exist.*

and so:

> *Wovon man nicht sprechen kann, darüber muss man schweigen.*

which was translated in Ogden's 1922 version as *Whereof we cannot speak, thereof we must be silent*. As lovely as this sounds, it gives the unfortunate impression that Wittgenstein is expressing some form of metaphysical aphorism. He is not. He is simply saying that if something cannot be said, it cannot be discussed.

Language games

In the *Philosophical Investigations*, Wittgenstein introduced the notion of a language game (*sprachspiel*). While in the *Tractatus* he had thought of language as having only one way of connecting with the world – essentially that of dividing the world into facts - in the *Investigations* he came to think of this as only one of several possible language games.

This does not mean that anything goes. A *sprachspiel* has rules of logical grammar like the rules of a game. Saying something is like making a move in a game. Only correct moves are allowed. A move that is not within the rules ruins the game; makes a nonsense of it. Rules in any language game have to be mutually understood and obeyed or we cannot talk to each other.

> *If language is to be a means of communication there must be agreement not only in definitions but also (queer as this may sound) in judgements.*

The connection between Wittgenstein's earlier and later works is that there is no language game in which I can claim the existence of something without there being, in principle at least, a way of testing that claim. So no wonder the sentence that we used above, *I believe in the Devil*, is odd. It uses the word *believe* in a very tricky way. It uses *believe* to mean *know without any evidence or possibility of evidence* rather like the word *gnosis*, which the Gnosis Society says is:

> The knowledge of transcendence arrived at by way of interior, intuitive means.[1]

But does this make any sense? It seems to be saying that there are types of knowledge that do not meet the criteria for being knowledge - a self-contradiction. If you disobey the rules for using the words, then you cease to communicate; what you say may sound splendid but it doesn't mean anything.

The views I have used here are not unique to Wittgenstein. They were also held by Francis Bacon (1561-1626), seen as the founder of scientific method. He wrote:

> The syllogism is made up of propositions, propositions of words, and words are markers of notions. Thus if the notions themselves (and this is the heart of the matter) are confused, and recklessly abstracted from things, nothing built on them is sound. (Aphorism 14)

Until Bacon, truth had been sought via deduction from accepted truth or gnosis. After Bacon, truth is sought by what he refers to as induction, more normally today called hypothetico-deductive reasoning; that is, creating hypotheses from observation and testing them rigorously by prediction and experimentation.

Incidentally, Constant makes a similar distinction between knowledge and belief:

> We must separate certainties from beliefs and firmly distinguish between science and faith, recognising that we do not know things which we believe, and that we cease immediately to believe anything which we come actually to know. It follows that the essence of the things of faith is the unknown and the indefinite, while it is quite the reverse with the things of science.

An interlude's interlude

This part is purely for the masochistic among you. Wittgenstein's statement:

> Wovon man nicht sprechen kann, darüber muss man schweigen

has implications beyond what I said above. While Wittgenstein says that statements, such as *God exists*, cannot be discussed, he also says:

> There are indeed things that cannot be put into words. They make themselves manifest. They are what is mystical.

and

> It is not **how** things are in the world that is mystical, but **that it exists.**

Here he is referring to the experience of viewing the world as a limited whole, *sub specie aeterni*; standing outside the world and wondering at its very existence. For Wittgenstein, *talk* of god is pointless because:

> **How** things are in the world is a matter of complete indifference for what is higher. God does not **reveal himself** in the world.

---

[1] Drop the words *of transcendence* and the sentence becomes a little clearer.

The world is only about facts and facts are neither good nor bad; they just are. *God* is a value word, a word connected with *reasons why* but:

> *In the world everything is as it is and happens as it does happen. In it, there is no value - and if there were, it would be of no value.*

It is the observer who brings the value; the 'I' that sees the world.

> *What brings the self into philosophy is the fact that the 'world is my world.'*

> *The philosophical self is not the human being, not the human body, or the human soul with which psychology deals, but the metaphysical subject, the limit of the world - not a part of it.*

...or as I like to express it:

> *I am the point of view from which the world is seen.*

Descartes, (1596-1650) famously but mistakenly, takes *cogito ergo sum* to lead to *sum res cogitans* and thence, via the existence of a good and perfect god, to a proof of the existence of a world external to sense data. Of course, *I think therefore I am*, is no more logically important a statement than, *I play golf, therefore I am*. In both cases, it is the word 'I' that does the work, not as describing a specific form of being but as the point of view from which the world is seen. The 'I' views the world from the outside. Sartre's *La Nausée* expresses the sudden perception of the world existing quite separately from the observer.

> *And then all of a sudden, there it was, clear as day: existence had suddenly unveiled itself. It had lost the harmless look of an abstract category: it was the very paste of things, this root was kneaded into existence. Or rather the root, the park gates, the bench, the sparse grass, all that had vanished: the diversity of things, their individuality, were only an appearance, a veneer. This veneer had melted, leaving soft, monstrous masses, all in disorder - naked, in a frightful, obscene nakedness ... All these objects . . . how can I explain? They inconvenienced me; I would have liked them to exist less strongly, more dryly, in a more abstract way, with more reserve. The chestnut tree pressed itself against my eyes. Green rust covered it half-way up; the bark, black and swollen, looked like boiled leather.*

Chapter four: The Search for Horns

Jon Ronson's book 'The Men who Stare at Goats' recounts, if you believe such things, the story of the US Army's attempts to use psychic powers. One such attempt was to see if a soldier could kill just using his mind. At first the plan was to test it out on dogs but this upset the soldiers. So they used goats instead.

So what is so bad about goats? In this chapter, we seek to answer this question and discover how and where the negative image of the goat arose.

Constant refers to his engraving as the Goat of Mendes and so we journey first to Ancient Egypt, learning about the 'ba' and ghosts as we go. We will find rams rather than goats but also a connection between the two. We will also discuss modes of thought; how come anyone would think that the flooding of the Nile was caused by a person or indeed think that the sun was pulled across the sky by a chariot.

From Egypt, we follow a god to classical Greece, handle the concept of a mytheme and distinguish between fauns and satyrs. We then go off to that curious time when the Romans took command of an Egypt run by the Greeks to meet Cleopatra - in fact several Cleopatras.

We will hear from Herodotus and recall to mind that moment of blessed memory when Eric Morecambe and Ernie Wise met Glenda Jackson. We will touch upon Cyrus, King of Persia, Croesus, the Rosetta stone, Homer, Troy, Greek plays and a curious tale known as a hapax. (No, you have to read on to find out what that means.)

The chapter is followed by short interlude on Euclid and the Regius Poem.

The goat of Mendes

The *goat of Mendes* is one of the names that Constant gives his engraving and he gives it with a warning.

> We approach the mystery of Black Magic. We are about to confront, even in his own sanctuary, the black god of the Sabbath, the formidable goat of Mendes. At this point those who are liable to fear should close the book; even persons who are a prey to nervous imaginings will do well to divert their attention. We have undertaken a task, and we must complete it.

I trust you are ready for it!

Mendes was the Greek name for a city in the Nile Delta in the north of Egypt, known to the Egyptians as Djedet. There a ram, not a goat, was worshipped as the incarnation of the god *Banebdjedet* and he had a ram's head. Archaeological studies led by Professor Donald Redford[1] have shown that in ancient times Mendes was an active port, known particularly for its trade in wine and perfumes, serving Greece and later Rome. Much of the city was destroyed around 2200 BCE with great loss of life. Although rebuilt, it is a ruin again today. In the north-west of the city, a burial place of the sacred rams of Mendes has been uncovered.

Modes of thought

The River Nile is just over 4,000 miles long, similar in length to the Amazon. As the White Nile it rises somewhere still unknown in Rwanda or Burundi. As the Blue Nile, it rises in Ethiopia. It flows north into the Mediterranean and has always been the most significant element in Egyptian life. Geraldine Pinch writes:

> The habitable part of Egypt was effectively a giant oasis created by the Nile and its annual flood ... Every year a combination of melting snows and monsoon rains in the mountains of Ethiopia caused a huge increase in the amount of water in the Nile. When the swollen river reached Egypt, it flooded all the low-lying land in the Nile Valley and Delta, depositing a thick layer of silt.
>
> As the floods went down, the fields were planted and crops such as emmer wheat and barley grew very quickly in the moist, fertile soil. In a good year, the Egyptians could grow more grain than they needed to feed the population. In bad years, the flood might not be high enough to reach all the fields, or it might be too high and sweep away villages and towns and drown thousands of people.

It was a severe drought which was to blame for the collapse of the Old Kingdom, the prosperous period often called the age of the pyramids, and resulted in the long civil war during which Mendes was razed to the ground. It is no surprise, therefore, that the Nile was central to Egyptian religion.

In *La Pensée Sauvage*, the anthropologist Claude Lévi-Strauss makes a distinction between the *bricoleur* and the engineer. The engineer brings in the right materials and the right tools to get the job done. The *bricoleur* is a sort of Mr Fixit, a jack of

---

[1] Professor Donald Redford is Professor of Classics and Ancient Mediterranean Studies at Pennsylvania State University and Director of the Mendes expedition. For a report see *Archeology* Vol 6 March 2012, *Archaeological excavations at ancient Mendes.*

all trades, who uses whatever tools and materials he has to hand. At its worst, it is bodging; at its best it is an art form.

> *The bricoleur is skilled in executing a wide range of different tasks but, unlike the engineer, his achievement of each of them does not depend upon obtaining specific raw materials and tools created especially for the project.*

Lévi-Strauss argues that in pre-scientific thought, solutions to problems can be drawn only from a limited range of pre-existing ideas.

> *... the characteristic of mythical thought is that it expresses itself by use of a motley repertoire which, although extensive, is nevertheless limited. It has to use this repertoire, whatever the task in hand, because it has nothing else at its disposal. Mythical thought is therefore a kind of intellectual bricolage.*

To take an example, early thinkers sought to explain why the sun moved across the sky each day. In their repertoire of explanations of movement, they had only human causation to use. Thus, if something moved, someone must have moved it; the sun crossed the sky because someone towed it behind a chariot.[1] The people of ancient Egypt had little or no understanding of the science of the flooding Nile and again, in an attempt to explain it, had to use the repertoire of thought at their disposal. If sometimes the flood was good and sometimes it was bad, someone was making it so.

One of the most important of the ancient gods was Osiris. The god of the underworld and the dead, it was he who was also responsible for the flooding of the Nile and the fertile land it produced. He was thus seen as the creator of new life and is usually portrayed with an appropriately green skin and holding a farmer's crook and a flail used for threshing. In keeping with the cycle of Nile floods and the seasons, Osiris was thought to die and rise from the dead each year.

Introducing Banebdjedet

The god, Banebdjedet, whose worship was centred on Mendes, was not an individual being in his own right but a *ba*, in fact the ba of Osiris. His name, Ba-neb-djed-et, means *The ba of the lord of the djed.* In Egyptian religious thought, the ba was a perfectly normal derivative of a man or woman which maintained his or her personality after death. Geraldine Pinch describes the ba as a mobile manifestation of a dead person and it is usually shown as a

---

[1] Newton proposed a new thought. The natural state of things is motion. Things move unless they are stopped.

human-headed bird. To attempt to use words with which we are familiar, a ba is less like a soul and rather more like a ghost, particularly those in American movies, an intangible version of the person when alive.

Myth making is more often associative than deductive and the word *ba* sounded very much like the word for *ram* in the language of the time, thus a reason for Banebdjedet being depicted as having a ram's head, often four of them.[1] The djed part of the god's name refers to a special form of pillar, a ceremonial rather than structural item. It represented not only the spine of Osiris but also the river Nile, itself the spine of Egypt. Since Osiris died each year, his ba was often called upon and, as the ba of Osiris, Banebdjedet was also associated with the cycle of life, death and re-birth.

Khnum - Banebdjedet's alter ego

Khnum

Mendes was in the north of Egypt but Banebdjedet also appears in the south, there known as Khnum, whose worship was centred on Elephantine,[2] an island upstream from Thebes. Khnum also had a ram's head and his name derives from the word for *create* or *build* - close to *stability*. Khnum was also involved with the Nile flood and in particular with the silt and clay that the flooding brought, enriching the fields for cultivation. He was envisaged as a potter, using the clay from the river to create human life which he placed in women's wombs. As Pinch writes:

Khnum made life with his sexual power, by releasing the Nile flood that caused crops to grow and by crafting bodies on his potter's wheel.

In this, he was often assisted by his wife, Heqet the frog-goddess, who breathed the *ka* or life force into the clay bodies.[3] Frogs were symbols of fertility in Egypt and Heqet was invoked by mothers-to-be to avoid a still-birth.

---

[1] He was also taken to be the ba of three other gods as well - Geb, Shu and Ra-Atum - who together with Osiris were said to be the first four gods to rule Egypt.

[2] Just as the burials of rams have been found at Mendes, so mummified rams have been found on the island of Elephantine.

[3] By some accounts, Khnum did this himself; by still others, a birth-goddess Meskhenet. The Egyptian civilisation lasted a very long time and myths changed.

Virility

We are beginning to see a connection. Osiris was the creator of new life through his association with the flooding of the Nile. Banebdjedet, whose worship gave rise to the term *Goat of Mendes*, was a derivative of Osiris and was also Khnum, the potter creating the bodies of children. Banebdjedet was often called the *lord of sexual pleasure* and the description of the ram god on the Great Stela[1] of Mendes includes a similar reference. The stone declares that it was erected on the orders of Ptolemy II (284-246 BCE),

> *... who loves the ram, who is the lord of the city of Mendes, the great god, the life of Ra, the generator, the prince of young women ... the original male power of gods and men.*

The stone also describes a festival during which Ptolemy II installed a new ram in place as the living incarnation of the god. Another stone in the Ramesseum[2] records the story of the god Ptah (*He who set all the gods in their places and gave all things the breath of life*) taking the form of Banebdjedet to copulate with a mortal woman so she would conceive Ramesses II.

The god Khnum was also known as Min in the pre-dynastic period. He is often referred to (for example in Ian Shaw's *Oxford History of Ancient Egypt*) as the *ithyphallic Min*[3] and George Hart in his dictionary of Egyptian gods and goddesses mentions a coffin text describing the *woman hunting Min*. Yet another Ram-god was prominent in Middle Egypt and was named Heryshef, god of the riverbanks. He too was seen as a creator and fertility god.

The ram gods were associated with virility and the horns of the ram are associated with male sexual ability.[4] Constant's reference to the *obscene god of Mendes* stems from this association with virility but it takes a shift to Greece to understand why he also uses the term *goat* of Mendes.

Alexander the Great

I have already remarked how we tend to think of history in separate chunks when in reality they overlap. Here is another example. We tend to see the Egyptian, Greek and Roman civilisations as one following the other in a serial manner. In reality they overlapped to such an extent that Ptolemy I, the Pharaoh of Egypt, was Greek and Cleopatra, a descendent of Ptolemy, was wooed by Julius Caesar and by Mark Anthony, both of whom were Roman.

Alexander (356-323 BCE) was the Macedonian leader of the Greeks who conquered most of present day Turkey, Syria and Persia, now of course, Iran. His army penetrated as far as Samarkand, Islamabad, Lahore and the Punjab. Then a Persian possession, Egypt, including what is now Israel and Lebanon, became part

---

[1] A standing stone.

[2] Funerary temple of the Pharaoh Rameses the Great.

[3] The *Oxford Dictionary* is a little coy about the word. *Pertaining to the phallus carried in procession at the Bacchic festivals; grossly indecent.* It refers to the erect penis.

[4] The word *horny* is not that old. Meaning *lustful*, it dates from the late 19th century, although the expression *to have the horn*, descriptive of male sexual arousal, seems to be rather earlier.

of Alexander's conquest by default. He established Alexandria in Egypt in 331 BCE and his body was brought there by Ptolemy after his death.

Alongside Alexander throughout his campaigns, Ptolemy was his second-in-command in the Zagros Mountains in their last battle. Alexander's successor, Perdiccas, handed out parts of the empire to the more influential military leaders, primarily to keep them all well away from Greece, and Ptolemy received Egypt. Fighting off various attempts to dislodge him, Ptolemy established a dynasty that lasted 200 years.

Cleopatra(s)

The famous Cleopatra, who was essentially the last Pharaoh of Egypt, was the seventh ruler of that name, most of the others also being powerful women. Cleopatra II, for example, married Ptolemy VIII but led a revolt against him in 131 BCE. When her own choice of king was murdered by her ex-husband, Cleopatra II became ruler of Egypt herself. She was later reconciled with Ptolemy VIII and ruled jointly with him and Cleopatra III for eight years until she died.

With the exception of the famous Cleopatra, who saw herself as the reincarnation of the Egyptian goddess Isis, the Ptolemys spoke only Greek. This incidentally explains why the Rosetta stone was written in Egyptian hieroglyphs, Demotic script and Greek. During the Ptolemaic period, hieroglyphic writing was used mainly for religious purposes, demotic script[1] for writing business and legal documents and Greek was the language of the court.

When Pompey was defeated by Julius Caesar in 48 BCE, he took ship to Egypt. There Pompey was betrayed and his head presented to Caesar when he arrived in turn. Cleopatra later bore a son whom she called Caesarion.[2] After the battle of Philippi, where Mark Anthony and Octavian defeated Brutus, Cassius and the other conspirators against Caesar, Anthony went to sort out the eastern part of the Roman Empire and asked for Egyptian assistance. He thus met Cleopatra, which was wonderful for Elizabeth Taylor and Richard Burton but most rapturously for Eric Morecambe, Ernie Wise and Glenda Jackson.

After Octavian's victory over Anthony, Egypt became a directly ruled province of Rome. The third Prefect, Gaius Petronius, cleaned up the neglected irrigation canals which led to a sustained period of prosperity. Brian P Copenhaver writes:

> *The Nile Valley supplied as much as a third of Rome's grain, and Egypt was also a rich producer of grapes, olives, dates and other foods … under the Romans the population reached its peak in antiquity, numbering as much as eight million.*

Even earlier relationships

In 660 BCE, 300 years before the time of Alexander, the Pharaoh Psamtik hired Greek mercenaries to drive out the Assyrian[3] invaders and the Greek historian

---

[1] *Writing of the people* as Herodotus termed it. The Egyptians referred to it as *document writing*.

[2] Who seems to have been assassinated by Octavian.

[3] From Northern Mesopotamia (Greek: *between the rivers;* the Euphrates and Tigris) encompassing what is today Iraq, eastern Syria and south-eastern Turkey.

Herodotus[1] writes that Greek Spartans and Egyptians were both involved in the war between King Croesus of Lydia[2] and Cyrus, King of Persia. After Cyrus met Croesus in an inconclusive battle around 546 BCE, Herodotus writes that Croesus tried to create a coalition:

> *... having it in his mind to call the Egyptians to his help according to the oath which they had taken ... and to summon the Babylonians as well ... and send a message to the Lacedæmonians[3] bidding them to appear at a fixed time.*

The attempt was not successful. With the onset of winter, Croesus dismissed his Greek mercenaries, deciding to winter in Sardis until the next fighting season but, as Paul Davis writes:

> *Sure that Croesus would want to keep his mercenaries off the payroll during the winter ... after waiting sufficient time for Croesus to get home and dismiss his forces, Cyrus launched a forced march through Anatolia ... Not until the Persian forces appeared at the city gates did Croesus believe what was happening.*

Cyrus routed Croesus. Maybe Croesus was not as rich as we think, or perhaps he was just mean.

From Banebdjedet to Pan

What is clear is that relationships between Egypt and Greece were well established by the seventh century BCE. Lucas Livingston writes of the,

> *... blossoming trade relations between the Greeks and Egyptians, the cultural and political setting of the Mediterranean in the late 7th to 6th centuries ... perfect for the transference of artistic and architectural notions between the Egyptians and Greeks.*

So, given the considerable contact between the two cultures, there was plenty of time for a ram-headed god to mutate into a goat-headed one and re-surface in Greece. It should be no surprise to us to see Banebdjedet become Greek.

Pan - *a voluptuous and sensual being* writes Aaron Atsma - appears in the *Homeric Hymns[4]* but his very earliest mention is in one of the *Odes* of Pindar (522–443 BCE) where the poet is somewhat cheekily commenting on the religious affiliation of young ladies.

> *But I, for my part, want to offer a prayer to the Mother, the revered goddess whose praises, with those of Pan, girls often sing at night beside my doorway.*

The Greeks knew of Banebdjedet himself through trade with the port of Mendes and in a curious passage in the *Histories*, Herodotus goes so far as to claim Pan to be an Egyptian god:

> *... Pan is represented in Egypt by the painters and the sculptors, just as he is in*

---

[1] Writing between 450 and 420 BCE.

[2] The Anatolian Peninsula in western Turkey.

[3] Another name for the Spartans.

[4] Written between 500 and 450 BCE, not by Homer but in his style. The Hymn to Pan (number 19) is thought to be one of the later hymns.

> *Greece, with the face and legs of a goat … The Mendesians hold all goats in veneration, but … one is venerated more highly than all the rest, and when he dies there is a great mourning throughout the Mendesian canton. In Egyptian, the goat and Pan are both called Mendes.*

Herodotus can only be referring to Banebdjedet even though Pan had the lower body of a goat while Banebdjedet had the head of a ram. The *Histories* of Herodotus are a very readable and often gossipy but not always accurate account of the landscape, history, customs and religions of the places and people he had heard about and often visited. He spent several months travelling in Egypt, one of the first tourists, going as far south as Aswan and he seems to have the idea that almost all the Greek gods came from Egypt, their being translatable from one language to the other: the Egyptian *Isis* becomes the Greek *Diameter*; *Oros* becomes *Apollo* and *Osiris* becomes *Dionysos*.

We might be able to understand this more if we make a leap in our imagination of some 2,500 years back to the fifth century BCE and consider that to Herodotus the gods were present, actual and real beings. Since there were gods in Egypt whose habits and actions were similar to those of the Greek gods, it might seem quite reasonable to him to treat them as the same.[1] To him history and myth were the same. For example:

> *Now the Dionysos who is said to have been born of Semele the daughter of Cadmos, was born about sixteen hundred years before my time, and Heracles who was the son of Alcmene, about nine hundred years, and Pan who was born of Penelope, for of her and of Hermes Pan is said by the Hellenes to have been born, came into being later than the wars of Troy, about eight hundred years before my time.*

The phrase *before my time* somewhat endearingly shows that he thinks of all these figures to be as real as himself. They form quite a mixture.

Semele was a mortal woman, the mother of Dionysos by Zeus; one of the many liaisons that the amorous king of the gods had with mortals.

Cadmos was a mortal who was said to have introduced the alphabet into Greece and to have founded Thebes, a city north-west of Athens.

Heracles (Hercules to the Romans) was another son of Zeus, this time with Alcmene who was described by the poet Hesiod[2] as the tallest and most beautiful woman ever born to human parents.

Penelope was the wife of Odysseus, in Homer's *Odyssey*.

---

[1] I refuse to go into the question of the *identity* of a god! The question of how we know that Mr Smith is the same Mr Smith we met years ago, even when Mr Smith, as the result of an accident, now looks different, speaks differently and behaves differently, is one thing but add to that the impossibility of using physical characteristics, family history or documentation and the question of identity becomes very fraught.

[2] Hesiod himself was composing his most important work, the *Theogony*, in about 700 BCE. A theogony is a sort of family tree of gods.

Hermes, who will be important to us later, was known to the Romans as Mercury, and was yet another son of Zeus[1], this time by a goddess.

Troy is today identified with remains found on the north-west coast of Turkey.

Manfred Korfmann, Director of the excavations at Troy and Professor of Archaeology at the University of Tübingen writes:

> *According to the archaeological and historical findings of the past decade especially, it is now more likely than not that there were several armed conflicts in and around Troy at the end of the Late Bronze Age. At present we do not know whether all or some of these conflicts were distilled in later memory into the Trojan War or whether among them there was an especially memorable, single Trojan War.*

There is no agreement on whether Homer as a person existed but there is agreement that the poems were not originally written down but delivered orally from memory. This view dates as far back as Josephus:

> *Now some say that he did not leave his poems in writing, but that they were committed to memory as songs and put together afterwards, and this is the reason why they have so many variations.*

A very sensible approach to Homer is taken by Oliver Taplin, writing in the *Oxford History of the Classical World*:

> *The conclusion that the Homeric world is ... a poetic amalgam is in no way inconsistent with its having exerted a powerful influence on the real life of the Greeks over the next 1,000 years after its creation. Homer provided one persuasive, universally known, and inspiring model of heroism, nobility, the good life, the gods. Homer affected history.*

Whether we conclude that Herodotus was right or wrong in believing Pan to be an Egyptian god, there were certainly gods in Egypt who had features in common with Pan. Banebdjedet is one of these. Many of the features that go to make up Pan were communicated from Egypt to Greece and, in this sense, Banebdjedet becomes Pan.

Mythemes and satyrs

Pan was *a sexy beast* as was Banebdjedet. The idea of horns being representative of male reproductive ability may be an example of what Lévi-Strauss calls a *mytheme* – a continuing element of meaning that is independent of any one myth but acts as a constituent part of many. We have evidence of something like this with satyrs.

Plays about satyrs were very popular in Greece around the middle of the 5th century BCE. The plays were short and full of *double-entendres* - rather like the TV comedies of Benny Hill, but even more obscene - and they provided light relief after a Greek tragedy. Satyrs had a constant desire for alcohol and sex. Their stage costume usually featured an erection, a wine skin, a thyrsus (stick) and a musical

---

[1] On one count, I made it 56 gods/goddesses and 52 mortals who were offspring of Zeus.

pipe. They were connected with Dionysus, the god of divine ecstasy, who dispelled care through excess of wine.

With human bodies and feet, long and rather trim beards, pointed ears and bushy tails, satyrs had no goatish features and did not look in the least like our image of Pan - but there were other creatures, known as fauns, that did.

Satyr plate from about 500 BCE

Fauns were shy creatures of the woodlands and pastures, not above playing tricks on men in wild, remote places but the only sex involved was the ability of the god Faunus to make cattle fertile. Fauns were goats from the waist down and had horns. The mytheme got to work and satyrs and fauns became conflated. Satyrs had the sex and fauns had the goatish looks. The result is that the goatish faun is now the way that everyone sees satyrs.[1]

---

[1] There is a theory that the Greek word *tragoidia* means *goat song*. A goat was the prize for the winning playwright at the Athenian Festival. Sophocles won 24 times, Aeschylus 13 and Euripides 5 but this has nothing to do with our search. Goats were sometimes simply lunch.

Pan himself seems to have started out as a faun. The Homeric Hymn emphasises his pastoral side:

> *Hermes came to Arkadia, the land of many springs and mother of flocks, there where his sacred place is as god of Kyllene. For there, though a god, he used to tend curly-fleeced sheep in the service of a mortal man, because there fell on him and waxed a strong melting desire to wed the rich-tressed daughter of Dryopos, and there he brought about the merry marriage. And in the house she bore Hermes a dear son who from his birth was marvellous to look upon, with goat's feet and two horns - a noisy, merry, laughing child.[1]*

Self portrait as a faun. Johfra (1919-1998)

Pan started out as a god of wild nature, forests and mountains, of hunting and rustic music and, like other fauns, he too frightened people who journeyed through wild, remote places. As with Osiris, Pan's farming connections led to him becoming associated with the natural cycle of birth and death and so Pan became associated with fertility and sex.

The mytheme did its work and Pan became a satyr. Its appearance stolen, the faun disappeared into formless obscurity and its name is now only and wrongly used as another name for a satyr.

The death of Pan

A curious event is recorded by Plutarch towards the end of the first century CE.

> *Epitherses, who lived in our town and was my teacher in grammar ... said that once upon a time, in making a voyage to Italy, he embarked on a ship carrying freight and many passengers. It was already evening when, near the Echinades Islands, the wind dropped, and the ship drifted near Paxi.[2] Almost everybody was awake, and a good many had not finished their after-dinner wine. Suddenly from the island of Paxi was heard the voice of someone loudly calling 'Thamus', so that all were amazed. Thamus was an Egyptian pilot, not known by name even to many on board. Twice he was called and made no reply, but the third time he answered; and the caller, raising his voice, said, 'When you come opposite to Palodes, announce that Great Pan is dead.'*

> *On hearing this, said Epitherses, all were astounded and reasoned among themselves whether it were better to carry out the order or to refuse to meddle and let the matter go. Under the circumstances Thamus made up his mind that if there should be a breeze, he would sail past and keep quiet, but with no wind and a*

---

[1] Translation HG Evelyn-White, Loeb Classics 1914

[2] This event seems to have taken place in the Ionian Islands on the West coast of Greece. The island of Paxi is just south of Corfu.

smooth sea about the place he would announce what he had heard. So, when he came opposite Palodes, and there was neither wind nor wave, Thamus from the stern, looking toward the land, said the words as he had heard them: 'Great Pan is dead.'

Even before he had finished there was a great cry of lamentation, not of one person, but of many, mingled with exclamations of amazement. As many persons were on the vessel, the story was soon spread abroad in Rome, and Thamus was sent for by Tiberius Caesar. Tiberius became so convinced of the truth of the story that he caused an inquiry and investigation to be made.[1]

This odd story is a *hapax*, something quite unique. As Philippe Bourgeaud writes:

Not a single parallel, variant or commentary has been handed down from Graeco-Roman polytheism to aid the interpreter.

Moving on

The death of Pan, which Plutarch dates to Tiberius's reign as Emperor (14-37 CE), was used by the Christian apologist Eusebius of Caesarea:[2]

... it is important to notice the time at which he says that the death of the demon took place. For it was the time of Tiberius, in which our Saviour, making his sojourn among men, is recorded to have been ridding human life from demons of every kind. You have therefore the date of the overthrow of the demons.

Banebdjedet's next transformation is to become a demon.

---

[1] Translation Harold Cherniss, Loeb Classics.

[2] 263-338 CE, most famous for his *Life* of Constantine and his history of the early church. His account of the death of Pan occurs in his *Praeparatio Evangelica*.

Interlude: Euclid and the *Regius* Poem

Often taken to be the father of geometry and thus someone who ought to be more prominent in freemasonry than he is, Euclid is said to have worked in Alexandria during the reign of Ptolemy I (367-283 BCE). The *Regius Poem* claims, with some degree of accuracy, that Euclid found geometry in Egypt and, with a great deal less accuracy, that he became a teacher of the art there and in other lands.

> *The clerk Euclyde on thys wyse hyt fonde,*
> *Thys craft of gemetry yn Egypte londe.*
> *Yn Egypte he tawghte hyt ful wyde,*
> *Yn dyvers londe on every syde;*

Proclus,[1] writing in the 5th century CE, said:

> *According to most accounts, geometry was first discovered among the Egyptians, taking its origin from the measurement of areas. For they found it necessary by reason of the flooding of the Nile, which wiped out everybody's proper boundaries.*

A bundle of papyrus, found in ancient rubbish in Egypt, contains the oldest surviving version of Euclid's theorems, dating from 75-125 CE and thus 350 or so years after Euclid. This fragment includes a diagram which accompanies the fifth proposition of Book II:

> *If a straight line is cut into equal and unequal segments, then the rectangle contained by the unequal segments of the whole together with the square on the straight line between the points of section equals the square on the half.*

---

[1] One of the last of the classical Greek philosophers, he wrote *Wherever there is number, there is beauty*. A suitable thought for a freemason perhaps?

The *Regius Poem* dates from about 1390 CE and is the earliest document that we have indicating a *speculative* element to the operative craft of masonry. It is part of that great flowering of the English language which generated Chaucer's *Canterbury Tales* and the Wycliffe translation of the Bible. The poem claims Euclid as the originator of masonry.

> *Bet this grete clerke more ordent he*
> *To him that was herre in this degre*
> *That he shulde teche the symplyst of wytte*
> *In that onest craft to be parfytte*
> *And so vchon schulle techyn othur*
> *And love togedur as systur and brothur.*

He ordered those who were more experienced to teach others, no matter what their standing, to perfect themselves in the honest craft of masonry so that each may teach another and all live in harmony and affection as sisters and brothers. It was many years afterwards, you understand, that the craft came to this land. It came to England, they say, in the time of good King Athelstan:

> *Mony erys afterwarde, y understonde,*
> *Er that the craft com ynto thys londe,*
> *Thys craft com ynto Englond, as y gow say,*
> *Yn tyme of good kynge Adelstonus day.*

Bertrand Russell was rather rude about Euclid.

> *It has been customary when Euclid, considered as a text book, is attacked for his verbosity or his obscurity or his pedantry, to defend him on the ground that his logical excellence is transcendent, and affords an invaluable training to the youthful powers of reasoning.*

> *This claim, however, vanishes on a close inspection. His definitions do not always define, his axioms are not always indemonstrable, his demonstrations require many axioms of which he is quite unconscious.*

Russell wrote this for the *Mathematical Gazette* in 1902, more than 2,000 years after Euclid, so we might with some justice say, *Give him a break!*

Chapter five: You'll never get to Heaven

Mount Sinai

To understand our heroes' transition to evil, I am afraid that we are going to have to get to grips with a bit of theology. In particular, we need to take account of polytheism, henotheism and monotheism. I need to establish the rise of the afterlife and how and when it arises as a divine promise because we will find it was the afterlife that guaranteed monotheism and turned our heroes into the devil by inventing the concept of sin.

It may come as some surprise to learn that, outside of Egypt and its Book of the Dead, the afterlife is a comparatively late development. The Greeks and the Romans had little concept of it but its arrival had a major effect on religion, if less on morality than has been thought.

The rise of monotheism was a gradual process and one that we can observe actually occurring in the Old Testament. We will examine how and when the Old Testament was written, focusing primarily on its authors and editors as human beings (who can always make mistakes.) We will hear two stories of burning bushes and the ten (actually 613) commandments, visit King Solomon and touch on scrolls versus books, the 14th hole at St Andrews and literalism in Bible reading.

This chapter takes us back to Cyrus the Great and to his return of believers to their native lands. Since this is of greatest interest to Royal Arch Masons, I will reserve the detail for the interlude that follows - but we start with a bit of rock'n'roll.

Great balls of fire

My Boy Scout troop in Walderslade, Kent was amazingly lucky. We had our very own forest camp ground and we really did sing songs around the camp fire. One sticks in my memory from 50-odd years ago: *You'll never get to heaven.* You might know it. I think the chorus went something like:

> *I ain't gonna grieve, my lord,*
> *I ain't gonna grieve, my lord,*
> *I ain't gonna grieve, my lord, no more.*

One verse was a quite improper comment on Ford's quality control:

> *You'll never get to heaven in an old Ford car*
> *'Cos an old Ford car, won't get that far*
> *Oh you'll never get to heaven in an old Ford car*
> *'Cos an old Ford car won't get that far (Chorus)*

There were dozens of verses:

> *You'll never get to heaven on roller skates.*
> *'Cos you'll roll right past those Pearly Gates.*
> *...*
> *You'll never get to Heaven in powder and paint,*
> *'Cos the lord don't like you as you ain't.*

and my masonic brother Lawrie's favourite:

> *You'll never get to heaven in a baked bean tin,*
> *'Cos a baked bean tin's got baked beans in.*

Oh dear, simpler days. Mind you, we were about to discover rock'n'roll and, sorry, I can't resist it. What is your top twenty from the late 50s? Here's mine.[1]

Jerry Lee Lewis	Great Balls of Fire
Gene Vincent	Be-Bop-A-Lula
Little Richard	Good Golly, Miss Molly
Buddy Holly	That'll Be The Day
Little Richard	Tutti-Frutti
Buddy Holly	Rave On
Bill Haley	See You Later Alligator
Elvis Presley	Hound Dog
Everly Brothers	Bye, Bye Love
Buddy Holly	Oh, Boy!
Little Richard	Lucille
Ritchie Valens	La Bamba
Little Richard	Long Tall Sally
Jerry Lee Lewis	Breathless

---

[1] I once saw Screaming Lord Sutch and Gene Vincent on successive nights.

Buddy Holly	Peggy Sue
Bill Haley	Rock Around The Clock
Gene Vincent	Rocky Road Blues
Chuck Berry	Johnny B.Goode
Jerry Lee Lewis	Whole Lotta Shakin' Going On
The Coasters	Yakety Yak

Your list is going to be different. Mine will be tomorrow.

The top twenty is not entirely an aside. Freemasonry is not the only institution attacked by what we might call the 'unusual opinion' web sites. Here is Jesus-is-savior.com on the topic of rock'n'roll:

> *Satan is the spiritual power behind ALL rock music, including so-called Christian rock. Rock-n-roll is a religion of immoral sex, drug abuse, and demonic powers summonsed through the music itself. Brian Wilson, lead singer of the Beach Boys, even admitted that he was trying to create witchcraft music.*[1]

So how do you get to heaven? Clearly not by following Eddie Cochrane's posthumous three steps (covered by Showaddywaddy in 1975.)

Henotheism

Garth Fowden describes polytheism as a belief that,

> *... the divine realm is populated by a plurality of gods of broadly comparable status, not fully subordinated to or comprehended within a single god of higher status.*

On this basis, henotheism might be described as a belief that the divine realm is populated by a plurality of gods who are subordinated to but not comprehended in a single god of higher status. The word is from the Greek, εις and θεός - *hen* meaning *one* and *theos* meaning *god*.[2] Not good, is it? It connotes monotheism. How about τοπ - meaning top. Topotheism? Top god?

The most familiar examples of religious systems in Egypt, Greece and Rome, are polytheistic but examples of henotheism (or topotheism) are more common than one might think. In Egyptian, Greek and Roman beliefs, gods had locations where they were most often found and where their worship was strongest. The presence of a local god did not preclude worship of other gods and in many cases s/he represented them. One might see this as local henotheism, the local top god acting for and on behalf of the others, a sort of divine agency system.

Henotheism and Cyrus the Great

Cyrus first became king in 559 BCE when his kingdom was only a small part of what is now south-east Iran. Within thirty years, he had created the Achæmenid

---

[1] There is a whole subculture of these sites, each given to virulently attacking the others.

[2] Perhaps the best, and certainly the funniest, embodiment of henotheism is to be found in Terry Pratchett's *Small Gods*. As Stephen A. Haines wrote in reviewing the book, *The basic theme is a simple, but rarely recognized, truth. Gods are created by people. The fewer the believers, the smaller and weaker the god. When belief fades or believers are eliminated, the gods cease to exist.*

Empire, the largest the world had ever seen. He was killed in 530 BCE while campaigning along the Syr Darya River, but his successors - his son Cambyses II, Darius and Xerxes - further extended the Empire so that it stretched from the borders of India to Libya and from Sudan to Bulgaria. Fowden writes that the Empire lasted until conquered by Alexander and, since Alexander saw himself as the heir of Cyrus, through his reign as well, a total of 236 years.

The Syr Darya River, where Cyrus died, is top right.

An empire that large could not have been run as a dictatorship. It spread through too many different countries and cultures and over too great a distance for direct control, certainly in those days. Cyrus practised what Tom Peters and Robert Waterman Jnr have called *loose-tight* management. He was insistent that the subject countries paid due homage and taxes to him but all other matters he left to the local people to decide. He was what we would today call a liberal in religious affairs. He and his successors, Fowden writes,

> *... on the whole respected and even drew inspiration from the diversity, including cultural diversity, of their subjects. They did this, though, not out of weakness but because they believed that all gods should be worshipped in their own countries, and that maintenance of order among their many subject races was the mission entrusted to the Achæmenids by god.*

It is generally thought that the Achæmenids followed Zoroastrianism; a henotheistic belief system. It had one top god, *Ahura Mazdā*[1], alongside lesser supernatural beings and Cyrus, having conquered Babylon, was quite happy to deal with

---

[1] The priests of the religion were known as *Magi* and some commentators say that the wise men of Matthew's Gospel were from Iran.

Marduk, the top god of Babylon, confident that Marduk was subordinate to Mazda. He would see Marduk as a locally important god, worth keeping in with.

According to the Cyrus Cylinder, a clay object dating from around 538 BCE and now to be found in the British Museum, the god Marduk made the kings from all around kiss Cyrus's feet and bring '*weighty tribute*' to the capital of Babylon. As a result, Cyrus had,

> *... sent back to their places to the city of Assur and Susa, Akkad, the land of Eshnunna, the city of Zamban, the city of Meturnu, Der, as far as the border of the land of Guti - the sanctuaries across the River Tigris - whose shrines had earlier become dilapidated, the gods who lived therein, and made permanent sanctuaries for them.*

The Cyrus Cylinder - the marks are writing in Babylonian cuneiform

This is in keeping with Fowden's view that Cyrus was keeping the local gods happy while confident in his god as number one. The Achæmenid's religion was not a proselytising one. It did not see the need to persuade others to believe in Mazda. As Fowden writes:

> *The Achæmenid Empire had no cultural motive, no mission to Iranize, only the militarily, politically, and economically motivated goals of preserving order and the Iranian elite's domination.*

The Book of the Dead

The afterlife in some religions is taken to be conscious eternal life, retaining one's personality characteristics such that one is recognisable to family and friends arriving later or indeed already there. Entry into the afterlife is commonly a reward for behaviour consistent with a god's rules. So common is a belief in the afterlife that it may come as some surprise to learn that, outside of Egypt, it is a comparatively late development. Zoroastrianism, for example, contained no teachings about the afterlife.

The Egyptians certainly believed in the afterlife and it can seem that the whole of their normal life was spent getting ready for it and ensuring that they got there. As their guide to eternity, the Egyptians had the *Book of the Dead*. For as long as they prepared properly, had the spells beside them in their tomb and said them at the right time to the right god, they got through to eternity no matter what their mortal life had been like.

The heart of the scribe Ani being weighed. Book of the Dead of Ani, circa 1275 BCE.

It is true that the weighing of the heart figured in the eventual destination of an Egyptian after death. The heart was weighed on scales against a feather, representative of truth, order and justice and known as *Maat*. If the heart was heavy with sins, the deceased was condemned to nothingness. If it was light as a feather, the deceased entered the afterlife - and this is where spell 125 came in. It was guaranteed to ensure your heart weighed appropriately, although for obvious reasons few sought to get their money back. Spell 125 is very long but begins:

> *Homage to you, great god, the lord of the double Maat!*
> *I have come to you, my lord,*
> *I have brought myself here to behold your beauties.*
> *I know you, and I know your name,*
> *And I know the names of the two and forty gods,*
> *Who live with you in the hall of the two truths,*
> *Who imprison the sinners, and feed upon their blood,*
> *On the day when the lives of men are judged in the presence of Osiris.*

> *You are the twin sisters with two eyes, the daughters of the two truths.*
>
> *In truth, I now come to you, and I have brought Maat to you,*
>
> *And I have destroyed wickedness for you.*
>
> *I have committed no evil upon men.*
>
> *I have not oppressed the members of my family.*
>
> *I have not wrought evil in the place of right and truth.*
>
> *I have had no knowledge of useless men.*
>
> *I have brought about no evil.*
>
> *I did not rise in the morning and expect more than was due to me.*
>
> *I have not brought my name forward to be praised.*
>
> *I have not oppressed servants ...*

and so on. Spell 30 helped things along as well, particularly when inscribed on a scarab amulet wrapped close to the heart:

> *O my heart that I received from my mother, my heart that I have had since birth, my heart that was with me through all the stages of my life, do not stand up against me as a witness! Do not oppose me at the tribunal! Do not tip the scales against me in the presence of the Keeper of the Balance! Go forth to the hereafter.*

At first the preserve of the wealthy, copies of the *Book of the Dead* were later produced in less expensive formats. In about 650 BCE, the book was standardised and the spells given numbers.

Greece, Rome and the afterlife

In Greek mythology all the dead went to Hades, a somewhat uninviting and colourless place where the only vegetation seems to have been the pale grey asphodel. While we should not expect consistency of belief in myth, Homer describes the dead as,

> *... pathetic in their helplessness, inhabiting draughty, echoing halls, deprived of their wits, and flitting about uttering batlike noises.*

To get into Hades, you had to have had a proper burial with sufficient coinage to pay Charon, the boatman, to take you across the River Styx. Another and useful river in Hades was the Lethe, whose waters would erase memory and thus make things easier to bear. The dead who had no money or whose burial rites were incomplete haunted the living. The most terrible sinners were consigned to Tartarus, originally commissioned as a prison for the Titans, the giants who fought against the gods. The sinners and their punishments in Tartarus are however essentially poetic constructions, stories with a moral. Tantalus, whose name is the origin of the word *tantalising*, was chained, perennially hot and thirsty with water and grapes just out of reach. Sisyphus was condemned eternally to roll a huge rock uphill. As it neared the top, the rock rolled back down again no matter what he did.

Later, the idea of the Elysian Fields gained ground. At first only the greatest heroes were allowed in but things became more democratic as time went on. Nevertheless, the Elysian Fields and Tartarus played a very small part in mainstream Greek mythology. The Greeks were not very interested in the afterlife as such.

Hell's Bunker, beyond which lie the Elysian Fields. 14th hole on the Old Course at St Andrews

The relationship of the Romans to their gods was even less personal than it was for the Greeks and their views on the afterlife were even more vague. Sacrifices and other religious observances were carried out as if they were part of a commercial contract. The gods helped out in daily life for as long as the correct religious observances were made and the people expected the gods to behave properly when they were. A very similar theology obtains in many parts of Africa today. The philosopher, Kwasi Wiredu, argues that:

> There is no such thing as salvific[1] eschatology in African thought about the post-mortem destiny of humankind.

Beliefs regarding the afterlife are mainly to do with ancestors whose job it is to look after the well-being of the living. There are spirits beside ancestors but:

> Rituals and worship in connection with these 'gods' are in fact ways of establishing good relations with them with an eye to their services.

The Ghanaian historian JB Danquah explained that such gods are treated with respect if they deliver the goods and with contempt if they fail.

Religion and morality

The afterlife for the Egyptians, Greeks and Romans, and indeed in modern Africa, has little to do with moral excellence. In polytheism, morality is distinct from reward. The gods are immortal and certainly very powerful but the fate of any human after death is a matter of no great concern to them and so nothing humans do affects their access to any afterlife. One does what is right because it is right.

---

[1] Leading to salvation. *Salvific eschatology* is a teaching of salvation after the end of the world.

Few Greeks, Egyptians or Romans believed that what the gods did was to be emulated. They viewed the affairs of the deity rather as people today enjoy TV soap operas or the love life of 'celebs'. Copenhaver puts it in a more upmarket way when he says that the Greeks rejoiced in the grace and radiance of the immortals. That may be so but, like *East Enders*, the myths are more about sex and violence than grace and radiance.

People did pray and sacrifice to the gods but it was largely to ensure that they did not make things difficult in this life. The gods were not seen to be necessarily interested in human affairs (perhaps concentrating on their own) and it was often necessary to call their attention to what was going on down below. As Pinch writes:

> *One of the main functions of Egyptian art was to provide temporary bodies for deities in the form of statues, drawings or hieroglyphs. Much of the ritual that went on in Egyptian temples was aimed at encouraging the gods to inhabit these bodies so that their presence could benefit humanity.*

By contrast, in monotheism what is right becomes what the god says is right if only because he decides on access to the afterlife. A believer obeys the monotheistic god to get to heaven. If one was being a little crude, one might say that the latter is a sort of bankers' philosophy. *I do what gets me the reward. Questions of right and wrong are irrelevant.*[1] The movement from polytheism to monotheism was thus a shift, not just in the number of gods but in the purpose of life and the justification of morality.

Proselytising

You will remember that Zoroastrianism was henotheistic and that as long as the populace paid their taxes and acknowledged him as boss, Cyrus was easy going. His subjects were not particularly rebellious, perhaps as a result. Egyptian, Greek and Roman religions were polytheistic, with a little local henotheism. None of these religions were given to proselytising. It would not have made much sense. They had lots of gods and a few more wouldn't make much difference. Judaism is monotheistic but not only does it not seek converts, it has often seemed opposed to them. This is primarily because the objective of religious obedience in Judaism is the well-being of the Jewish people. The reward for correct behaviour is not personal. Yahweh sets out what he wants and if the people deliver it, the nation of Israel prospers.

Christianity is a proselytising religion and therefore its monotheism must be somehow different from Judaism. Several questions occur, including why and how monotheism arose, what it is that makes Christianity want to proselytise and how that turned Banebdjedet and Pan into devils. I think we will find some of the answers we are looking for in the development of the Old Testament.

A warning: literal truth

There are many people for whom the Bible is literal truth. In this section, we will be looking at the Bible not as a sacred text but as something written by human beings. I would like to stress that no disrespect to any literal beliefs is intended.

---

[1] Or as Ivan Boesky (almost) said, *Greed is good.*

According to Karen Armstrong, an exclusively literal interpretation of the Bible is a 19th century development. She writes:

> *For centuries, Jews and Christians relished highly allegorical and inventive exegesis, insisting that a wholly literal reading of the Bible was neither possible nor desirable. They have rewritten biblical history, replaced Bible stories with new myths and interpreted the first chapter of Genesis in surprisingly different ways.*

The whole idea of a canonical Bible, a standard collection of texts, is itself something that only comes about around 800 CE. Even then the standard collection contains surprises: two stories of the creation, of the flood and of Moses and the commandments; a book, the *Song of Songs*, which is widely taken to be nothing more than a collection of erotic poetry and whose *metaphors show a freedom and boldness we should not allow ourselves today;*[1] a book, featuring Boaz and Ruth, whose religious significance is not immediately evident; and even a book whose author, as we shall see later, has been described as *a splendid liar.*

The Old Testament was written over a period of some 700 years which gives rise to another of those unexpected overlaps. The very earliest books of the Bible include *Hosea, Amos* and *Micah* which date from around 775 BCE. Hesiod was writing about the same time, the Homeric poems were created some 150 years before and the *Book of the Dead* was already more than 700 years old by then.

The Pentateuch

The *Pentateuch*, consisting of the first five books of the Old Testament *(Genesis, Exodus, Leviticus, Numbers* and *Deuteronomy)* was put together by an unknown editor some time after the exile of the Israelites to Babylon (roughly 597-538 BCE) and about the time (449-432 BCE) that the Parthenon and Acropolis were built in Athens and Euripides won his first festival prize for a tragedy. Fox argues that when the Israelites[2] went into exile, some unknown hero:

> *When faced with fire and destruction, for the first time in history ... preferred books to ... precious metals and saved the contents of a library ... the book of the law was among the bundle, but, so too, were old texts of songs, royal deeds and prophetic sayings, from Amos to Isaiah and perhaps some recent words of Jeremiah.*

The sources that the Pentateuch editor used no longer exist but masons ought to be aware of the possibility of recreating lost documents. It is generally agreed that the *Old Charges*, which today appear in an abbreviated form in the front of the *Book of Constitutions*, were once used during the initiation or *making* of a Mason. A copy was prepared for each initiate, used in the meeting and given to him as a memento. We have extant the actual copy, dated 16th October 1646, used[3] for the initiation of Elias Ashmole. Referred to as *Sloane 3848 MS*, this copy belongs to the Sloane family of manuscript *Old Charges*. Each family shows variations in content and each member of a family has minor variations as the copyist made errors or inserted his own material. By tracing these families and variations, scholars can arrive at a text

---

[1] HH Rowley, writing, it has to be said, in 1937.

[2] It seems to be the custom to refer to the *Israelites* before the exile and the *Jews* after.

[3] I suppose the words *almost certainly* ought to be inserted here.

which no longer survives but which all the versions must stem from. In his Prestonian Lecture, Wallace McLeod provides an account of the methodology and what he refers to as *a tentative text* of the *Standard Original*. It is well worth study.

Robin Lane Fox, New College Oxford.
Extraordinary Lecturer in Ancient History,
Garden Fellow, Reader in Ancient History.

Thus, the sources of the *Pentateuch* can be identified and the oldest stem from sometime in the 8th century BCE. They are known as J (*Yahwist*) and E (*Eloist*) after their preferred names for god. The authors differ in their descriptions of the deity. Armstrong shows that J describes god in human terms. He strolls about the Garden of Eden, shuts the door of Noah's ark, gets angry at things and changes his mind. E's god rarely speaks and communicates through angels.

While J and E are mainly responsible for *Genesis* and *Exodus*, two later sources, D (*Deuteronomist*) and P (*Priestly author*) were largely responsible for the rest of the *Pentateuch*. Responsible for most of *Numbers* and *Leviticus*, P also wrote the sabbatical creation story (so-called because in this version, god rests on the seventh day), the promise to Noah, one story of the flood,[1] the covenant with Abraham and the second account of Moses on Sinai. D is described by Fox as a *natural and fervent speech writer*.

> For the first time, long speeches reinforced the themes of a historical narrative, and like the later historians of Greece, D knew how to place them at climactic points in his story. Naturally, they are his own invention: nobody knew what, if anything, had once been said.

The burning bush(es)

Sometimes two authors wrote accounts of the same event and, when putting together the material from his sources, the editor included both without reconciling their differences. This is also why the Bible contains two different stories of the creation, of the flood, and of Moses and the Ten Commandments.

The burning bush appears first in *Exodus* 3:2. Investigating this phenomenon, Moses hears his name called and is told to remove his shoes *for the place whereon thou standest is holy*. The voice then announces itself to be that of the *god of thy father, the god of Abraham, the god of Isaac, and the god of Jacob*. At this point, *Moses hid his face: for*

---

[1] P's version has god instructing Noah to bring into the ark *two* of every kind of animal, bird etc. (*Genesis* 6:19-20) while in the other version god calls for *seven* of every clean animal and *two* of every unclean animal (*Genesis* 7:2-3.)

he was afraid to look on god. God then gives a number of promises to Moses, works various miracles, famously including dividing the waters to facilitate the Israelites' escape from Pharaoh's army, and then dictates a long list of rules among which are the ten commandments (*Exodus* 20:3-17.)

He then dictates another list of the gifts he wants in exchange for looking after Israel. These include the Ark, the Table, the Lampstand, the Tabernacle, the Altar of Burnt Offering, the Courtyard, the Basin for Washing etc. Then Moses returns down the mountain with the tablets of stone. Apart from the fact that Moses met with Yahweh at the top of Mount Sinai and not at the foot of *Mount Horeb in the wilderness of Sinai*, as in Royal Arch ritual,[1] everything is fine. However, at about 33:7, the story starts all over again. At 33:19, Yahweh is again about to show *his glory* to Moses but this time Moses does not cover his eyes. Instead Yahweh warns him that *you cannot see my face for no-one may see me and live* and tells him:

> *There is a place near me where you may stand on a rock. When my glory passes by, I will put you in a cleft in the rock and cover you with my hand until I have passed by. Then I will remove my hand and you will see my back; but my face must not be seen.*

Royal Arch Masons might note that while the first account fits with the Royal Arch story, the second account would be rather difficult to handle. It would make a bit of a nonsense of the first part of the Mystical Lecture.[2] Then in a section which is so clumsy as to be really quite risible, the editor tries to link the two accounts together by inserting the explanation[3] that Moses broke the first two tablets and had to go back for a new set.

> *The lord said to Moses, 'Chisel out two stone tablets like the first ones, and I will write on them the words that were on the first tablets, which you broke.'*

One cannot help feeling that a couple of un-divine words are missing at the end: something like, *You twit!* If it can be said that the commandments appear at all in the second version, they do so in a different form. Instead we get a statement of Yahweh's jealous nature and an instruction that the Israelites should destroy the holy artefacts of other religions to focus on the sacrifices that he requires. We then get, yet again, the list of offerings that he wants, including the Ark, the Table, the Lampstand, the Tabernacle, the Altar of Burnt Offering, the Courtyard, the Basin for Washing etc.[4] A major difference is that the dividing of the waters is missing in the second account.

The Chronicler and Hiram Abif

The authors of the Bible are not always above political concerns. *Chronicles* is mostly the work of an author known as C (*the Chronicler*) writing in about 350 BCE, about

---

[1] Sinai and Horeb are taken to be two names for the same mountain in the south of the Sinai Peninsula.

[2] What might further complicate that lecture is Karen Armstrong's view that *I am that I am* is not an ontological statement as the lecture assumes it to be but a refusal to discuss such matters: *never you mind who I am.*

[3] *Exodus* 34:1

[4] Interestingly, there is no mention of the escape from Egypt in the second account.

the time of Alexander the Great. Most of his work is a re-hash of other material and it is he who Fox describes as a *splendid liar*. The American historian and archeologist Charles Cutler Torrey wrote:

> *No fact of Old Testament criticism is more firmly established than this, that the Chronicler as a historian is throughly untrustworthy. He distorts facts deliberately and habitually: he invents chapter after chapter with the greatest freedom and what is most dangerous of all, his history is not written for its own sake, but in the interests of an extremely one-sided theory.*

The Chronicler sets out to prove that the centre of the Israelite religion was continuously in Jerusalem, so that the Jews returning from exile were the genuine heirs of Moses and the Samaritans, northerners who had not been exiled, had no claim to leadership. C seeks to justify Zerubbabel's rejection of the help the Samaritans offered in the rebuilding the temple. Opposing C was the argument that after Jerusalem had been destroyed by Nebuchadnezzar, the priestly families had moved north so that the Samaritans were the genuine heirs to temple leadership. HGM Williamson writes:

> *The author's purpose ... is both positive and polemical. On the one hand he is concerned to trace lines of continuity between the restored community and the Israel of pre-exilic times, between the second and first temples, and so on. Legitimacy is clearly a fundamental issue. On the other hand, he goes to considerable pains to justify the rejection of the offer of northern participation in the restoration itself.*

As an example of C's political trickery, take the story of Hiram Abif, a tale dear to freemasons. There are two accounts of the original building of Solomon's temple, one in *Kings* and one in *Chronicles*. In *Kings*, Hiram Abif's mother is said to be of the tribe of Naphtali, a northern tribe. C changes this so that in *Chronicles* she is said to be of the tribe of Dan, a southern tribe. Judaism is matrilineal so in changing his mother's birth place from north to south, C makes it seem that Hiram Abif was also a southerner - and that no northerner was involved. As I said in the prelude, C would have been most upset to discover that the origin of the sacred name was Samaritan - and northern.

The Volume of the Sacred Law (the Bible) is always open in lodge, usually at an account of Solomon's temple, the central story on which the allegory of the Craft is based. Since there are two accounts, freemasons have frequently been uncertain which to choose. The great masonic historian, Harry Carr, opts for *I Kings vii 13-21*. Fox and Torrey would certainly agree, given their views on the Chronicler.

Imagination and legend

Many parts of the Bible are not historical accounts. Solomon lived around 1000 BCE, and, with no written records from that time, his legend derives from a great deal of imagination. There may have been a King Arthur, although few of the stories about him can be true. There may have been a Robin Hood, but it is very unlikely that he was the romantic character of the films. Likewise, there may have been a King Solomon but not the person of legend. Fox asks us to imagine Solomon returning perhaps around 3 BCE.[1]

> *Suppose that King Solomon had come back ... He would never have credited it. Here were his descendants, venerating texts which he was supposed to have written ... He had never composed a word of it. One of them said that he had uttered three thousand proverbs and his songs were a thousand and five; it was amazing to be thought so clever. There were even people who thought that he had written the Song of Songs; it would have looked to him like a collection of straightforward love poetry (his Egyptian wife had known plenty of bits like it.)*
>
> *... It was good to see that people remembered all the horses, the Temple and the women, but they grossly exaggerated the numbers. The bits about the Queen of Sheba also sounded intriguing, even if they failed to specify her gifts and hard questions; in real life, he had never had such a visitor.*
>
> *True, he had sacrificed on the high places, but some of the most conspicuous altars to foreign gods and goddesses had been the idea of his girls. He himself had never imagined that all the other gods should be chased off the hills round Jerusalem or that Yahweh was the only one. Nor, in his view, had Yahweh: he had been quite amenable for years on end, and a large, single kingdom had persisted.*
>
> *Look at Israel nowadays: the North had disappeared completely; there was no king and the Romans controlled Judæa ... There must be something annoying Yahweh: did he, perhaps, want honours for his consorts? Was he angry that his name had gone ex-directory and that he himself was being worshipped alone?*

Fox's view on Solomon's polytheism is supported by Karen Armstrong:

> *In the Temple was a huge bronze basin, representing Yam, the primæval sea of Canaanite myth and two forty-foot pillars, indicating the fertility cult of Asherah.*[2]

Solomon's temple was built according to the then current ideas of what a temple ought to look like. As we have said, ideas do not appear out of thin air.

Fiction

According to most scholars, the most recent books of the Old Testament are the most fictional. *Jonah* is dated between 400-300 BCE; *Ruth*[3] about 433-424; *Esther* around 200 and *Daniel* just after 164 BCE. Thus, *Esther* and *Daniel* were written about the time of the Rosetta stone and about 50 years before Cleopatra (the famous one) becomes Queen of Egypt. When *Esther* was being written, Hannibal was defeating the Roman army at Cannae in the second Punic war.

The Book of *Daniel* is interesting because, while it was written very late, the story is set in the time of the exile, Daniel being among those carried off to Babylon. The

---

[1] The Israelites did expect a great figure from the past to return. They did not expect Jesus.

[2] Asherah was a fertility goddess, one of the consorts of Ba'al.

[3] The Book of *Ruth* tells how Boaz, who has fallen in love with Ruth, cleverly uses the obscure Judaic law of levirate marriage to gain her hand. It is a sort of legal love story. Their child is Obed who in turn is the father of Jesse, the father of David.

Jewish religion was not static and by the time that *Daniel* was written, the idea of an immediately present god with whom the Israelites had day to day contact had faded. As Armstrong writes:

> *It had been tacitly agreed that after the exile, the era of prophecy had ceased. There was to be no more direct contact with God: this was only achieved in the symbolic visions attributed to great figures of the remote past, such as Enoch and Daniel.*

Only by using a figure from antiquity could a later author write about visions.

What is in the Bible?

If you think about it, scrolls do not lend themselves easily to being collated and held together. While a number of scrolls may be tied together by a ribbon, the set or collection can be changed simply by adding or removing scrolls from the bunch. The ribbon may come undone and then all notion of there being a set of documents disappears.

The idea of a fixed collection of texts occurred only when books became widely available but books are not just easier to use than scrolls; they change the nature of what is written. A collection of scrolls presents no fixed order in which they are to be read but a book has a beginning and an end. What is in the book is fixed as soon as it is bound. Bindings do come adrift but, even then, the book may lose no more than a page or two.

Bound books are a late invention. The first books, known as *codices* (singular *codex*), were bound in wooden or lead covers and written on sheets of papyrus, a paper-like material made from a plant of the same name and date from the 1st century CE. Even then, it was not until the 4th century that books overtook scrolls as the favoured method of publication. So while today, we think of the Old Testament as having fixed content from early times, Fox writes:

> *Our earliest full copy of the Hebrew scriptures nowadays is a manuscript known as the Leningrad Manuscript, which was written in AD (CE) 1009. The form of its Hebrew text can be traced back further, to groups of Jewish scholars who were working in the eighth and ninth centuries AD (CE), especially in Palestine. They are known as the Masoretes ('masorah' is the Hebrew word for tradition) and it is to their efforts that we owe the traditional text of the Old Testament.[1]*

The discoveries at Qumran have shown that the Masoretic text is just one line of development. While many of the finds bear a fairly close relationship to the Masoretic text, others do not. Fox again:

> *There is a version of the book of Jeremiah which is an eighth shorter than our Bible's, a text of Samuel which is not so very close to the text from which our Samuel is translated, variants in the text of Job, a doctored text of Ecclesiastes, two different Isaiahs and many other complexities ... quite a variety of readings for bits of Deuteronomy, a text of Leviticus whose differences resemble no known tradition and an intriguing cluster of readings in a copy of Exodus.*

We have to accept that what we have is not a book that was written and bound to be the same for all time. The Old Testament that we read is only one possible set of

---

[1] The Jewish canon, known as the *Mishnah*, was settled between 135 and 160 CE.

texts, each of which has several versions. It contains material written, copied, edited, abbreviated and extended by a number of authors over a period of 600 years or so. Some of its contents were lost to the desert winds, some buried in caves, others used to wrap the Babylonian equivalent of fish and chips and some added when thought to be important or holy, even when not. Over time, the stories changed in whole or in part and the use of scrolls facilitated the process.

Qumran showing the cave in which scrolls were found.

A developing story

Given the foregoing, it would be very surprising if the Bible contained a consistent story. Karen Armstrong goes so far as to ask whether Abraham and Moses even worshipped the same god:

> *But who is Yahweh? ... J says that men had worshipped Yahweh ever since the time of Adam's grandson but in the sixth century, P seems to suggest that the Israelites had never heard of Yahweh until he appeared to Moses in the burning bush. P makes Yahweh explain that he really was the same god as the god of Abraham, as though this were a rather controversial notion: he tells Moses that Abraham had called him El Shaddai and did not know the divine name Yahweh.*

Armstrong points out that we automatically assume that Abraham, Isaac and Jacob were monotheists but they probably had polytheistic beliefs:

> *It is probably more accurate to call these early Hebrews, pagans who shared many of the religious beliefs of their neighbours in Canaan. They would certainly have*

believed in the existence of such deities as Marduk, Ba'al and Anat.[1]

She considers it possible that the patriarchs worshipped separate gods and thinks it likely that the god of Abraham was *El*, the high god of Caanan, known as *El-Shaddai* (El of the mountain) and *El-Elyon* (most high god) and whose name is preserved in *Isra-El* and *Ishma-El*. El is a very mild and friendly deity, while Yahweh is a terrifying god, appearing to Moses in the middle of a volcanic eruption.[2] He may have been the god of others before taking on Israel. Fox dates the very first intimations of Judaic monotheism to around 530 BCE when,

> ... *an unknown prophet (Second Isaiah) is very insistent that Yahweh is the only god, whereas the heathen gods are not gods at all: they are merely idols, bits of wood or stone. There were Jews, no doubt, who thought otherwise: monotheism, the belief in Only One, was born from tensions in this period.*

The Jews took little notice of this prophet and other early monotheistic claims were treated in much the same way. The *heretic King Akhenaten*, as Pinch describes him, (1352-1336 BCE) tried to establish the sun god *Aten* as the only god in Egypt. In rather the way that Henry VIII abolished the monasteries, Akhenaten had a go at the images and temples of all other gods. He even abolished the plural of the word *god*. The Egyptian economy nosedived towards the end of Akhenaten's reign and his successor, the famous Tutankhamen, reversed Akhenaten's policy to appease those gods who had clearly been offended. This may be the first example of the adage, *It's the economy, stupid*.

The first commandment

When thinking about this subject, the first commandment immediately comes to mind. The standard work on this is the monograph by Stamm and Andrew. In their study of the first commandment, *You shall have no other gods beside me*, they offer two alternative translations: *Thou shalt not prefer other gods to me*, and, since the Hebrew words carry a hostile overtone, *Thou shall not have other gods in defiance of me*, and they are clear that the wording of the commandment does not,

> ... *deny the existence of other gods, but only refuses to recognize their legitimacy for Israel.*

Part of the argument is the prescription in *Exodus 34:14*, *You shall worship no other god, for Yahweh, whose name is Jealous, is a jealous god*. This would make no sense if there were no other gods to be jealous of. Armstrong and Fox agree that there is no implication of monotheism in the first commandment and the Emperor Julian, known as the *apostate* because he sought to revive polytheistic beliefs, shares that opinion. Of the statement, *I am a jealous god*, he writes:

> *Then if a man is jealous and envious you think him blameworthy, whereas if god is*

---

[1] Marduk and Ba'al we know about. Anat, the daughter of El, was another fertility goddess and another consort of Ba'al.

[2] It has been suggested that Yahweh was originally a god of volcanoes worshipped in what is now Jordan. While the area contains no active volcanos today the geology shows the result of eruptions, especially in the Pleistocene era. The Bible mentions earthquakes and related activity in *Isaiah*, *Zechariah* and *Jeremiah* as well as in the New Testament. The Jordan Valley is a rift and is subject to frequent earthquakes. A volcano erupted in the Yemen in 2007.

called jealous you think it a divine quality? ... For if he is indeed jealous, then against his will are all other gods worshipped, and against his will do all the remaining nations worship their gods. Then how is it that he did not himself restrain them, if he is so jealous and does not wish that the others should be worshipped, but only himself? [1]

The story of god's covenant with Israel has been dated from the eleventh to the seventh century BCE, the latter more probable. In the covenant, the Israelites' promise to ignore all other gods and worship Yahweh alone and Yahweh promises to look after them in return. An analogy is single sourcing in business. Customer (C) may agree to buy only from supplier (S) if in return S agrees s/he will deliver goods of consistent quality such that C can dispense with goods inward inspection. This only makes sense if there are alternative suppliers for C and the Israelites' deal makes sense only if there were other deals that might have been done. Armstrong writes:

Whatever its date, the idea of a covenant tells us that the Israelites were not yet monotheists, since it only made sense in a polytheistic setting.

Of course, it may well be more a matter of henotheism. While other gods exist, Yahweh is the top god as far as the Israelites are concerned. On many occasions the Israelites reneged on their part of the bargain and were punished for doing so. They had agreed to ignore all other gods but yielded to temptation especially when under stress. Hunger can override covenants. As Armstrong writes:

Yahweh had proved his expertise in war but he was not a fertility god. When they settled in Canaan, the Israelites turned instinctively to the cult of Ba'al, the Landlord of Canaan, who had made the crops grow from time immemorial.

Yahweh may not always have been top god either. According to many scholars, Psalm 82, known as the *Psalm of Asaph*, shows Yahweh, speaking in a council meeting chaired by El. The psalm gives difficulties to translators. The New International Version uses special inverted commas in an attempt to avoid the polytheism/henotheism but just makes it harder to read:

God presides in the great assembly. He renders judgment among the "gods". 'How long will you defend the unjust and show partiality to the wicked? Defend the weak and the fatherless, uphold the cause of the poor and the oppressed. Rescue the weak and the needy, deliver them from the hand of the wicked.' The "gods" know nothing, they understand nothing. They walk about in darkness. All the foundations of the earth are shaken. I said, 'You are "gods". You are all sons of the most high but you will die like mere mortals; you will fall like every other ruler.' Rise up, O god, judge the earth, for all the nations are your inheritance.'

---

[1] A very successful general and administrator, he was made Emperor in 361, following Constantine whose half brother he was. Gore Vidal wrote: *Julian has always been something of an underground hero in Europe. His attempt to stop Christianity and revive Hellenism exerts still a romantic appeal.* Simon Baker writes: *Julian the Apostate was so called because, though brought up an orthodox Christian, he had retro-converted to an intellectual form of paganism. But, by his day, to be a philhellene pagan or polytheist was to be a reactionary, raging impotently against the dying of the light of the pagan gods and their suppression by the one true god of Catholic (universal) Orthodox (correct-belief) Monotheism (one-god-ism).*

Monotheism and the afterlife

There was no official teaching regarding the afterlife in traditional Judaism. This stems from the nature of the deal with Yahweh. It was not a personal one but a deal with the Israelitish people; that is to say a population, a nation or a state, but not any or each individual. The people, as a whole, would continue and prosper, generation by generation, for as long as they did what they had agreed to do: worship only Yahweh and obey only his commands. The promise is in no way that anyone who obeys the laws will thereby become immortal nor does it matter what non-Jews do. Their actions in no way affect Yahweh's deal with Israel - although quite possibly they may affect any deal that they have made with their own god.

At some time, the henotheistic Jewish beliefs gave way to monotheistic ones and this seems to have been when the ideas of the afterlife as personal reward surfaced. Fox places this in the 160s BCE when the Jews were engaged in a war of rebellion against King Antiochus IV:[1]

> *Previously, there were Jews who had believed in a new age to be brought about by god: some also thought of a shadowy afterlife of uncertain scope. In the 160s the belief hardened. During the Jews' great war of resistance, martyrs were dying valiantly, but surely they were not dying forever?*

In *Daniel* (12:2-3), written about this time, we read:

> *And many of those that sleep in the dust of the earth shall awake, some to everlasting life, some to shame and everlasting contempt. Those who are wise shall shine like the brightness of the firmament: and those who lead many to righteousness like the stars for ever and ever.*[2]

In 2 Maccabees 12 there is an argument that the actions of Judas Maccabæus, the leader of the Jewish revolt in 167 BCE, showed that he must have believed in eternal life as the reward for a life of godliness. Discovering that those who had fallen in battle were wearing a forbidden token, he did everything he could to persuade god to forgive them.

> *In doing this he acted very well and honourably, taking account of the resurrection. For if he were not expecting that those who had fallen would rise again, it would have been superfluous and foolish to pray for the dead. But if he was looking to the splendid reward that is laid up for those who fall asleep in godliness, it was a holy and pious thought. Therefore he made atonement for the dead, that they might be delivered from their sin.*

The comments rather indicate that rising from the dead is a novel idea but now, and for the first time, there is a personal reward for obeying Yahweh: immortality. At which point the question of all other gods becomes irrelevant. After all, if one

---

[1] Of the *line in the sand* fame. When Antiochus (216-164 BCE) led an attack on Egypt, he was halted by the Roman Ambassador Popillius, who told him that unless he withdrew a state of war would exist between him and Rome. When Antiochus tried to play for time, Popillius drew a circle in the sand around Antiochus and told him that he must answer before crossing it. The implication was that Rome would declare war unless Antiochus backed down, then and there. He did.

[2] New King James Version with minor amendment for clarity.

god is offering immortality, one cannot see any other products in the market place competing. The offer of an afterlife guarantees monotheism. It also led to proselytising. After all, if someone is about to miss out on the afterlife through a mistaken belief, it surely is the done thing to tell them so - and if there is only one god, any beliefs they have to the contrary have to be wrong. This had major repercussions - although such changes take a while to happen.

Interlude: Cyrus and the Royal Arch

The *dramatis personae* of the Royal Arch story are Zerubbabel, Prince of the People, Haggai the Prophet, and Joshua the son of Josedech the High Priest, supported by Ezra and Nehemiah, lectors and expounders of the Sacred Law and attendants on the Grand Sanhedrin.

The story starts with Nebuchadnezzar, King of Babylon. Having captured Jerusalem and destroyed the first temple which had been built by King Solomon, he took a large number of the Israelites into exile in Babylon with King Jehoiachin their King, no doubt to prevent organised resistance. Some time later, in the story seventy years, Cyrus conquered Babylon and gave the Israelites permission to return to Jerusalem:

Thus saith Cyrus, King of Persia: 'All the kingdoms of the earth hath the lord god of heaven given me: and he hath charged me to build him a house in Jerusalem, which is in Judah. Who is there among you of all his people? The lord his god be with him and let him go up.'[1]

Cyrus - born probably 575 BCE, died 530 BCE

For Royal Arch Masons, the comforting aspect of the story is that it is true. Well, true-ish. Cyrus did give such a proclamation; Zerubbabel did go up to Jerusalem with the intention of rebuilding the temple; Haggai was around then and prophesied that god would enable Zerubbabel to carry out the work. Joshua was the High Priest at the time and Ezra and Nehemiah were indeed lectors and expounders of the Sacred Law. They both read the riot act to those who had ceased to obey the laws.

Of course, there are a few details which don't square with history. For example, Cyrus died in 530 BCE and the weight of scholarly opinion is that Nehemiah's activities take place in 445 BCE, some 85 years after Cyrus, and that Ezra was even later, around 398 BCE.[2] The first person to go up to Jerusalem on temple rebuilding business was not Zerubbabel but an otherwise unknown Sheshbazzar. However, one might still argue that the Royal Arch story has a basis in fact.

---

[1] From the Royal Arch ritual. The original appears in 2 *Chronicles* 36:23 and *Ezra* 1:2, 3.

[2] In the opinion of Fox, Nehemiah came up to Jerusalem from Babylon in 445 BCE and Ezra in 398. Rowley's dates are almost the same: 444 for Nehemiah and 397 for Ezra.

The history

In dealing with this story, we need to know that there are two kings of Judah with very similar names and that during the relevant period Judæa was frequently caught in the crossfire in a continuing war between Egypt and Babylon.

In the summer of 605 BCE, Nebuchadnezzar wins the battle of Carchemish on the Euphrates against the forces of Egypt. The following year, no doubt consolidating his hold on the area, Nebuchadnezzar defeats Jehoiakim (with a *k* and an *m*) and takes Jerusalem. Three years later, following another battle between Egypt and Babylon, this one being fought to a standstill, Jehoiakim revolts temporarily from Babylon. He dies in 598 and his son Jehoiachin (with a *ch* and an *n*) takes over. Almost immediately, the Babylonians besiege Jerusalem.

Largely following Fox, here is the sequence with the Royal Arch story, as I see it:

March 597 Nebuchadnezzar, King of Babylon from 605 to 562 BCE, and reputedly the builder of the Hanging Gardens, captures Jerusalem. He appoints Zedekiah as a client king and levies heavy tribute. The ex-King Jehoiachin is taken captive to Babylon, probably with a retinue.

595 Psamtik II becomes Pharoah in Egypt. He encourages and supports rebellion in Judæa, a policy continued by his son Apries who sends a force to Jerusalem in 588, encouraging Zedekiah to join the Egyptian side.

587 Nebuchadnezzar returns and destroys the city and the temple. He carries prominent Jews into exile: 832 right away and another 745 some five years later. (Accounts of numbers vary.)

539 or 538 Cyrus, King of Persia, conquers Babylon and is said to issue an edict encouraging Jews to go home. This may not be strictly true. The *Cyrus Cylinder* sets out only a general policy regarding religions in general.

538 In keeping with this policy, Sheshbazzar[1] goes to Jerusalem to rebuild the temple, funded by Cyrus. We hear no more of him.

530 Cyrus is killed beside the Syr Darya River. Cambyses II takes over.

522 Cambyses II dies. Darius takes over.

Early **522** Babylon in revolt against Darius

July-August **522** Zerubbabel arrives in Jerusalem, taking advantage of the interregnum and using Cyrus's general proclamation as authority. *Ezra* contains letters defending the Jew's right to rebuild the temple and a decree from (the late) Cyrus is mentioned, specific to Jerusalem. In my view, the story of the letter is an invention of the infamous Chronicler. (*See later.*)

Autumn **521** Second revolt in Babylon. Early betting is Darius to lose.

October **521** The prophet Haggai announces that he has been commanded by the lord to tell Zerubbabel and Joshua the son of Jehozadak (Josedech), the

---

[1] There have been suggestions that Sheshbazzar can be identified with Zerubbabel, but this is generally thought unlikely.

high priest, to start work on rebuilding the temple. Zerubbabel starts laying foundations for the new temple.

Late November **521** Darius wins.

Early December **521** Not having heard the result, Haggai issues a second announcement that the Lord has chosen Zerubbabel and that the Gentile armies, presumably those of Darius, will be destroyed. End of Haggai.

February **520** The prophet Zechariah reports the vision of the man on the red horse who says, *We have walked to and fro through the earth, and behold, all the earth sitteth still, and is at rest*, the implication being that Darius is now settled as king. Zechariah prophesies (*4:6-10*) that Zerubbabel, having laid the foundations of the temple, will complete it. Nothing more is heard of Zerubbabel, although the new temple (which Armstrong calls *a rather modest shrine*) was completed around 520-515 BCE. There is silence on the subject for some sixty years.

465 Artaxerxes I becomes King of Persia.

445 Nehemiah intercedes with Artaxerxes I and is given support to go to Jerusalem and work on rebuilding the walls of the city which are in ruins. He is upset by the behaviour of the Israelites and calls for a strict enforcement of the Sabbath and for the prohibition of foreign wives. Nehemiah remains as Governor of Judæa for twelve years.

404 Artaxerxes II becomes King of Persia.

398 Ezra goes to Jerusalem with the support of Artaxerxes II and with gifts for the temple. He reads the Law of Moses to the Jews.[1]

There is poetic licence in the ritual but many a Hollywood movie has done worse.

The letter and the infamous C

The story that Cyrus wrote a letter specifically permitting the Jews to rebuild the temple at Jerusalem appears in the book of *Ezra* which was written by the Chronicler. It is a most confusing story, but to summarise:

> Zerubbabel refuses when other tribes, largely northerners who had not been exiled to Babylon, ask to be allowed to help rebuild the temple.

> The northerners hire lobbyists to cause a fuss during the reigns of Cyrus, Darius and Ahasuerus (taken to be Xerxes who came after Darius.) A letter is written to Artaxerxes (after Xerxes) accusing the builders of intending not to pay any taxes. Artaxerxes orders the building to cease.

> Haggai prophesies and Zerubbabel recommences building. The Governor comes by and asks who gave them permission to do this. He tells them to stop building until Darius decides.

> They write to Darius asking him to search for a letter in which Cyrus gave specific permission for the temple at Jerusalem to be rebuilt. For some reason he does so.

---

[1] Williamson is of the opinion that Ezra preceded Nehemiah. The view I present here is that of Fox. It seems that Nehemiah made two trips, the second fifteen years after the first.

The letter is found at Achmeta in the province of the Medes. Darius gives permission for the building to go ahead and the temple is completed in the 6th year of his reign.

Masada today, overlooking the Dead Sea. The second temple lasted until the Jewish revolution in 66 CE. The city, including the temple, was destroyed by Roman forces under Titus, later Emperor of Rome. The last of the Jewish revolutionaries died at Masada in 73 CE. The ramp built by the Romans to attack the fortress on top of the mountain can still be clearly seen on the right.

Hercule Poirot would have found the little grey cells much exercised by this tale!

> How come the letter is found in an obscure library in the province of the Medians? It's the wrong way. It is west of Babylon and Jerusalem is east.

> How do the lobbyists cause a fuss during the time of Cyrus who has been dead for 8 years and the time of Xerxes who did not come to the throne for another 37 years?

> How do the lobbyists write to Artaxerxes to stop the building? Artaxerxes did not ascend the throne until fifty years after the temple was completed.

The Chronicler is not a very skilled liar. He gets his dates and kings horribly mixed up. The provenance of the letter is very dubious indeed and, in my view, it is highly likely to be a fabrication.

Chapter six: Sex and the Devil

Francisco Goya, The witches sabbath, 1797/8.

Sex has given problems to many religions, none more so than Christianity in its early days when an understanding of hormones was sadly lacking. It attracts and repels in almost equal measure as indeed does Pan: a sexy beast at one moment, poetically inspiring the next. As an example of this we look at the poetry of Elizabeth Barrett Browning. It was sex that caused Pan to become the devil and while the story of the death of Pan was a factor in him being pictured as the devil, that did not happen immediately. We will look at the different concepts of immorality, sin and evil. I shall seek to show that while our heroes may be figures of sin, they cannot genuinely be seen as figures of evil.

Dualism in religious terms is the belief that there is an equal and opposite power to god. The problem of evil and the heresy of dualism are intractable problems for a monotheism that seeks to show its god as good. We will look at this problem in the company of St Augustine. As examples, we will look at some dreadful events in the Bible and in history, with specific reference to the Crusade against the Cathars, discussing the devil and his place in the drama.

I touch on the Royal Arch Mystical Lecture and Fawlty Towers and finish the chapter with some erotica and with the wholly (perhaps) innocent institution of cheerleading. The interlude that follows the chapter discusses the issue of translating the Bible and the question of Satan: name or job description?

Sex and early Christianity

So, having seen the arrival of monotheism and how it arose, let us now return to Pan and Banebdjedet, our heroes, and investigate how they became seen to be evil. You will recall that Eusebius castigates the Egyptians for their animal gods, explicitly the *he goat at Mendes* and was upset about Banebdjedet and later Pan because of their sexual shenanigans. That sort of thing seems to have been a continuing problem for early Christianity. About a hundred years after Eusebius, St Augustine, in his *Confessions*, thanked god that:

> *Thou didst deliver me out of the bonds of desire, wherewith I was bound most straitly to carnal concupiscence.*

Augustine's account of the eating of the apple[1] has Adam and Eve immediately:

> *... confounded at their own wickedness; and therefore they took fig-leaves ... and covered their shame; for though their members remained the same, they ... experienced a new motion of their flesh, which had become disobedient to them ... For the soul was ... deprived of the command it had formerly maintained over the body and ... neither could it hold the flesh subject, as it would always have been able to do ...*

Pan would have found this very funny (and to be honest, it is) while the Egyptian ladies of Mendes, to whom Banebdjedet was *the prince of young women*, would have wondered what the fuss was about. However, St Augustine was deeply saddened by the way that libidinous desires so easily overcome the proper love of god:

> *The guilt of original sin was transmitted to Adam's descendants through the sexual act: when our reasoning powers were swamped by passion, god was forgotten, and men and women revelled shamelessly in one another.*

St Augustine is not the first to be very hot on the *motions of the flesh*. In 172 CE Tatian was leader of the *Aquarii*, a sect who abstained from wine even in the Eucharist. He considered even marriage to be fornication[2] and all Greek art, and even the Greek language, deceitful and immoral.

Justin Martyr (100-165 CE) called for people to cease to worship,

> *... Bacchus, the son of Semele and Apollo the son of Latona, who in their loves with men did such things as it is shameful even to mention, and Proserpine and Venus, who were maddened with love of Adonis ...*

and dedicate themselves to a god,

> *... of whom we are persuaded that never was he goaded by lust of Antiope or such other women, or of Ganymede.[3]*

Significant for our search, Justin Martyr says:

---

[1] *City of God*. Strictly speaking no *apple* but the *fruit of the tree of the knowledge of good and evil*.

[2] A man needs sex and a woman needs protection for herself and her children, so marriage is a deal like prostitution. Such statements tell more about the speaker than his subject.

[3] *Apologies* 1:25. Antiope was seduced by Zeus in the form of a satyr. Zeus abducted Ganymede, the most beautiful of mortals, to be his cup-bearer.

> *Those who believe these things we pity, and those who invented them we know to be devils.*

St Anthony's third century hormone-free vision has the devil groaning:

> *I am the friend of fornication. I lay my snares before the young to make them fall into vice ...*

Eusebius himself was extremely important in the early history of the church. He was Constantine's advisor and biographer and applauded him for his miraculous ability to spot sin:

> *And as the keen-sighted eagle in its heavenward flight is able to descry from its lofty height the most distant objects on the earth, so did he, while residing in the imperial palace of his own fair city, discover as from a watch-tower a hidden and fatal snare of souls in the province of Phoenicia.*

> *This was a grove and temple ... dedicated to the foul demon known by the name of Venus. Here men undeserving of the name forgot the dignity of their sex, and propitiated the demon by their effeminate conduct; here too unlawful commerce of women and adulterous intercourse with other horrible and infamous practices, were perpetrated ...*

The meaning of Pan

So sex was bad and Pan, whose enjoyment of it was legendary, was really, really bad, encouraging those *libidinous desires* that so horrified St Augustine. One might blame St Paul for this but he has so often been misquoted. What he says is:

> *Now to the unmarried and the widows I say: It is good for them to stay unmarried, as I do. But if they cannot control themselves, they should marry, for it is better to marry than to burn with passion.*

The last two words at least soften what he is so often quoted as saying. While preferring celibacy, he can be fairly realistic (in his terms) about married life. Replying to a letter from the church in Corinth, he writes:

> *It is good for a man not to have sexual relations with a woman. But since sexual immorality is occurring, each man should have sexual relations with his own wife, and each woman with her own husband ... Do not deprive each other except perhaps by mutual consent for a time, so that you may devote yourselves to prayer. Then come together again so that Satan will not tempt you.*

Eusebius might see Pan as a demon but Rabelais[1] saw him as Christ himself. Friedrich Nietzche saw the religions of Greece and Rome as *collective manifestations of exuberant imagination* and saw polytheism as an expression of individuality. In his majestic analysis of the myth, Philippe Borgeaud writes of Pan that:

> *His is the fusion, in one body, of the beast and the immortal; the coincidence of music and noise, of desire and fear, of seduction and repulsion. Be he the good*

---

[1] 1494-1553. French Renaissance writer, most famous for his comic novels *Gargantua* and *Pantagruel*. He writes about human greed and stupidity using grotesque jokes. He was thought to be attacking the political and church authorities and his work was officially banned.

shepherd or the stinking lascivious goat, the seductive musician or the amorous animal from whom the nymphs are put to flight ... it makes no difference. The result remains that Pan ... ends up being translated for us at one time as demon, at another as saviour.

As an example of this, let us take Elizabeth Barrett Browning and her poem *The Dead Pan*. For two-thirds of the poem she mourns:

Gods of Hellas, gods of Hellas,
Can ye listen in your silence?
Can your mystic voices tell us
Where ye hide? In floating islands,
With a wind that evermore
Keeps you out of sight of shore?
Pan, Pan is dead.

...

Have ye left the mountain places,
Oreads wild, for other tryst?
Shall we see no sudden faces
Strike a glory through the mist?
Not a sound the silence thrills
Of the everlasting hills:
Pan, Pan is dead.

From stanzas 24 to 26, she repeats Plutarch's story in a cry of despair.

Calm, of old, the bark went onward,
When a cry more loud than wind
Rose up, deepened, and swept sunward
From the piled Dark behind;
And the sun shrank and grew pale,
Breathed against by the great wail,
'Pan, Pan is dead.'

And the rowers from the benches
Fell, each shuddering on his face,
While departing Influences
Struck a cold back through the place;
And the shadow of the ship
Reeled along the passive deep.
Pan, Pan is dead.

And that dismal cry rose slowly
And sank slowly through the air,
Full of spirit's melancholy
And eternity's despair!
And they heard the words it said,
PAN IS DEAD, GREAT PAN IS DEAD,
PAN, PAN IS DEAD.

> *And that dismal cry rose slowly*
> *And sank slowly through the air,*
> *Full of spirit's melancholy*
> *And eternity's despair!*
> *And they heard the words it said,*
> *PAN IS DEAD, GREAT PAN IS DEAD,*
> *PAN, PAN IS DEAD.*

At this point the poem switches from poetry to pious versifying. She ends:

> *O brave poets, keep back nothing,*
> *Nor mix falsehood with the whole!*
> *Look up godward; speak the truth in*
> *Worthy song from earnest soul:*
> *Hold, in high poetic duty,*
> *Truest Truth the fairest Beauty!*
> *Pan, Pan is dead.*

Browning thinks she should disapprove of Pan but the legends of the Greek gods and the energy of Pan clearly inspire her.

Whence the evil?

It need not be a matter of either/or as John Donne shows. His poetry went through a similar change of focus from love to religion but avoided descent into versifying. Compare the strength of the tenth of his *Divine Poems* that starts:

> *Death be not proud, though some have called thee*
> *Mighty and dreadful, for thou art not soe,*

A slow enough opening in all conscience but then the power is unleashed and in the last four lines he despatches death with a rapier stroke:

> *And poppie, or charmes can make us sleepe as well,*
> *And better than thy stroake; why swell'st thou then?*
> *One short sleepe past, wee wake eternally,*
> *And death shall be no more; death thou shalt die.*

There is as much passion and power in this religious verse as there is in his love poetry, say, *The Canonization*, with its explosive opening:

> *For god's sake hold your tongue, and let me love,*
> *Or chide my palsy, or my gout,*
> *My five grey hairs, or ruin'd fortune flout,*
> *With wealth your state, your mind with arts improve.*
> *Take you a course, get you a place,*
> *Observe his Honour, or his Grace,*
> *Or the King's real, or his stamped face*
> *Contemplate, what you will, approve,*
> *So you will let me love.*

Donne did not see love and sex as evil but as much a part of life as death. Donne combines both with equal power as in the quintessentially beautiful *A Nocturnall upon S. Lucies Day, Being The Shortest Day*, written after the death of his wife. It begins:

> 'Tis the yeares midnight, and it is the dayes,
> Lucies, who scarce seaven houres herself unmaskes;
> The Sunne is spent, and now his flasks
> Send forth light squibs, no constant rayes;
> The world's whole sap is sunke;
> The generall balme th'hydroptique earth hath drunk,
> Whither, as to the beds-feet, life is shrunke,
> Dead and enterr'd; yet all these seeme to laugh,
> Compar'd with mee, who am their Epitaph.

The last stanza returns us to our goat:

> But I am None; nor will my Sunne renew.
> You lovers, for whose sake, the lesser Sunne
> At this time to the Goate is run
> To fetch new lust, and give it you,
> Enjoy your summer all;
> Since shee enjoys her long nights festivall,
> Let mee prepare towards her, and let mee call
> This houre her Vigill, and her Eve, since this
> Both the yeares, and the dayes deep midnight is.

Sexual love was not evil for the Egyptians, Greeks or Romans. They didn't admire celibacy. There was no particular reason for them to do so. Sexual love did not bring with it the risk of the fires of hell. It is only when it does, as in early Christianity, that celibacy becomes advisable. Pan's death is more than the end of a god, more than the end of pantheism. In place of the gods as explanations of events, as natural processes or indeed as *collective manifestations of exuberant imagination*, we find a god who demands obedience:

> Who, having defined for our instruction the limits of good and evil, will reward or punish as we have obeyed or disregarded his divine commands.[1]

So Banebdjedet and Pan were caught up in a change. Their behaviour was sometimes exciting and romantic but at others times sexy and naughty - or *naughty but nice* as some would have it. In the either/or form of monotheism, you can't have nice naughtiness. St Theophilus, bishop of Antioch around 180 CE, wrote:[2]

> As a burnished mirror, so ought man to have his soul pure. When there is rust on the mirror, it is not possible that a man's face be seen in the mirror; so also when there is sin in a man, such a man cannot behold god.

---

[1] Explanation of the working tools in the third degree of craft masonry.

[2] *Apology* (1:2)

It is easy, therefore, to see why the devil was depicted by early Christians as a figure resembling Pan - except he wasn't.

Picturing the devil

Peter Stanford argues that no artist's impression of the devil exists before the sixth century. Thereafter he is depicted in many different and sometimes very funny ways but rarely as having much in the way of goatish or ram-like features. The devil is represented by a menagerie of evil and violent creatures with no consistency. In Luther Link's view, it is this very lack of consistency that characterises portraits of the devil; *a mask without a face*, as Link calls him.

A picture from a French manuscript, dated to between 1450 and 1470.
Every chicken's nightmare and surely deliberate humour.

In 1542, as Wilfred Schoff tells us, the Spaniard Pedro Mexia published in Seville a compilation of marvellous tales entitled *Silva di Varia Leccion*.[1] One of the tales he included was Plutarch's story of Pan. The book was a best seller. A French edition went into four reprints. Guillaume Bigot (1502-1550) picked up the story and his friend, Rabelais, used it in his famous *Gargantua and Pantagruel*.

---

[1] *A miscellany of various lessons*

It would be interesting to know (writes Schoff) *how fully the writings of Eusebius were available to the medieval church in Western Europe. Greek, after the days of Charlemagne, was practically a forgotten language ... and it is quite possible that the Pan story slept throughout the dark millennium.*

Schoff argues that the story disappeared until Mexia's book. Following its resurfacing, the devil does appear as Pan, but not often. In their illustrations of *Paradise Lost*, both William Blake and Gustav Doré show a human devil while Guido Reni uses the powerful image of a balding rather than horned figure.

Archangel Michael defeating Satan.

Sin, immorality and evil

Sin is a word that operates, properly, only within a religious context: a matter of transgressing against a god's laws. It is not the same as immorality. An atheist cannot be said to sin because s/he has no divine laws to disobey but atheists still have a concern with morality. Among the sins, adultery seems to take up undue airtime. A panel of bishops in 2003 said that the Church of England appeared to have *an unhealthy obsession* with sexual sin. One is reminded of Oscar Wilde:

> *To be good, according to the vulgar standard of goodness ... merely requires a certain amount of sordid terror, a certain lack of imaginative thought, and a certain low passion for middle-class respectability.*

In common parlance, the subject of adultery is not always treated very seriously.

Wills's Cigarettes

Elinor Glyn

The recent series of women's novels commencing with *Fifty Shades of Grey*, is nothing new. Elinor Glyn (1864-1943) created the mass market for women's erotic fiction as long ago as 1908, leading to the famous rhyme:

Would you like to sin
With Elinor Glyn
On a tiger skin?
Or would you rather err
With her
On some other fur? [1]

It is the subject of many jokes:

On his return from the mountain, Moses found a crowd waiting for him. 'How did you get on Mo? What's the deal?' they shouted. 'Well,' he replied, 'The good news is I got him down to ten. The bad news is adultery's still in.'

In most people's eyes, sin is not the same as evil. It is unlikely that many people today would apply the word *evil* to the breaking of religious ordinances. Working on a Sabbath is not normally described as evil, nor is taking the lord's name in vain by the silly texting *OMG*. Evil acts are those which are extreme and not easy to comprehend: the pogroms in the Soviet Union under Stalin, the Inquisition, Japanese prisoner-of-war camps, My Lai and other obscenities of the Vietnam War, ethnic cleansing, Abu Graib, the twin towers, the crusades, the slave trade and, although to mention it in a list seems obscene, the holocaust.

Evil events also include natural disasters in which large numbers of people suffer from no fault of their own: a Tsunami in Sumatra or Japan, an earthquake in Haiti,

---

[1] The rhyme is anonymous.

a volcano in Chile, hurricanes in the Caribbean and the USA or a school bus crashing in flames. The connection between evil acts and natural disasters is, oddly enough, religious. A natural disaster is an act of god.

The occurrence of natural disasters was no logical problem for the Egyptians, Greeks and Romans. Such an event might indeed be the result of a god's behaviour and the reasons for it varied. On many occasions it was just like a traffic accident: the god did not notice what s/he was doing; humans just got in the way. At other times, it was a matter of whim: the god just felt like it or was upset for good or bad reasons with the local populace. Some gods were more likely to be inimical to humans than others but all could be dangerous or supportive as and when they felt like it, and the purpose of prayer and sacrifice was to put them in a good mood. It was not a theological issue; simply a practical one. You needed to identify gods who are about to cause trouble and sacrifice to them in time - a bit like car service.

The problem of evil

Once there is only a single god, omnipotent and omnipresent, evil becomes a problem. How can a being, we ask, thought to be beneficent, omniscient and omnipotent allow dreadful things to happen to creatures who are entirely innocent? The Scottish philosopher David Hume (1711-1776) wrote:

> *Is he willing to prevent evil, but not able? then is he impotent. Is he able, but not willing? then is he malevolent. Is he both able and willing? whence then is evil?*

Earlier, St Augustine had expressed the problem as:

> *Either god cannot abolish evil or he will not. If he cannot, he is not all-powerful; if he will not, then he is not all-good.*

A full treatment of the argument might run:

- *To be omniscient is to know everything, including knowing what is about to happen.*
- *To be omnipotent is to be able to do anything, including preventing things about to happen.*
- *Someone who is omniscient would know that an event in which innocent victims will suffer horribly was about to happen.*
- *Someone who is omnipotent would be able to prevent an event in which innocent victims will suffer horribly.*
- *An omnipotent being who knows that a dreadful event is about to happen but does not act to prevent it cannot be beneficent.*
- *Dreadful events do happen.*
- *God cannot be omniscient, omnipotent <u>and</u> beneficent.*

The theologian Hans Jonas held that after Auschwitz, a belief in an omnipotent god was impossible while Charles Darwin wrote:

> *I cannot persuade myself that a beneficent and omnipotent god would have designedly created the Ichneumonidae (parasitic wasps) with the express intention of their feeding within the living bodies of caterpillars.*

St Augustine's answer

Most Christian apologists to the modern day follow Augustine's answer, in *The City of God*. He divides evil into three categories: evil as the result of free will; evil as the result of original sin and evil that looks so to us but is not really so.

He argues, firstly, that god's creation is not evil but what we make of it may be. We have the free will to choose and some people chose wrongly.

> *Lovely and charming objects, are not evil, only the heart that inordinately loves sensual pleasures, to the neglect of temperance.*

The problem with this is that free will conflicts with the idea of omniscience. If god knows what is going to happen, then what is going to happen has already been decided, which leaves no room for free will. If we have free will and can choose what we do, then god cannot know before we choose[1] and is thus not omniscient.

Adam and Eve, Jan Gossaert

Secondly, Augustine argues that evil enters into the world through the fall of Adam and original sin,

> *... and the dreadful penalty entailed thereby on his sinful posterity, no less than death.*[2]

Augustine writes,

> *... human nature was in (Adam's) person vitiated and altered to such an extent that he ... became subject to the necessity of dying. And what he himself had become by sin and punishment, such he generated those whom he begot; that is to say, subject to sin and death.*

This does not seem to solve the problem of beneficence. Why would a good and loving god blame and punish people for something that their ancestors did? The problem is the combination of all three virtues.

It seems that you can have any two of these attributes but never all three of omniscience, omnipotence and beneficence. Even allowing that these logical problems could be overcome, we are still left with the problem of natural disasters; those *acts of god,*

---

[1] Although he may well have a good idea.

[2] Royal Arch ritual.

and even more so those genuine acts of god reported in the Old Testament. As an example, take *Ezekiel 9*, the story of the man with the masonically famous writer's inkhorn. You may recall that the story is one of god punishing idolators. He tells the inkhorn bearer to:

> Go through the midst of the city, through the midst of Jerusalem, and put a mark[1] on the foreheads of the men who sigh and cry over all the abominations that are done within it.

He then orders soldiers to:

> Go after him through the city and kill; do not let your eye spare, nor have any pity. Utterly slay old and young men, maidens and little children and women; but do not come near anyone on whom is the mark.

When Ezekiel remonstrates with god he replies,

> The iniquity of the house of Israel and Judah is exceedingly great, and the land is full of bloodshed, and the city full of perversity,

and for this reason he will, he says,

> ... neither spare, nor will I have pity, but I will recompense their deeds on their own head.

Fair enough, you might say. A deal's a deal. The Israelites were supposed to obey god's laws no matter what in return for his special care, so the Israelites have brought it on themselves - but what about those *maidens and little children*? Did they understand the deal? Did they have a part in the perversities? Would they have been old enough to know a perversity if they saw one? Would they be able to *sigh and cry over all the abominations*? It seems difficult to believe.[2]

Ezekiel is of course a series of visions but there are similar reports in more historical accounts, for example in *Numbers 31*. Here is an abridged version:

> And they warred against the Midianites, as the lord commanded Moses; and they slew all the males. And the children of Israel took all the women of Midian captives, and their little ones, and took the spoil of all their cattle, and all their flocks, and all their goods. And they burnt all their cities wherein they dwelt, and all their goodly castles, with fire. And Moses was wroth with the officers of the host, with the captains over thousands, and captains over hundreds, which came from the battle.

It is no surprise to us that Moses was angry at the behaviour of his soldiers. What is a surprise is that far from castigating them for their dreadful actions, he was angry that they had not done even worse.

> Have ye saved all the women alive? Behold, these caused the children of Israel ... to commit trespass against the lord ... Now therefore kill every male among the little ones, and kill every woman that hath known man by lying with him. But all the

---

[1] Said in the Royal Arch ritual to be the *tau*.

[2] From my observation, when maidens sigh it has little to do with abominations - unless you consider *Take That* or *Westlife* to be abominable.

women children, that have not known a man by lying with him, keep alive for yourselves.[1]

If the deal is *obey the rules and Israel gets looked after*, this is what you have to accept. But do you? A god who demands this behaviour is morally repulsive. Surely the morally correct thing to do is to refuse, no matter what. Of course, few believers can stomach such an argument and so there is an attempt to show that whatever god wants, however nasty, is really morally good after all. St Augustine argues that such events, and indeed natural disasters, appear evil only to our inadequate vision. This is his third explanation of evil that we must praise god whatever happens because we cannot see the whole of his purpose.[2]

> *And to thee is nothing whatsoever evil: yea, not only to thee, but also to thy creation as a whole ... But in the parts thereof, some things, because unharmonising with others, are accounted evil ... Far be it then that I should say, 'These things should not be' for should I see nought but these, I should indeed long for the better; but still must praise thee even for these ... because with a sounder judgment I apprehended that the things above were better than these below.*

Such an argument is difficult to sustain in the face of our examples - murdering children and enslaving women are not, in themselves, actions difficult to understand - and, in any case, it is no explanation. It says no more than we should stop thinking about it. This answer continues to be used; for example, Peter Kreeft writes:

> *A child on the tenth storey of a burning building cannot see the firefighters with their safety net on the street. They call up, 'Jump! We'll catch you. Trust us.' The child objects, 'But I can't see you.' The firefighter replies, 'That's all right. I can see you.' We are like that child, evil is like the fire, our ignorance is like the smoke, god is like the firefighter, and Christ is like the safety net.*

The analogy does not hold. We are not children. We think, analyse and consider. We have a moral sense. To say that we should not use our powers of thought and moral judgement is no answer. Moral questions are asked and do have to be answered. Typical of such questions is the one that the Emperor Julian asks:

> *What could be more irrational, even if ten or fifteen persons, or even, let us suppose, a hundred ... ventured to transgress some one of the laws laid down by god; was it right that on account of this one thousand, six hundred thousand should be utterly destroyed? For my part I think it would be altogether better to preserve one bad man along with a thousand virtuous men than to destroy the thousand together with that one.*

Charles Mathewes writes,

> *The picture ... of a perfectly good and omnipotent god not only seems wildly at odds with what evidence we can comprehend, as Hume points out; it also, as Nietzsche suggests, hints that there is something more than merely theoretical interest in the problem - that 'something more' being ... the compound of desperate utopian hope ... which Nietzsche called 'slave morality.'*

---

[1] King James Version.

[2] *Confessions* 7:13:9

The world seems cruelly inappropriate for the sort of account Christianity proposes and the protestations of millennia of theologians, seemingly so blind to the blatant refutation of their theories by concrete cases, seem suspicious, motivated by interests other than surface theoretical concerns. In this situation to say 'God is love' can seem like handing daisies to a psychopath.

Tough-minded answer

One way to approach the problem of evil is to confront it head on, giving a tough minded answer. It doesn't have to matter whether god is good or not. He just is.

What is an electron? Is it a wave? Is it a particle? Is it a bird? Is it a plane? If you measure it as a wave, it will behave as a wave. If you measure it as a particle, it will behave as a particle. It is conceivable, and even likely, that an electron is neither a wave nor a particle. It isn't really like anything in the Newtonian world and using a Newtonian ruler to measure the spin of an electron, doesn't make much sense. The Newtonian world makes certain assumptions about reality, few of which hold in the quantum universe.

By analogy, our moral perception makes certain assumptions about intentionality and ethical understanding. One might argue that measuring god makes no more sense than using a Newtonian ruler with quanta. The nature of electrons is a bit of a puzzle but quantum mechanics works. The fact that we cannot explain it, doesn't alter this. God just is and it doesn't matter a row of beans whether you like what he does or not. If you are a believer[1] then you believe that following god's commands gets you into heaven. Why, doesn't matter. It works. Most of the time, it means doing good things:

> *So that by square conduct, level steps and upright intention we hope to ascend to those blessed mansions from which all goodness emanates.*[2]

Sometimes it is not goodness that emanates but less pleasant things but so what? Sh*t happens. Heaven is what you want and obedience is the route.

Masonic aside

There is an echo of the tough minded answer to the problem of evil in the first part of the traditional Royal Arch Mystical Lecture; one which is heavy on original sin and the need for humility, contrition and resignation. The message of this lecture is that we are made as servants to god and that the criterion of what is good is what benefits him. If we give him what he wants, we gain his favour,

> *... by which means alone we hope to pass through the ark of our redemption into the mansions of eternal bliss.*

Despite the fact that god made us, we need his constant help to deliver what he wants, otherwise *we must have ever remained unprofitable servants in his sight*. If we fail, god will exact extreme retribution. Offending against his *mighty will and power* means being *cut off from the land of the living*. While memorising that lecture, I was constantly

---

[1] If you are not a believer, you might find the Old Testament god to be a very unpleasant person. But then, if you are not a believer, it doesn't matter. It's only a book.

[2] From the explanation of the Working Tools in the second degree.

put in mind of the *Fawlty Towers* episode, *Gourmet Night*, in which Basil's car breaks down and he thrashes it with a branch of a tree as punishment. After all, he had given it fair warning about its behaviour! Maybe this accounts for why the Mystical Lecture is so hard to learn.[1]

It's the devil wot done it

One way out may be to blame the devil; to hold that it is the devil from whom all evil stems. That would appear to get god off the hook. God does the good things and the devil the bad things - but there is a problem.

- If the devil is subordinate to god and acts by god's command (or permission as in the Job story), then the devil cannot carry the blame. If god commands him to act then the blame stays with god. (Mind you, the excuse, *I just did what I was told,* has become less and less acceptable. It is quite a thought that the devil, as the servant of god, might be obliged to refuse to obey god's commands because they were immoral.)

- If the devil is independent of god and acts of his own free will, god's goodness can be saved but only at the expense of his omnipotence or omniscience. If the devil can do evil things that god would wish not done, then god either cannot prevent them or did not know they were going to happen. The devil's independence and power limits that of god. We still find we can have two but not all three.

Augustine indulges in a wriggle to avoid this conclusion, arguing that in god's *most excellent scheme of things*, anything the devil does may only *appear* bad; that whatever the devil does, god has arranged things such that there will be a good outcome in the end. If terrible things happen to wicked people then the devil is just delivering god's justice and if terrible things happen to good people, then they are taught perseverance and thus come closer to god. This is merely a wriggle. The devil is still doing what god wants him to do and so god is still the author of the terrible things.

The second part of the claim, that the torments of the righteous bring them closer to god, is an empirical statement; it is a matter of fact whether it is true or not. Since the existence of evil is often said to be the main reason why people do not believe in god, the empirical data would appear to say that Augustine is factually wrong.

Of course, with the tough-minded answer, the devil is unnecessary. When god is seen as the author of both good and evil, there is no need of a cosmic enemy and, indeed, the god of the Old Testament does not seek to be nice. In his book on the devil, Darren Oldridge refers to *Isaiah 45:7* which he says is *especially stark*.

> *I form the light, and create the darkness: I make peace, and create evil: I the Lord do all these things.*

---

[1] Bernard E Jones tell us that the lectures date from no earlier than 1835. They do not appear in American working nor Bristol or Irish working. They seem to be the work of the Rev. GA Browne, at the time Grand Superintendent for Suffolk. The new alternative version of the Mystical Lecture is less heavy on the original sin and is a bit, but not a lot, better.

If god does not need to be seen as benevolent, the existence of evil presents no logical problem. We know we can have omniscience and omnipotence without benevolence - but that is not what the Christian wants.

Dualism

Dualism, in theology but not in philosophy or psychology,[1] is the view that there are two supernatural beings in conflict. We met an example of this in Cyrus the Great and the beliefs of the Achæmenids which held, as the *Encyclopædia Iranica* puts it:

> ... there was an adversary of god, like him uncreated and in this respect his 'twin'. This is the Hostile Spirit, Angra Mainyu. Zoroastrian tradition states ... that Ahura Mazdā became the Creator ... to destroy Angra Mainyu, and so to achieve a universe that was wholly good.

The belief that god and the devil are quite separate beings in conflict provides at least one meaning and purpose to prayer. The *Zohar*, a thirteenth century work by Moses de Leon, says that prayer, ritual acts, and even the rejection of sinful thoughts give strength to the divine in its conflict with the evil powers. Prayers are not just shopping lists for god; they power some kind of force-field.

Perhaps the most well-known example of dualism is Manichæism. An Iranian who lived from 216-276 CE, Mani created a religion which was a serious competitor to Christianity and which survived his death for at least 600 years. Augustine himself was a Manichæist for a while. Its central and very complex myth is of a war between good and evil, a war which like that in Zoroastrianism gives rise to creation. Manichæism is not really a variant of Christianity, but it was still treated as a virulent heresy and came to be the brand name of any dualist belief.

The Cathars

The Bogomils, a sect that arose in the first Bulgarian Empire,[2] believed that the world was created not by god but by the devil, who was an opposite and equal force. The devil was god's first-born son who became jealous of the way that his father favoured his brother, Michael.[3] In retaliation, the devil created the earth as his own empire and so, to the Bogomils, everything in creation was evil. As a consequence, they rejected every material pleasure.

Like the Bogomils, whom in many respects they followed, the Cathars believed that the physical and visible world in which we live is evil. The *Liber de duobus principiis* (Book of two principles), a Cathar text,[4] presents an argument in line with the problem of evil. Section IV is entitled, *A Compendium for the instruction of beginners* and I quote from this.

In *IV.5*, the author writes that god cannot be nor can create evil:

---

[1] In the latter case, dualism is the view that the mind and body are not identical; that mental events cannot be reduced to physical events in the brain. It is opposed to materialism.

[2] The first Bulgarian Empire reached its height in the mid 900s CE and was defeated by the Byzantine Emperor Basil II in 1018.

[3] Who appeared on earth as Jesus.

[4] Said to have been written by Jean or Giovanni de Lugio, a *True Christian* (as the Cathars referred to themselves) writing around 1240 in Northern Italy.

In *IV.5*, the author writes that god cannot be nor can create evil:

> *Therefore, it is firmly to be believed that because there exists in god no potency for evil by which he might bring evil things into existence, there is another principal, one of evil, who is potent in evil. From that one flow all evils which were, are, and shall be.*

In *IV.13*, which seems directly aimed at *Ezekiel 9* and the story of inkhorn man, the author deduces that a world containing evil cannot be the work of a benevolent, omniscient and omnipotent god:

> *... it is quite evident that he cannot be a true creator who, in the temporal world, caused the manifest and merciless destruction of so many men and women with all their children. For it does seem incredible that in the case of the children, since they had not the knowledge rightly to distinguish good from evil, nor the free will, that the true Creator could in this temporal world have destroyed them pitilessly by a most revolting death; especially when the Lord had said through Ezekiel, 'The son shall not bear the iniquity of the father, but the soul that sinneth, the same shall die.'*

In *IV.17*, the author concludes that the world was created by an evil force:

> *Therefore ... there is an evil god, lord and creator; he is the source and cause of all the evils ...*

The world, containing evil as it does, must be the work of the devil and all matter, the stuff of the material world, must be corrupt. The Canadian author, Stephen O'Shea writes:

> *The god deserving of Cathar worship was a god of light, who ruled the invisible, the ethereal, the spiritual domain: this god, unconcerned with the material, simply didn't care if you got into bed before getting married, had a Jew or Muslim for a friend, treated men and women as equals, or did anything else contrary to the teaching of the medieval Church.*

While in practice, most Cathars acted according to normal moral codes, what an individual did was up to him or her:

> *Worldly authority was a fraud, and worldly authority based on some divine sanction, such as the church claimed, was outright hypocrisy.*

The Cathars' religious view of reincarnation was like Bill Murray in *Groundhog Day*; reincarnation repeated until the individual led a spotless life. As O'Shea says:

> *To be saved ... meant becoming a saint. To be damned was to live again, on this corrupt Earth. Hell was here, not in some horrific afterlife dreamed up by Rome to scare people out of their wits.*

The only escape from the cycle of reincarnation was to become a *Perfect*,

> *... to abstain from any form of sexual intimacy, pray constantly and fast frequently. When allowed to eat, they had to avoid all meat and any byproduct of reproduction ... cheese, eggs, milk or butter. One slip in this strictly enforced regimen - be it as minor as a nibble of veal or a stolen kiss - and the status of Perfect vanished.*

Poster for the 1993 movie starring Bill Murray and Andie MacDowell.

The Cathars were entirely heretical; so much so that the Church exterminated them to prevent their beliefs endangering the souls of good Christians.

The greatest evil

Most people know about the crusades to the Holy Land but perhaps fewer know that there were many other crusades or crusade-like actions: against the Moors in Lisbon, the Arabs in Tunis, by the Germans and Danes against the Wends in the Rhineland, in Egypt, in Prussia, Estonia, Russia, Finland and Byzantium, with Orthodox Christianity as its national religion. Simon Lloyd writes:

The crusade, the most potent weapon in the papacy's formidable arsenal, increasingly emerged ... as an instrument to be applied as and when popes saw fit, and against whomsoever and wherever its use was appropriate.

Some crusades were religious, some were little more than land grabs, but none were as murderous as the Albigensian Crusade which commenced in 1209 and officially ended in 1229. In fact, the fighting went on until 1244 and the Inquisition executed its last Cathar in 1321. During the destruction of the city of Béziers, when asked how the soldiers could identify the Cathars among the good Christians in the city, the Papal Legate is popularly supposed to have said, *Caedite eos. Novit enim Dominus qui sunt eius* (Kill them all. God will know his own.) The city was set on fire and everyone, *from graybeard Cathar Perfect to newborn Catholic baby was put to death*. The Legate reported to the Pope:

> *Nearly twenty thousand of the citizens were put to the sword, regardless of age and sex. The workings of divine vengeance have been wondrous.*

It seems to be common in Christian religions for each to believe that it is the only correct one. In this way, a religion may not itself be evil but, in its anxiety to save souls, it can be, and often is, a vehicle for evil. If in the minds of the believer, the greatest evil is to lead someone away from a belief in god and thus to endanger an immortal soul, then just about any action is legitimate to prevent this. Religions have done terrible things to force believers in other religions or none, to convert. The events of the period from 1209 to 1321 were wholly evil.

The title of Christopher Frayling's book and 1995 TV series, subtitled *a journey through the middle ages,* seems most appropriate: *Strange Landscape.*

Not evil enough

The devil-as-goat figure is brought back into our consciousness by Pedro Mexia and his book. It is used by Francisco Goya in 1798. Corrado Giaquinto gives us a delicately horned devil in his *Satan before God* (c. 1750). The question therefore arises of why Guido Reni, William Blake and Gustav Doré did not use it. The horrors that we have witnessed in this chapter are truly what we would term *evil* in any normal use of the word. If we were able to use the notion of a devil, it would most certainly be possible to all see this as his work - but impossible to see it as that of Pan or Banebdjedet.

Goya's pictures are of nothing more sinister than a bunch of ladies, old enough to know better, flashing a goat and neglecting their children and grandchildren. So adultery? Quite possibly. Sex? Yes. But murdering twenty thousand innocents and seeing this as the workings of divine vengeance; slaying old and young men, mothers and little children but keeping every virgin alive for yourself; burning the cities in which they lived; Abu Graib, slavery and the holocaust? No. These are not the actions of Pan or Banebdjedet. For real evil, you need an image far stronger than a nice-but-naughty one. A human figure would do, of course.

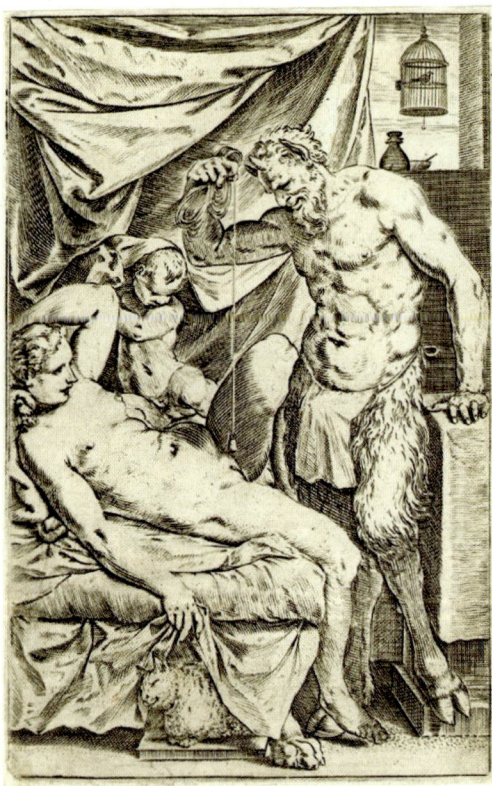

Erotica

Before departing from this theme, with some hesitation I draw your attention to this engraving. Many artists, even great ones, have made money out of erotica. Titian's work is well known. The painter Agostino Carracci (1557-1602), who also painted religious themes, made copies of the *I Modi* (The ways), an erotic book first published in 1520. The originals were destroyed on the orders of the Pope but the Carracci copies survive, including this curious example entitled *The Satyr Mason*.

It was the apron that brought this work to my attention. I have tried to discover a masonic connection but without success. Working masons' aprons were much larger than the one in the picture and there is no suggestion that speculative masonry existed in Italy in the early 1500s. Despite the presence of the plumb-line, it seems that the apron simply serves the function of covering while declaring an erection.

So horns were still identified with sex. Despite the fact that neither Banebdjedet nor Pan will serve as figures of evil, particularly of those we have witnessed, they will suffice as figures of sin - specifically the sin of adultery and the mytheme still works today. The NFL team, the St Louis Rams, has cheerleaders once known as the *Embraceable Ewes*. All right! Now this is more like our Pan! Very naughty-but-nice.

Interlude: Satan or satan in the Bible

When reading the Bible in the normal way, one does not think very much about the difficulties of translation but it can raise important issues. Let us take a non-controversial example: *Isaiah* 13:21. The King James Version reads:

> *But wild beasts of the desert shall lie there; and their houses shall be full of doleful creatures; and owls shall dwell there, and satyrs shall dance there.*

I was attracted to this verse by the possibility that satyrs were known to the Israelites in the time of *Isaiah* but the 1984 *New International Version* of the Bible does not use the word:

> *But desert creatures will lie there,*
> *Jackals will fill her houses;*
> *There the owls will dwell,*
> *And there the wild goats will leap about.*

Instead of satyrs dancing, we have goats leaping. We still have owls but now jackals instead of doleful creatures. The *Amplified Version* of the Bible reads:

> *But wild beasts of the desert will lie down there, and the people's houses will be full of dolefully howling creatures; and ostriches will dwell there, and wild goats [like demons] will dance there.*

Back to the doleful creatures who are now howling, poor things, but the owls have become ostriches and the wild goats are now letting loose on the dance floor. The 19th century *Young's Literal Translation* seeks to give the straight meaning of words without reference to religious views. It reads:

> *And Ziim have lain down there,*
> *And full have been their houses of howlings,*
> *And dwelt there have daughters of an ostrich,*
> *And goats do skip there.*

Now we have ostrich offspring; perhaps the same size as owls. The source of the howling is now unknown and the goats have calmed down a bit. Young does not try to translate *Ziim* but *Barnes Notes*[1] on the Bible says it *denotes properly those animals that dwell in dry and desolate places* - which seems to fit. Finally the *Great Isaiah Scroll*, found near Qumran in 1947, reads:

> *And their houses shall be filled with jackals and relatives of the owl shall dwell there and wild goats shall dance there and island hyenas shall cry in widows' houses and serpents in their pleasant halls.*

No satyrs after all. Just a degree of disagreement on the menagerie present. Of course, this does not matter much. No religious belief will hang on owls, ostriches or their offspring, nor even on the terpsichorean ability of goats but suppose we take a more controversial example - the word *satan*.

---

[1] Albert Barnes (1798-1870) was an American Presbyterian church minister in New Jersey and Philadelphia. His notes are still popular despite being in fourteen volumes.

Is there a devil in the Bible? While few people would be agitated by the choice between owls and ostriches, some people may get very upset about whether or not Satan appears in the Bible. Translating the Bible is not just a matter of translating words. The question of *belief,* in the specific sense of that word, comes in as well.

I was surprised to discover that the word *satan* appears in relatively few places in the Old Testament: only three in the New International Version and four in the King James. The most famous appearance of Satan is in the Book of Job where, as an agent of god, he tries Job's faith. He is acting, if you will forgive the pun, like the devil's advocate, once known as the *Promoter of the Faith*[1] in the Catholic Church, whose job it was to find every reason why a candidate should not be made a saint. In the Book of Job, one might say that Satan is god's employee, just doing his job, if that were not just too terrible a pun.

It is generally accepted that the word *satan* comes from the Hebrew *ha-Satan*, which is taken to mean *the opposer* or *the accuser.*

The question is whether the word *satan* is the name of a unique being or the job title of one of the angels.

The decision is not going to be made entirely on linguistic grounds. We know how to translate the word but the real issue is whether one wants to believe in an incarnation of nastiness. The belief will drive the translation.

Gustave Doré, 1866 Illustration for Paradise Lost. Luke 10:18 gives Milton another source for his fallen angel: I beheld Satan as lightning fall from heaven.

---

[1] The role was abolished in the 1980s.

Chapter seven: It's Magic

Le Conjurer, Heironymous Bosch (1450-1516.) Notice the pickpocket far right!

Let's take a break from the heavy stuff for a while and talk about magic: the wonderful tale of raising the dead for a mysterious lady, folk cures, necromancy, potions, divination, the Grand Grimoire and Astral Light.

Today medicine is a matter of science. We seek to understand what causes conditions in the body and what can be done to prevent or ameliorate them. This understanding is rooted in chemistry, biochemistry and, most importantly, the scientific method. In earlier times there was no such understanding and cures were mysterious with little distinction between magic, medicine and religion.

We will look at the nature of claims of success for magic, and whether Constant really believed what he wrote. I will ensure an appropriate measure of gothic horror, bewitchment and fortune telling (since you have crossed my palm with silver by buying this book) including a foolproof way of finding celestial horoscopes by onomancy (which you have always wanted) ... oh, and I will give a mention to sexual magic.

During all this, I shall be seeking what gives Constant's engraving its persuasiveness; why it is seen as anything more than a figure with a goat's head. Now far away from its incarnation as Banebdjedet or even Pan at his most naughty, the goat image is becoming sinister and we need to discover why. As Constant says:

EVERYTHING IS POSSIBLE TO HIM WHO WILLS ONLY WHAT IS TRUE.

Raising the dead

The aim of the magician, as you will recall Constant saying, is:

> *Être toujours riche, toujours jeune, et ne jamais mourir.*

Constant was never rich nor did he maintain his youthful figure and I fear, as with all mortals, he died. This was ratified when he was dug up and re-buried in unconsecrated ground. A failure then? Not at all, says Constant.

> *... to those who ask, 'If you possess the secrets of a force which can transform the world, why do you not make use of them?' I answer that such knowledge has come too late for me and I have expended all the energy with which I might have applied the knowledge in gaining its acquisition in the first place. So I freely offer it to anyone who can avail themselves of it ... solely for the good of humanity, asking nothing in exchange.*[1]

As if to prove his qualifications, he tells us a story.[2]

> *In the spring of the year 1854 I had undertaken a journey to London, that I might escape from internal disquietude and devote myself, without interruption, to science.*

Despite his wish for freedom from interruption, one day,

> *... returning to my hotel, I found a note awaiting me. This note contained half of a card on which I recognized at once the seal of Solomon. It was accompanied by a small sheet of paper on which was pencilled, 'Tomorrow at three o'clock in front of Westminster Abbey, the second half of this card will be given you.'*

He kept the assignation and there,

> *... found a carriage drawn up and, as I unaffectedly held the fragment of card in my hand, a footman approached, making a sign as he did so, and opened the door of the equipage. It contained a lady in black wearing a thick veil. She motioned to me to take a seat beside her, showing me at the same time the other half of the card.*

The occupant of the carriage swore him to secrecy and then invited him to view a remarkable magical cabinet.

> *I made the required promise and keep it faithfully by not divulging the name, position or abode of this lady, whom I soon recognized as an initiate, not exactly of the first order, but still of a most exalted grade.*

This lady persuaded him to invoke the *divine Apollonius.*[3] Not a problem:

> *We must meditate for twenty-one days on his life and works, form an image of his appearance, converse with him in our minds, imagining his answers. We must keep his portrait or at least his name about us, while following a vegetarian diet for these twenty-one days with a severe fast during the last seven.*

---

[1] Elsewhere he writes, *What use is money to those who can make gold?*

[2] Here mostly in AE Waite's translation.

[3] A follower of Pythagoras, himself often associated with magic, Apollonius is a first century CE figure, seen as a miracle worker and as the pagan equivalent of Jesus.

We must next construct the magical oratory and see that all light is excluded therefrom. The magic lamp must be so situated that its single ray shall fall upon the altar smoke. The chafing-dish with the sacred fire should be in the centre of the oratory and close to the perfumed altar. The adept must face east to pray, and west to invoke. He must be alone or assisted by two others in the strictest silence; he must wear magical vestments and be crowned with vervain (the enchanter's plant) and gold.

He must bathe before the invocation, and his undergarments must be completely intact[1] and scrupulously clean. The ceremony must start with a prayer suited to the nature of the spirit about to be invoked; one to which he would have given his approval when still alive. In our ritual of invocation of Apollonius, we read the Magical Philosophy of Patricius, which contains the teachings of Zoroaster and of Hermes Trismegistus.

All this he did, and then recited,

> *... the Nuctemeron[2] of Apollonius in Greek with a loud voice conjuring with the words, 'Let the father of all advise and thrice-great Hermes guide us.'*

As he spoke, the flame went out *leaving the smoke still floating white and slow about the marble altar.* The earth shook and, as he heaped more perfumed twigs on the chafing dish, the flame lit again and he briefly saw the figure of a man. Redoubling his efforts, he invoked Apollonius again and the figure re-appeared.

> *I felt strangely cold, and when I tried to question the spirit I could not utter a syllable. I put my hand upon the Pentagram and pointed my sword at the figure, commanding it to obey. It immediately disappeared. I ordered it to return, and something touched the hand which held the sword and my arm was numbed to the elbow.*

> *I understood that the sword disturbed the spirit, and I therefore pointed it downwards. The figure reappeared immediately, but I experienced an intense tiredness in all my limbs and fainted into a deep sleep. The apparition did not speak to me, but I found the questions I had intended to ask had been answered in my mind.*

It is something of a pity that, faced with the opportunity of asking a first century sage about the events of that tumultuous period, Constant could only ask whether,

> *... reconciliation and forgiveness were possible between two persons in my thoughts.*

Spiritualism has always seemed so depressingly domestic as if the *other side* is wholly preoccupied with gossip, the heavenly equivalent of *Coronation Street.*

---

[1] No holes in your knickers! Sorry, but it is impossible to read this stuff with a straight face. His throwaway lines still remain superb. I love lines such as: '*not exactly of the first order, but still of a most exalted grade*' and '*as I unaffectedly held the fragment of card.*'

[2] *The Day of God Shining in the Darkness.* Twelve cryptic aphorisms which enable the day of god to dawn in an adept's life. Quite.

Indefeasibility and comedy

Glendower:	*I can call spirits from the vasty deep.*
Hotspur:	*Why, so can I, or so can any man;*
	But will they come when you do call for them?

Shakespeare was writing at the very beginning of the scientific age and one of the major planks of scientific discovery is that any experiment must be capable of being performed by another scientist with the same results. Constant would no doubt agree and say that any other adept should be able to raise a spirit using his methodology - for as long as he carried it out correctly.

An indefeasible proposition is one that admits no empirical evidence to disconfirm it. For example, Sigmund Freud said that dreams were about sex but if a dream appeared to be solidly not about sex, the dreamer was repressing sexual thoughts. Heads I win, tails you lose. Constant's claim to be able to raise spirits from the dead has, of course, the same indefeasible nature. Challenged by any would-be adept who used his methods but failed to raise Apollonius or any other dead notable, he would have replied that the failure was the result of incorrect preparation: insufficient fasting, a misaligned oratory or even inadequate underwear.[1] In effect, Constant's argument amounts to: *If you do x correctly, y will occur. If y does not occur, you did not do x correctly.*

The *incorrect preparation argument* provides amusement in the case of the transmutation of metals into gold. Sir Keith Thomas writes in *Religion and the Decline of Magic*:

> Alchemy was a difficult spiritual quest since transmutation could not be accomplished until the adept had purged himself of all vices, particularly covetousness; that is to say, he could not make gold until he has ceased to want to do so.

Indefeasibility becomes low comedy when Constant discusses necromancy.[2]

> There are necromantic processes of tearing earth from a grave with one's nails, digging out bones to be worn in the form of a cross on the breast and during midnight mass on Christmas Eve, rushing out of the church just before communion calling, 'Let the dead rise from their graves!'

> Taking a handful of earth from the grave, one places the bones in the form of a cross at the door of the church just as the congregation exits having been alarmed by the clamour and shouting once again, 'Let the dead rise from their graves!'

> If the adept avoids arrest and the mad house, he must then take four thousand, five hundred steps at a slow pace in a straight line, if necessary climbing over walls. He then lays down on the ground as if in a coffin and repeats in deathly tones, 'Let

---

[1] The James Randi Educational Foundation (JREF) offers a one-million-dollar prize to anyone who can show, under proper observing conditions, evidence of any paranormal, supernatural, or occult power or event. There is a log of attempts to win the prize at forums.randi.org/forumdisplay.php?f=43. To date, no one has passed even the preliminary tests but the nature of the attempts and of the measurement criteria are instructive.

[2] The process of communicating with and summoning the dead.

the dead rise from their graves!' Finally he calls three times on the person whose apparition he desires.

The process described is so ludicrous that it must be an example of Constant poking fun at such forms of magic, especially given the comment which follows:

No doubt anyone who is mad and wicked enough to do all this is already disposed to see all manner of chimæras and phantoms.

Constant follows this *ludicrum* with a mock serious remark:

The Grand Grimoire is most efficacious, but we advise none of our readers to test it.[1]

The spell in the grey box, right, is from the Grimoire, although one might well ask what the result has to do with magic. Few of his readers appear to notice Constant's humour. AE Waite always takes him seriously and neither Christopher McIntosh nor Robert Uzzel appear to see Constant's tongue ever in his cheek.

With a straight face, Uzzel reports that Pascal Beverly Randolph, an American occultist and creator of a system of *sexual magick*,[2] claimed that Constant installed him as *Supreme Grand Master of the Western World* of a Rosicrucian organisation. Constant must have invented both society and title on the spot *pour faire une blague*. I am sure he was highly amused when Randolph took it seriously.

Early medicine and magic

It is not easy to understand how an educated person like Waite could believe in magic in the 19th century but such belief is easier to understand

Take a gold ring that is studded with a small diamond that has not been worn by anyone. Wrap it in a piece of green fabric and for nine days and nine nights wear it against your skin over your heart. On the ninth day, before the Sun rises, engrave the word Scheva inside the ring with a new tool.

Obtain three hairs of the person who you want to love you, unite them with three of your own hairs, while saying: 'Body, that you could love me, that your desires could be as passionate as mine, by Scheva's most potent virtue.'

Tie the hairs in a love-snare knot around the ring. Wrap the ring in a piece of silk, and wear it against your skin over your heart for another six days. On the seventh day, fast. On an empty stomach, unwrap the ring and give it to the person you desire to love you.

If your ring is accepted then you can be certain to be loved by that person. If the ring is refused, rest assured that the heart of that person belongs to another and in that case, you should seek your fortune elsewhere.

---

[1] The *Grand Grimoire* claims to originate from the writings of King Solomon.

[2] *The ejective moment, therefore, is the most divine and tremendously important one in the human career as an independent entity; for not only may we launch Genius, Power, Beauty, Deformity, Crime, Idiocy, Shame or Glory on the world's great sea of Life, in the person of the children we may then produce, but we may plunge our own souls neck-deep in Hell's horrid slime, or else mount the Azure as coequal associate gods; for then the mystic Soul swings wide its Golden gates, opens its portals to the whole vast Universe and through them come trooping either Angels of Light or the Grizzly Presence from the dark corners of the Spaces.*

in earlier times. Up to the mid-1800s,[1] medical practice was almost completely useless and life expectancy had not increased since the Stone Age. The Black Death reduced the world population by about 25% between 1348 and 1350, and was one of many outbreaks of Bubonic Plague, now known to be the result of a complex process involving the bacterium *Y. pestis*, carried by fleas in turn carried by rats. In the 150 years leading up to its last occurrence there in 1665, London experienced only a dozen plague free years.[2]

No one knew what caused the plague nor were any genuine cures available. Amulets, toads, vinegar, rosewater, roasted shells of new laid eggs, marigolds, clay and violets were among remedies variously put forward. Add to the plague smallpox, influenza, typhus, dysentery, vitamin deficiencies and frequent harvest failures, and it is amazing that anyone survived at all. No cures worked and it is no wonder that people grasped at any possible help. Having no understanding of the causes of diseases or even much understanding of the notion of a cause, people turned to magic and to religion for cures in ways that were not always distinguishable from each other. Thomas writes,

> ... the essential difference between the prayers of the churchman and the spells of a magician was that only the latter claimed to work automatically; a prayer had no certainty of success and would not be granted if god chose not to concede it. A spell, on the other hand, need never go wrong, unless some detail of ritual observance had been omitted or a rival magician had been practising stronger counter-magic.

Folk cures

John Aubrey wrote of Thomas Hobbes,[3] who lived to the age of 91, that:

> He was wont to say that he would rather have the advice or take physic from an experienced old woman that had been at many sick people's bedsides, than from the learnedst but unexperienced physician.

Francis Bacon shared that opinion, saying that *old women were more happy many times in their cures than learned physicians*. There was some empirical basis to the old woman's physic while there was none for the prescriptions of the physician. The old woman's physic was not magic of course, but lessons orally transmitted from generation to generation:

> The crust of the bread is good for you; it contains more antioxidants.
>
> A tomato is good for soothing burns; it is has an anti-inflammatory effect.

---

[1] Pasteur (1822-1895) and microbiology; Ignaz Semmelweis (1818-1865) and handwashing; John Snow (1813-1858) and epidemiology. The flush toilet was first exhibited at Crystal Palace in 1851. The lowest average life expectancy at birth today is around 32 years in Swaziland, a country beset by HIV but it was not HIV that reduced life expectancy in 1800. It was infant mortality and death in childbirth caused primarily by insanitary conditions.

[2] It hit Scandinavia in 1709-1713, Marseilles in 1720, and remained active in the Middle East until 1800. An outbreak in China around 1850 spread to India and killed over 10 million people. Bubonic plague still kills today.

[3] Aubrey (1616-1697) was an archeologist, folklorist and author of *Brief Lives*. Hobbes (1588-1679) was a great political philosopher whose major work was *Leviathan*.

Dandruff is inhibited by cider; it reduces the yeast on the scalp.

Garlic relieves stomach upsets; it is a natural antibiotic.

Sage cures a sore throat; it contains anti-bacterial oils and soothes delicate membranes.

Willow bark reduces pain; it contains salicin, similar to Acetylsalicylic acid.

Miracles

Sufferers also sought the touch of holy relics; they invoked saints, received blessings and resorted to exorcism. The sick made pilgrimages to shrines and the saints' successes were sometimes impressive. Thomas writes:

> *Over 500 miracles were associated with Becket and his shrine and at the Holy Rood of Bromholm in Norfolk; thirty-nine persons were said to have been raised from the dead and twelve cured of blindness.*

He lists a goodly number of *ecclesiastical preservatives*.

> *The consecration of church bells made them efficacious against evil spirits and hence enabled them to dispel the thunder and lightning ... Alternatively one could invoke St Barbara against thunder or tie a charm onto the building one wished to protect ... As a protection against fire, there were St Agatha's letters, an inscription placed on tiles, bells or amulets ... there were exorcisms to make the fields fertile, holy candles to protect farm animals and curses to drive away caterpillars and rats and to kill weeds. The key of the church door was said to be an efficacious remedy against a mad dog ... even the coins in the offertory were credited with magical value.*

Oddly, William Tyndale (1492-1536)[1] wrote:

> *We worship saints for fear lest they should be displeased and angry with us and plague or hurt us ... Who dares deny St Anthony a fleece of wool for fear of his terrible fire, or lest he send the pox among our sheep?*

If for *saints*, one reads *gods*, these sentiments would not have been out of place in ancient Greece. The idea that a saint/god would harm someone who refused to worship him is more suited to Greek, Roman or Egyptian beliefs than Christianity.

Denunciation

Day to day magic was not always harmless. There were magical means of identifying wrong-doers. Thomas reports the technique of the sieve and shears:

> *Stick a pair of shears in the rind of a sieve and let two persons set the top of each of their forefingers upon the upper part of the shears, holding it with the sieve up from the ground steadily and ask Peter and Paul whether A, B, or C have stolen the thing lost; and at the nomination of the guilty person the sieve will turn round.*

Such superstition was usually ignored by authority until the 16th century when action was taken against it. Thomas points to the 1559 *Elizabethan Injunctions*.

---

[1] Executed for translating the Bible and publishing it in English.

> The Queen's most royal majesty, by the advice of her most honourable council, intending the advancement of the true honour of Almighty God, the suppression of superstition throughout all her highness's realms and dominions, and to plant true religion to the extirpation of all hypocrisy, enormities, and abuses (as to her duty appertaineth), doth minister unto her loving subjects these godly Injunctions hereafter following.

One doubts that Elizabeth had much interest in the injunctions, being herself more concerned to keep the peace between the various religious factions of her realm than to prevent superstition.[1] Nevertheless, the injunctions ordered that people,

> ... shall not set forth or extol the dignity of any images, relics, or miracles; but, declaring the abuse of the same, they shall teach that all goodness, health, and grace ought to be both asked and looked for only of God.

that congregations should be taught that,

> ... the works devised by man's fantasies, besides Scripture (as wandering of pilgrimages, setting up of candles, praying upon beads, or such like superstition), have not only no promise of reward in Scripture for doing of them, but contrariwise great threatenings and maledictions of God.

and that in general,

> ... no persons shall use charms, sorceries, enchantments, witchcraft, soothsaying, or any suchlike devilish device, nor shall resort at any time to the same for counsel or help.

It should not be thought that these denunciations were made on empirical grounds. The superstitions were simply seen as irreligious.[2]

Constant and cures

Magic was part of the culture into the Elizabethan age and for some time after that but Constant himself was writing in a time of the discovery of blood transfusions, general anæsthetics, antiseptic surgical methods, the germ theory of disease and vaccines. He knew that magic did not cure disease. He also knew that magical spells had no effect but he had no intention of giving up his claims to be a Magus. The way he deals with this lets us peek behind the curtain of the occult.

- Constant uses pop psychology to show how some apparently magical effects are produced. This enables him to deny the efficacy of common or garden spells and, at the same time, demonstrate his own sophistication.

---

[1] Elizabeth had been Queen for less than a year when the injunctions were published. It is generally held that she disagreed with them and that it was Henry Cecil who was behind the publication. Many presage the excesses of the Puritans 70 years later.

[2] Magic formed only a part of the Injunctions which were in general rules for approved religion. Such rules prevented ecclesiastical persons resorting to taverns or alehouses; created registers of births, marriages and deaths; set out means of paying for education; insisted on the use of English in church; allowed priests to marry *honest and sober* wives and enabled Sunday working.

- He describes spells and potions etc. as tricks that other magicians use. He is thus able to give the gothic and gory details and demonstrate his knowledge, while defending himself against the 19th century French equivalent of the Trades Description Act. He even pokes fun at such spells, apparently confident that his readers, who are already convinced of the efficacy of magic, will either not notice or share his disdain.

- He claims that his own results are gained by the use of forces unattainable by lesser beings. His superior tools are the Astral Light and the Tarot (which he wrongly thought was connected with Kabbalah, of which more later.)

One of his few straightforward lies is the story of the raising of Apollonius and, as we have seen, he prevents discovery if not suspicion by the indefeasibility of his claim and the impossibility of access to his witnesses.

Pop psychology

He writes:

> For example, you invite a woman, anxious to secure a husband, to be present at such and such a performance, telling her that she will see her sort of man there. You tell her that the man will also see her and oddly enough marriage may well be the result. You can count on the lady to attend. You can count on her seeing a man and believing that he has seen her. You may count on her thinking that marriage is on the cards. It may not come to that, but she will not blame you, unwilling to give up the illusion. On the contrary, she will diligently consult you again.

Whether you believe such a sexist tale or not, there is something in it to do with wish-fulfillment and self-deception. He also has some sensible comments to make on folk magic and alternative medicine:

> In medicine it is really faith that cures. There is scarcely a village which does not have its male or female occultist, and such people are far more successful than officially approved doctors.

He tells a couple of tales to exemplify this:

> An elderly and eccentric merchant ... retired from business to practise occult medicine, motivated by Christian charity. His only cures were oil, insufflations and prayers. When he was accused of illegally practising medicine, the publicity generated by the court case made everyone aware that he had cured ten thousand people over five years. His following increased dramatically.

and

> A demented nun cured diseases using an elixir and a plaster she had invented ... She was also prosecuted, but it was soon found necessary to allow her to work at least once a week. Sister Jane-Frances has been seen surrounded by people who have queued all night, sleeping on the ground to receive her elixir and plaster.

Of course,

> Since her remedy was the same for all complaints, she had no need to get to know her patients, but she always listened to them with rapt attention. Here was to be

found the magical secret ...

... and the explanation of the cures worked by alternative medicine in the modern day. Many people feel better when given attention and a listening ear. It is the attention that works, when it does, not the elixir, plaster, flower essence or the substances repeatedly diluted until no trace of the original remains.

Of course, if someone genuinely believes in magic, they are easy meat for the magician. Constant explains this with a simple tale.

> *During the civil war, a shopkeeper informed on one of his neighbours. As a result, the neighbour served a gaol sentence and lost his job. When he regained his freedom his only revenge was to walk past the informer's shop twice a day, stare at him, salute and continue on. This went on until the shopkeeper could bear it no longer. He sold his shop at a loss and left, ruined, leaving no forwarding address.*

Of this story, Constant says,

> *A bewitchment is real when it acts on the imagination of the victim, especially when victim has a belief in the occult and its unstated powers. The terrible menace of hell has created more nightmares, more unknown illnesses, more intense insanities, than all the vices put together.*

Magic potions

To establish his occult knowledge, Constant delves into the subject of *philtres* and *enchanted potions*, first teasing in his usual fashion:

> *We shall not go into the dangerous aspects of the practice, that which Cornelius Agrippa[1] himself called Venomous Magic. It is true that there are no longer bonfires for sorcerers, but now more than ever, there are penalties dealt out to wrongdoers. Therefore, let us restrict ourselves to recognising the reality of such powers.*

He refuses to describe:

> *... how plants are poisoned; how animals fed on these plants have their flesh infected which, when turned into food, causes death by poison, leaving no trace; how the walls of houses are impregnated; how the air is permeated by fumes, requiring the operator to use the glass mask of St. Croix.*

and then goes into detail:

> *Evil-doers distilled the venom of reptiles and the sap of poisonous plants. They extracted deadly narcotics from the fungus, the toxins of the plant* Datura stramonium, *poison from the pits of peach and almond which, placed on the tongue or in the ear, destroyed even the strongest living being in a lightning flash.*

> *The white juice of sea-lettuce was boiled in milk in which vipers and asps had been drowned. They pulverized flint, mixed the dried slime of reptiles with impure ash, made up hideous philtres with the blood of mares on heat; they mingled human blood with dreadful drugs, creating an oil the mere odour of which was fatal ...*

---

[1] Whom we will meet later.

Datura Stramonium is useful for asthma and as an anaesthetic but it is also hallucinogenic and fatal in doses only slightly more than recommended. The pits of peaches, plums and almonds are dangerous if bitten into. They contain cyanide.

Witchcraft

We cannot miss Constant on witchcraft and spells. Again he expresses his contempt for such matters:

> Sorcerers and necromancers have always sought the power of magnetism possessed by the true adept but they sought it only to abuse it. Their evil and primary goal was the power of bewitchment and death.

... before describing them with glee. Constant is very good on the gothic horror. You will remember his account of the bewitchments of the sorcerers who *procure hair or garments of the person whom they seek to destroy?* Well ...

> Another spell ... consists of consecrating iron nails to works of hatred through the foul fumigations of Saturn and invocations of evil spirits. They trace the footsteps of their victim and drive the nails into his footprints in the form of a cross.

> In an even more abominable practice, a fat toad is baptised with the name of the victim and then is given consecrated host, on which curses have been laid, to eat. The animal is then wrapped in magnetised objects, bound with the victim's hairs on which the adept has spat and buried under the threshold of the victim's door. The toad's spirit haunts the victim's nightmares as a vampire - unless he knows how to turn the spell back on the adept.

Constant also gives us baptismal oil and more consecrated host with which,

> *... apostate[1] divines create a model of their intended victim and dress it to look like him, calling down upon its head all the evils they can think of, torturing it daily to torment the victim by sympathetic magic.*

As Constant says:

> *Such bewitchment is more effective if the hair, blood and above all a tooth of the victim can be procured.*

Well, of course.

Divination and prediction

As we have seen, Constant can write beautifully. Here is his account of astrology:

> *Contemplation of the sky exalts our imagination and the stars respond to our thoughts. The imaginary lines drawn by primitive observers from one star to another provided the first ideas of geometry. The stars burn with menace or sparkle with hope as our soul is troubled or at peace. The sky is the mirror of the soul and when we read the stars, it is ourselves we discover.*

The end of divination is, he says:

> *To know the secret thoughts of men; to penetrate the mysteries of the past and future; to reveal exactly what will occur through precise knowledge of the causes.*

Astrology has a long and inglorious history. One Jerome Cardan predicted that the young King Edward VI would reign for forty-five years.[2] One might have thought that such failures, and of course they were frequent, would have brought astrology into disrepute. However, as Thomas writes:

> *... astrologers were deeply undaunted by failure. No human science was perfect, they reminded themselves, and astrology was certainly no worse than medicine. If different astrologers produced different results, then so did different theologians and lawyers. Everyone knew that some practitioners were better than others and that the profession was infested by charlatans and quacks.*

Constant agrees, arguing that it is the Magus and not the spell that works:

> *We repeat that it is magnetic intuition alone that gives value to astrological calculations; childish and uninformed when made without the inspiration of a powerful will.*

The Magus has no need of artifice but to help the beginner Constant gives *an exceedingly simple method of finding celestial horoscopes by onomancy.*[3] Cease reading when your eyes glaze over - although this is one of Constant's jokes.

> *Take a black card and cut in it the name of the person for whom the divination is required. Fix this card over the smaller end of a tube, to be read by the observer at the other end. Look through the tube towards the four cardinal points, beginning at the east and finishing at the north.*

---

[1] One who has turned his back on his religion.

[2] (1537-1553). He was crowned king at age nine and died six years later.

[3] A form of divination using only the letters of a name.

Take note of all the stars which you see through the letters. Convert the letters through which you have seen stars into numbers and add the numbers together. Renew the operation, this time counting the stars you have seen. Add this number to the result of the previous calculation. Write the sum of the two numbers in Hebrew characters. Renew the operation. Write down the names of the stars you have seen, using the planisphere to find their names. Classify them according to their size and brightness, choosing the most brilliant of all as the polestar of your astrological operation. Lastly, in the Egyptian planisphere, find the names and figures of the genii to which these stars belong.

You will learn in this manner the fortunate and unfortunate signs attached to the name of the person and the nature of their influence: in childhood, the name traced at the east; in youth, the name traced at the south; in mature age, the name at the west; in decline, the name at the north and for his or her whole life, the total sum of the letters and stars. This operation is simple and calls for few calculations.

Still there? Like the stage performer, Constant advises simple research to assist divination. Sympathetic questioning, he says, will reveal the subject's dreams, *the reflection of life, both interior and exterior.* Favourite colours and animals, he argues, will provide further insight. False, yes, but superficially convincing.

Those who like blue are idealists and dreamers; lovers of red are material and passionate; those who prefer yellow are fantastic and capricious; admirers of green are often commercial and crafty; the friends of black are influenced by Saturn; the rose is the colour of Venus.

Lovers of the horse are hard-working, noble in character, and at the same time yielding and gentle; friends of the dog are affectionate and faithful; those of the cat are independent and libertine. Frank speaking people hold spiders in special horror ... The face and its wrinkles, hands and their lines provide further information.

Astral Light

Constant's true adept uses no trickery but only the Astral Light, *that great book of divinations.* He seems to see the Astral Light as some form of ether, a substance that was once thought to fill space and within which everything occurred. As a theory in physics, it was shown to be false in 1887, twelve years after Constant's death.

His Astral Light is not quite the same as the physical theory of ether, being something operated upon by the will of the Magus. For example, the passes that the Magus makes with his hands or specifically the fingertips *where all nerves terminate,* he says will *diffuse or attract the Astral Light* which the Magus can control:

(He) communicates and directs at will the magnetic vibrations in the whole mass of the Astral Light, the currents of which he divines by means of the Magic Wand ... a perfected divining rod.

... and uses such currents to achieve his magical results:

A lucid will can act upon the mass of the Astral Light, and in concurrence with other wills which it absorbs and draws along, can create and control great and irresistible currents.

This is not a conscious process:

> *Divinatory vision operates only in a state of ecstasy, which is achieved only when doubt and illusion are rendered impossible by closing the mind to thought.[1]*

Now whether Constant actually believes this stuff is not easy to identify. Frankly, I haven't a clue what he is talking about and even his co-occultists could make little of it. Helena Petrovna Blavatsky, founder of Theosophy,[2] wrote:

> *That Astral Light, which the paradoxical Éliphas Lévi calls in one breath the body of the Holy Ghost and in the next Baphomet ... the androgyne Goat of Mendes, is the grand Agent Magique with him; undeniably it is so but only as far as black magic is concerned and then on the lowest planes of what we call Ether, the noumenon[3] of which is simply the older sidereal light of Paracelsus ...*

which does not seem to help much. (Although she gets Constant right when describing him as paradoxical. That is what he set out to be.) Paul Foster Case, the American occultist, wrote:

> *Einstein has advanced a theory that gravitation and electromagnetism are one and the same thing. By reviving this ancient doctrine, known to his Hebrew ancestors, the great mathematician brings closer that revolution in physics Éliphas Lévi predicted back in 1859 ...*

seeing Constant as a precursor of Einstein - without requiring all that tedious mathematics!

Waite's disappointment

Poor AE Waite, who really wanted to believe that Constant was on to something, had the greatest difficulty with Astral Light, eventually bringing himself reluctantly but honestly to say that he had reservations about it. The best he can say is:

> *I neither know or care whether such a fluid exists or ... whether it is applicable to the uses indicated.*

Waite was always in two minds about Constant. He writes of Constant's book, *L'Histoire de la Magie*, that it is the *most arresting, entertaining and brilliant of all studies on the subject* but he also says that Constant's work on Hermetic Magic leaves much to be desired; that his discourse on magic in India constitutes *the title-deeds of incompetence,* and that he had *little knowledge of those Kabbalistic texts ... about which he claims to speak with full understanding.*

Waite really wanted to believe that Constant was some form of Magus and, of course, this is how it works. People want to believe that the adept has magical powers and the magician seeks to sustain that credulity, often unconsciously drawing the listener in, suspending disbelief. The magician wants to share his audience's belief and this is the *folie à deux* which sustains the occult.

---

[1] The *Inner Game* of magic?

[2] The study of the *unexplained laws of nature and the powers latent in man*, a philosophy of psychic and spiritual evolution founded by Helena Blavatsky (1831-1891).

[3] *Noumena* are distinguished from *phenomena* by Kant; the latter can be perceived by our senses, the former not. Similar to Plato's world of ideas, they can only by known by reason.

So powerfully was Waite gripped by Constant's claims in *Dogme et Rituel* that he was bitterly disappointed with Constant's later disavowal of practical magic in *L'Histoire de la Magie*. He complains:

> *What has happened to the one science that is coeval with creation itself, to the key of all miracles and to the almost omnipotent adeptship?*

He really wanted to believe that Constant had discovered the secrets of the ancients during his studies, so much so that he put Constant's disavowal down to Constant's fear that he had said too much, so leading others into danger and himself into opprobrium. Surely the opposite is true. Constant is an engaging charlatan whose frequent warnings are part of his mystery making. His sense of fun does peek out on occasion and risks giving him away - but poor Waite never notices it.

A science of magic

Constant wants us to believe that his magical powers derive from no polyglot collection of spells, but from a deeper, more theoretical understanding; a science behind magic.

> *There is a formidable secret, whose revelation has already transformed the world, as testified by the tradition of Egypt, summarized symbolically by Moses at the beginning of Genesis. This secret is the knowledge of good and evil, and the consequence of its revelation is death.*

He cannot really give us the information.

> *Here I must pause, and I fear that already I have said too much. I testify, in fine, that there is one sole, universal and imperishable dogma, strong as supreme reason; simple, like all that is great; intelligible, like all that is universally and absolutely true ... one which confers on man powers apparently superhuman.*

Much of Constant's persuasiveness lies in his ability to marshall references; to make them sound as if they reveal hidden mysteries and truths. In this way, he seeks to add profundity to what he writes and to his engraving in particular. The only way to discover whether what he says is really profound is to unpack the references. At least in doing this, we will be taken into some fascinating areas.

> Dreyfus: Clouseau?
> Clouseau: Yes?
> Dreyfus: Are you wounded?
> Clouseau: No. Fortunately I was saved by the darkness.
> Dreyfus: So what we need is more light.

An example

Let us take Constant's description of the pentagram and unpack the references.

> *In Gnostic schools (the pentagram) is called the Blazing Star, the Star of the Magi, the sign of the Word made flesh; and, according to its points, represents order or disorder, the Divine Lamb of Ormuz and John, or the accursed goat of Mendes. It is initiation or profanation; it is Lucifer or Vesper, the star of morning or evening. It is Mary or Lilith, victory or death, day or night.*

You will remember that with one point up as in *le bouc de sabbat*, the pentagram is the sign of the Saviour; with two points, it is satanic. (Come on. Keep up!) We are aware of the accursed goat of Mendes and the Magi. The Divine Lamb of Ormuz is a further nod to Zoroastrianism whose god Mazda was also called Ormuzd or wise lord.

The word made flesh sounds like a simple reference to Christ but we will find that it has other meanings in gnostic creation stories which we will come on to. We have talked about Lucifer and the star of morning, if not Vesper[1], the star of the evening. Both are the planet Venus.

From Dogme et Rituel

The Divine Lamb of John is Christ (this John being the Baptist) and Mary is, as we have seen, a central figure in Constant's religious writings, so no problems there. Lilith is the first wife of Adam. The idea of Adam's plural wives may be a surprise. Very briefly, Moses de Leon, whom we have met as the author of the *Zohar,* writes:

> At the same time that the Lord created Adam, he created a woman, Lilith, who like Adam was taken from the earth. She was given to Adam as his wife. But there was a dispute between them about a matter that when it came before the judges had to be discussed behind closed doors.

The disagreement that could only be discussed in private is said to have concerned sexual equality and positions during intercourse. It turns out that there were two Lilliths; one the bride of *Samael, the great prince and great king over all the demons* and the other the bride of Asmodeus whom we have already met in the discussion of Pike. Lilith is thus seen as a female demon or as the first feminist, according to taste.

At this stage in the unpacking, you probably have the impression that Constant is not giving us an explanation of the pentagram so much as his reading list. I am not at all sure that this impression is incorrect but let us keep an open mind for the moment because we are about to be led into the fascinating subject of *Gnosticism.* This refers primarily to those fantastic and fabulous[2] religions that were initiated over what I call *the turning point,* the period from 200 BCE to 200 CE. I think that in its development, we will find Constant's *formidable secret, whose revelation has already transformed the world.* There are further clues in the exhortation:

> Rest in Nature, study, know, then dare; dare to will, dare to act and be silent! Such are the consequences of the philosophical dogma of Hermes; such has been

---

[1] Derived from the Greek, *Hesperos.*

[2] Using both these words in their original sense.

from all time the ethic of true adepts; such is the philosophy of the Rosicrucian inheritors of all the ancient wisdoms; such is the Secret Doctrine of those associations that are treated as subversive of the public order, and have ever been accused of conspiring against thrones and altars.

Listen out for Hermes and his philosophical dogma. Later still we will seek to understand those Rosicrucian inheritors and indeed those Kabbalistic texts of which Constant may or may not have full understanding.

Chapter eight: The Turning Point

The Western Wall in Jerusalem, the lower courses of which date from the time of Herod's rebuilding of the temple. Behind is the Dome of the Rock.

The rate of change in the 20th and 21st century may seem dramatic but really only in technological terms. The changes have done little to alter the certainties of our lives and perhaps only the rise of socialism and concern with human rights has done that. It may be that the most recent discovery genuinely affecting our lives is not the Higgs Boson but the fact that those in positions of authority cannot be trusted: that so many are either immoral or incompetent, or both.

In this chapter, we look at the often violent changes in and around the Mediterranean between 200 BCE and 200 CE. We might argue that these changes are more dramatic than any technological changes today. Our central focus will be gnosticism and by this focus I am setting up an understanding of the Corpus Hermeticum, basic to the ideas of Constant. In all of this, we will touch upon the Pharisees, Sadducees and early Christianity as well as Tecumseh and the Shawnee Indian nation.

The interlude which follows the chapter goes more deeply into Q and the Jesus people, something mentioned briefly in the chapter proper. I find it fascinating. I hope you do.

Religious experiment

During the *turning point*, the period from around 200 BCE to 200 CE, the religious world was in flux, packed with religious experiments. At a time when the presence of the divine was an everyday reality, such uncertainty must have been deeply disturbing, certainly more so than the invention of *Twitter*. Changes were taking place throughout the Graeco-Roman world, in Judaism, paganism and even in the nascent Christianity. None were exempt. It seemed that religious belief was up for grabs and the market responded. The uncertainty assisted Christianity and indeed one might say that without that uncertainty the new religion would not have flourished; not having to compete against fixed and firmly held beliefs, it could opportunistically find a place in the fluxfield.

The driver of change in paganism at the turning point stemmed from the very openness of polytheism. We have seen earlier that:

> *The Egyptians and the Greeks ... were entirely liberal about religious behaviour. They had lots of gods and discovering a few more in countries they came across did not make much difference.*

The key phrase here is *a few more*. As time went on, it ceased to be a matter of a few more but a matter of *far too many more*. Pagans increasingly found such a bewildering choice of gods that no one could be sure that they had placated all the relevant gods for where they were or where they might be travelling. The Roman insistence on the worship of the Emperor as a god was a further complication. We noted earlier the Copenhaver hypothesis that this over-supply of gods drove people towards monotheism. EP Sanders believes that the *philosophical attractiveness* of monotheism in the face of the over-supply was certainly a great help to Paul in his attempts to make converts to Christianity.

We should not over-egg this particular pudding. The pagan gods lasted for a long time. I am writing this passage not long after the end of the Olympic Games in London. The games themselves started in 776 BCE and took place during a sacred truce. They ended with sacrifices to Zeus and they continued in this manner until 395 CE when the Byzantine Emperor Theodosius I ordered all pagan celebrations be abolished. So paganism was alive and well four hundred years after the birth of Jesus even if the Olympic Games ceased to be, until their return in 1894.

Sectarianism and the loss of the temple

I have argued, with Robin Lane Fox, that Judaic monotheism dates from 160 BCE. On the surface this appears to be a major change dwarfing all others but, for all practical purposes, it mattered little whether Yahweh was the only god or one among others. For the Jews, Yahweh was their god, the only one that mattered to them.

In this sense the Jewish religion is straightforward. Yahweh sets out in apparent detail what he wants and if the people give him what he wants and obey his commands, the nation of Israel prospers. Whether there exist other gods or not, there is no room for them in this arrangement.

Despite the apparent specificity of his commands, what Yahweh wanted was always the subject of debate and never more so than during the turning point. Four primary religious groups passionately adopted varying views.[1]

The Roman born Jewish historian Josephus[2] (37-199 CE) writes that the **Pharisees** *live meanly, despise delicacies* and *follow the conduct of reason.* That is to say, they accepted those changes in the religious rules that seemed necessary. They also accepted predestination and somehow combined this with a belief in man's ability to do right or wrong. They believed in immortality; that *souls have an immortal rigour in them* and that *under the earth[3] there will be rewards or punishments according as they have lived virtuously or viciously in this life.* In the opinion of Josephus, these doctrines appealed to the people and the Pharisees' rules on divine worship, prayers and sacrifices were usually followed by the population at large. Paul is said to have been a Pharisee for part of his life, but as Sanders writes:

> The one activity which cannot be ascribed to Paul as a Pharisee with certainty is his persecution of the Christian movement. It is important to note that this had to do with Paul's zeal but not with his Phariseeism. Acts represents Gamaliel[4] as speaking in favour of tolerance for the Christian movement.

It was a **Sadducee** High Priest who employed Paul. Josephus says that the Sadducees were the direct opposite of the Pharisees. They did not accept immortality, holding *that souls die with the bodies.* They seem not to have accepted any form of reasoned debate and regarded *the observation of anything besides what the law enjoins* as unacceptable. They obeyed the established rules without question, whether or not changed times seemed to call for different interpretations. This did not make them popular and they seem to have been a much smaller sect.

The **Essenes**, Josephus says, shared many of the beliefs of the Pharisees in that *they teach the immortality of souls* and *esteem that the rewards of righteousness are to be earnestly striven for.* It was how they lived more than their beliefs which differentiated them. They practised a form of communism away from other people in what later became known as *kibbitzim* - collective settlements in which goods are held in common. They were self sufficient and, as Josephus puts it, *entirely addict themselves to husbandry.* Josephus writes that *they exceed all other men* in virtue and righteousness. A *rich man enjoys no more of his own wealth than he who hath nothing at all.* They do not *marry nor keep servants thinking the latter tempts men to be unjust and the former leads to domestic quarrels.* Karen Armstrong holds that Qumran, where the Dead Sea Scrolls were found in 1942, was the home of an extreme wing of the Essenes.

---

[1] The membership of these groups was not necessarily very large. We might think of them almost as pressure groups or political parties.

[2] His *Antiquities of the Jews* (written about 95 CE) is the only non-biblical mention of Jesus. *Now there was about this time Jesus, a wise man, if it be lawful to call him a man; for he was a doer of wonderful works, a teacher of such men as receive the truth with pleasure.* Josephus mentions that Jesus appeared to *those who loved him* after his crucifixion *alive again the third day.* He concludes by saying that *the tribe of Christians are not extinct to this day.* Scholars generally agree that the mention of Jesus, Pilate and the crucifixion are authentic although many see the rest of the passage as later interpolation.

[3] The Greeks also viewed the afterlife as underneath and not, as in the Christian view, above.

[4] The leader of the Pharisees.

Josephus adds a fourth group of which he says *Judas the Galilean[1] was the author*. He says that they largely agreed with the Pharisees but had *an inviolable attachment to liberty* believing *that god is to be their only ruler and lord*. Josephus says of this fourth group, who have been identified with the **Zealots**, that they had no fear of death or pain and that they were later responsible for the Great Revolt in 66 CE which led to the destruction of Jerusalem and the death of thousands of Jews. Today we might refer to them as fundamentalists.

The presence of these groups created instability in Judæa both in politics and religion and led finally to the ultimate change in Judaism, the destruction of the second temple, the centre of Judaism and the house in which Yahweh lived.

It had happened before

The Hebrew *Chronicles* have Yahweh speaking to David about his son, Solomon:

> *And it shall come to pass, when thy days are fulfilled that thou must go to be with thy fathers, that I will set up thy seed after thee, who shall be of thy sons; and I will establish his kingdom. He shall build me a house, and I will establish his throne for ever.*

When Nebuchadnezzar took the Israelites into exile, the promises made by Yahweh must have seemed empty. Most horrifically, the house of Yahweh - built by Solomon - whose throne would last forever, had been destroyed. The Israelites must have feared that Yahweh had left, never to return.

Their solution was to rationalise the event, to find a reason for the temple's destruction that could be fitted into their world view. After all, to accept that Nebuchadnezzar had simply won through *force majeure* would have been tantamount to accepting that his god was greater than Yahweh. So the Israelites took Nebuchadnezzar's actions to be Yahweh's punishment for their misbehaviour. As we have seen, Nehemiah and Ezra called for a reversion to traditional values, not an uncommon reaction among religious groups when things do not turn out as they had hoped. For example ...

Ten-squat-a-way

For some 300 years, the Shawnee Indian Nation had an itinerant existence, driven from one place to another by the Iroquois, Cheyenne, Chickasaw, French, British and finally the Americans. They were caught up in the French-English wars and in the War of Independence, frequently fighting battles, winning some and losing some. Ultimately they could not resist the flood of settlers as the frontier moved inexorably west. Just like the westward migration of such tribes as the Franks, Saxons, Vandals and Visigoths, the westward advance of the white man's frontier in North America was driven by forces beyond the control of any Indian or indeed American leader. The agreements made and broken by sometimes honest and often duplicitous politicians had little impact on that process.

In 1802, the Shawnee leader Tecumseh rejected yet another attempt by the American Government to dodge the terms of an earlier agreement and sought to

---

[1] Judas was a common name; this one led the revolt against the Romans in 6 CE.

create a confederacy of the western Indian tribes to resist yet more land being swallowed up by the settler machine. He is supposed to have said:

> *The only way to stop this evil is for the red man to unite in claiming a common and equal right in the land, as it was first, and should be now, for it was never divided. We gave them forest-clad mountains and valleys full of game, and in return what did they give our warriors and our women? Rum, trinkets, and a grave. Brothers, my people wish for peace. The red men all wish for peace but where the white people are, there is no peace for them except it be on the bosom of our mother.[1] Where today are the Pequot? Where today are the Narragansett, the Mahican, the Pokanoket and many other once powerful tribes of our people? They have vanished before the avarice and the oppression of the White Man, as snow before a summer sun.*

Ten-squat-a-way; the Open Door. The brother of Tecumseh, known as The Prophet,

Tecumseh's younger brother, Ten-squat-a-way, hitherto a drunkard and ne'er-do-well, experienced a vision in which the *Master of Life*, the Shawnee henotheistic god,

---

[1] A Shawnee belief personifies the earth as their mother.

told him that the evils they had experienced had come about because they had turned their backs on the old ways and taken up the white man's products and practices. The *Master of Life* promised that if they returned to their native customs, he would drive the white man from the land. Against his older brother's orders, Ten-squat-a-way attacked an American army led by William Harrison and was defeated.

Tecumseh himself had only partial success with his confederacy, but still gave American forces a bad time along the Ohio frontier for several years by uniting with British forces from Canada. Eventually, he too was defeated by Harrison[1] and died at the Battle of the Thames (1813), a battle that was really part of a war between the USA and Great Britain, a sideshow of the Napoleonic war, and which essentially ended with the Treaty of Ghent in December 1814. The demarcation between the USA and Upper Canada (now Ontario) was settled, the Indian Nations signed a peace treaty and the economy of Ohio, boosted by the war, took off. The *Liberty Hall and Cincinnati Gazette* gave its opinion.

> *The cession (sic) made by the Indians on this occasion nearly extinguishes their title to this state. The small reservations are but little consequence to us. The two great objects gained; the security of the North Western Frontier and an immediate settlement of the country ... will compel the few remaining Indians to adopt the habits of civilisation or to migrate to situations more congenial to savage life.*[2]

Ten-squat-a-way died aged 61, having retreated with most of the Shawnee to what is now Kansas. The reversion to traditional values hadn't worked for them.

Destruction again

Nor did it for the Jews. Despite Nehemiah and Ezra, the temple had now been destroyed a second time, which seemed like the end.

> *In 70 CE the emperor Vespasian finally conquered Jerusalem. When the Roman soldiers broke into the temple's inner courts, they found six thousand Jewish zealots there, ready to fight to the death. When they saw the temple catch fire, a terrible cry arose. Some flung themselves on to the Romans' swords; others hurled themselves into the flames.*
>
> *Once the temple had gone, the Jews gave up and showed no interest in defending the rest of the city but watched helplessly as Titus's officers efficiently demolished what was left of it. For centuries the temple had stood at the heart of the Jewish world and was central to Jewish religion. Once again it had been destroyed but this time it would not be rebuilt.*[3]

The destruction of the temple gave the nascent Christian sect an opportunity. As Armstrong writes:

> *Only two of the Jewish sects that had proliferated during the Late Second Temple period were able to find a way forward. The first to do so was the Jesus movement,*

---

[1] Harrison became the shortest serving President of the USA. He died after 32 days in office.

[2] Reported in R. Douglas Hurt's unsentimental account of the Ohio Frontier.

[3] Karen Armstrong.

which was inspired by the disaster to write a whole new set of scriptures.[1]

The Jesus people

Initially, of course, the Jesus movement was just a Jewish sect; another alongside those that Josephus describes, the difference being that they followed Yeshua (Jesus) of Nazareth.[2]

We can tell very little about the beliefs of the early Jesus people unless we accept the *Q theory* and the relevance of the *Gospel of Thomas* to it.[3] Put briefly, the *Q theory* is accepted by most academics to explain the fact that while *Matthew* and *Luke* have passages which appear in Mark, they also contain passages (nearly) identical to each other which do not appear in Mark.

The view is taken that *Mark* is the oldest gospel and that *Matthew* and *Luke* drew material from it. Those passages in *Matthew* and *Luke* which are *identical to each other* but *do not appear in Mark* are said to derive from another document, now lost, referred to as Q. Part of this document is thought to have been written during the life of Yeshua or soon after.

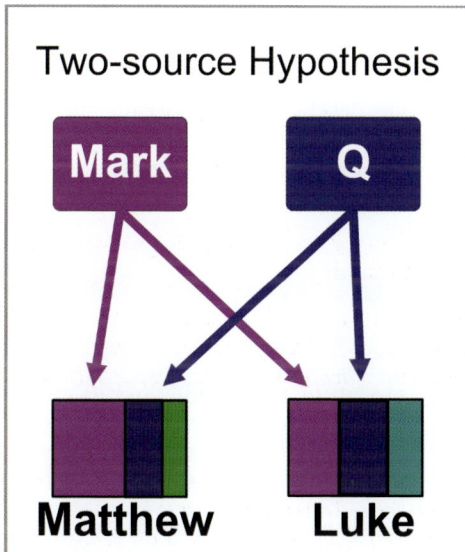

In this diagram, the coloured areas in the boxes indicate:

Purple - *derived from Mark*

Blue - *derived from Q*

Green - *unique to each gospel*

About 40% of Matthew and Luke is derived from Mark while about 25% is said to come from Q.

From the German *Quelle* meaning *source*, Q has been reconstructed from those common elements of *Matthew* and *Luke*. The reconstructed Q appears as a collection of somewhat gnomic sayings and announces the imminent arrival of the kingdom of god on earth although this message develops within the text.

---

[1] The other sect to find a way forward was that of the Pharisees.

[2] According to Burton Mack, the Jesus people were initially Galilean and Galilee was quite different from Judæa. It had no borders with Judæa and was a far more cosmopolitan society, exposed to many non-Jewish faiths.

[3] In the view of the Jesus Seminar, the gospel of Thomas may have more authentic material than the gospel of John. The Jesus Seminar was organised in 1985 *to discover and report a scholarly consensus on the historical authenticity of the sayings and events attributed to Jesus in the gospels.*

While Q is an assumption, the *Gospel of Thomas* does exist. A copy was found in the *Nag Hammadi* codices discovered near *Hamra Dum*, just north of Luxor in Upper Egypt in 1945.[1] Marvin Meyer writes:

> There is hardly any narrative in the Gospel of Thomas and the gospel does not tell a story of the life of Jesus. Rather, Thomas's Jesus is a teacher of wisdom and the value of Jesus lives in what he has to say and how his sayings lead to wisdom and understanding.

If we accept the theory that Q existed and that the *Gospel of Thomas* fits with it, then the early Judaic Christians thought of Yeshua/Jesus primarily as a Galilean teacher, and one within a tradition of such teachers. Burton Mack says of the early followers, that they,

> ... did not think of Jesus as a Messiah or the Christ. They did not take his teachings as an indictment of Judaism. They did not regard his death as a divine, tragic, or saving event. And they did not imagine that he had been raised from the dead.

These followers:

> ... did not form a cult of the Christ such as the one that emerged among the Christian communities familiar to readers of the letters of Paul. The people of Q were Jesus people, not Christians.

If Mack is correct, the belief in a divine Jesus develops later with Paul[2] although even Paul did not claim that Jesus was god. He used the description *son of god* which in Hebrew carries the meaning of someone with a special relationship with god, such as King David or a miracle worker, a charismatic exorcist able to dominate and purge unclean spirits. Geza Vermes writes:

> The identification of a contemporary historical figure with god would have been inconceivable to a first-century CE Palestinian Jew.[3]

The growth of Christianity

Whatever the truth of Q or Thomas, the growth of Christianity and its change from a Jewish activity to a world (and gentile) religion was a further cause of instability during the turning point. (Further discussion of Q takes us too far away from our theme and so I will leave it to the interlude that follows this chapter.)

The number of practising Christians in the Roman Empire was never large. Edward Gibbon, in *Decline and Fall of the Roman Empire*, estimated that by 250 CE, five per cent of Rome's inhabitants were Christian. However, Rome was an unusually cosmopolitan city, not unlike London today and the varied nature of London's religious and cultural life is unique in the UK.[4] Robin Lane Fox writes:

> Although we have so much incidental material for life in the Empire, the

---

[1] The actual material of the find probably dates from the second century CE although some of it is no doubt based on older content.

[2] The word *Christian* is first used in Acts 11:26. The view that Paul created Christianity goes back as far as 1845 in Ferdinand Christian Bauer's book, *Paul: his life and works*.

[3] The divine nature of Jesus arrives with the Johannine Gospel.

[4] The 2011 census showed less than half of London's residents to be 'White British'.

inscriptions, pagan histories, texts and papyri make next to no reference to Christians before 250: the two fullest histories, written in the early third century, do not even mention them.

Even in 400 CE, some seventy years after Constantine the Great made Christianity the official religion, it is estimated that no more than ten per cent of the population was Christian but, as Fox says:

Although Christians' numbers are elusive, the volume of their writings is conspicuous. In the later second and third centuries, most of the best Greek and Latin literature which survives is Christian and much more has been lost ... But we must not mistake eloquence for numerical strength ... To read these books is to attend to a small but extremely articulate minority.

Gnosticism

Further adding to the religious turmoil was the rise of *gnosticism*. The word *gnosis* itself is Greek, meaning *knowledge* but of a very specific kind. The ancients distinguished between knowledge derived from reason and knowledge derived from direct experience. While the latter sounds like empirical knowledge, it is nearer to the direct awareness of a vision - but not quite so.

And there mine eyes saw the secrets of the lightning and of the thunder, and the secrets of the winds, how they are divided to blow over the earth, and the secrets of the clouds and dew, and there I saw from whence they proceed in that place and from whence they saturate the dusty earth. And there I saw closed chambers out of which the winds are divided, the chamber of the hail and winds, the chamber of the mist, and of the clouds, and the cloud thereof hovers over the earth from the beginning of the world.

This paragraph is taken from the apocryphal *Book of Enoch*. It recounts a vision. It is perhaps fortunate that Enoch's visions remained apocryphal. Had they reached the Bible proper and become orthodox belief, they might have set the science of meteorology back years - and we have enough trouble with the weather already.

Gnosticism is more than a vision or dream. It implies comprehension: direct knowledge of the divine through personal perception. It is contrasted with knowledge worked out from the study of sacred texts or accepted authorities. Of course, the religious hierarchy recognised only knowledge derived from accepted teaching. Anything else would be a heresy and such heresies included both gnosis and science. Not only were gnostic beliefs considered heresy but so were Galileo's much later empirically based assertions about the solar system.

The name *gnosticism* is often taken to refer to those religious beliefs arising during the turning point although there were many later gnostic beliefs, including Bogomilism and Catharism. Gnosticism is said to thrive in times of uncertainty, as do fundamentalism and extremism which bear resemblances to it. Of course, having a personal experience of the divine is one thing, having the literary skill to turn it into something that someone else can believe is quite another. It is this that prevents the world being swamped with do-it-yourself religions.

According to Elaine Pagels, Tertullian,

... ridiculed the gnostics for creating elaborate cosmologies, with multi-storied

heavens like apartment houses, 'with room piled on room, and assigned to each god by just as many stairways as there were heresies: the universe has been turned into rooms for rent.'

Having read several gnostic accounts, I can sympathise with his view but, when you get down to it, the main gnostic accounts do not seem to be highly individual perceptions of the divine. On the contrary, they rather resemble each other; the driving force for most is the problem of evil and their answers to it are all dualist.

Marcionism

Marcion (about 85-160 CE) was a Roman Christian who was unable to reconcile the god of the Old Testament with the god of the New. He argued that the Old Testament god was the creator god, a god of the law, and an incompetent god at that. Why else had he afflicted women with the agonies of childbirth? Why else did he favour bandits and terrorists such as David, King of Israel? Marcion's New Testament god, on the other hand, was the supreme god of goodness and Jesus was the messenger of this latter god.

This is an instance of the dualism that is such a marked feature of the many gnostic accounts, here used to handle those dramatic and unpleasant events in the Old Testament we looked at earlier. GRS Mead recreates[1] what Marcion probably said about the relationship of Jesus with the creator god.

> *Then the Christ descended a second time, but now in the glory of his divinity, to plead with the god of the law. And the god of the law was compelled to acknowledge that he had done wrong in thinking that there was no higher power than himself. And the Christ said unto him: 'I have a controversy with thee, but I will take no other judge between us but thy own law. Is it not written in thy law that whoso killeth another shall himself be killed; that whoso sheddeth innocent blood shall have his own blood shed? Let me, then, kill thee and shed thy blood, for I am innocent and thou hast shed my blood.'*

> *And then he went on to recount the benefits he had bestowed on the children of the creator, and how he had in return been crucified; and the god of the law could find no defence, and confessed and said: 'I was ignorant; I thought thee but a man, and did not know thee to be a god; take the revenge that is thy due.' And the Christ thereupon left him, and betook himself to Paul, and revealed the path of truth.*

Elaine Pagels remarks that the Christian creed starts, *I believe in one god, father almighty maker of heaven and earth*, and that some scholars have suggested it was designed to exclude followers of Marcionism from orthodox churches.

Too many gods, too many Adams

Iraneus, a late second century Christian apologist, said that his main complaint against the gnostics was that they believed in gods in addition to the creator. Several texts found at Nag Hammadi would serve as examples including *Hypostasis of the Archons*, *The Secret Book of John* and *On the Origin of the World*, which share many

---

[1] While none of Marcion's writings survive, Mead says that *so many orthodox apologists wrote against Marcion after his death, that it is possible to reconstruct almost the whole of his Gospel.*

characters including Sophia and Yaldabaoth. The text, *On the origin of the world*, has the female Pistis Sophia at its centre.

> *(She) came and appeared over chaotic matter which had been expelled like an aborted foetus, without any spirit in it.*

Pistis Sophia is very upset about chaos and wants to make *this thing with no spirit into the likeness of the divine.* She blows into its face and a creature appears. *Young man come here,* she orders. He obeys and so she called him *Yaldabaoth*[1] and he creates the heaven and earth. A troublemaker tries to disturb matters so Pistis Sophia blows her breath again and imprisons the troublemaker. Yaldabaoth is now getting ideas above his station. He is unaware of any other creator and so he declares *I am god, and there is no other but me.* Very cross about this, Pistis Sophia *reveals her greatness* and puts Yaldabaoth back in his place.

Yaldabaoth's son, Sabaoth,[2] hears Pistis Sophia and sings such songs of praise to her that she is pleased and gives him her daughter, Zoe, meaning *life* in Greek. Sabaoth then creates thousands of angels, a firstborn called Israel and another called Jesus Christ *who sits at the right of Sabaoth on a remarkable throne.* As the story proceeds, Yaldabaoth becomes jealous and creates death. Light shines over the earth as the result of unrequited love. Eros appears and everyone falls in love with him so that sexual desire sprouts on the earth.

> *Woman followed the earth.*
> *Marriage followed woman.*
> *Birth followed marriage.*
> *Decay followed birth.*

At one point, we learn that Zoe's name is also Eve[3] and Pistis Sophia sends her to raise Adam, in whom there is no soul so that when,

> *... Eve saw her male partner on the ground, she felt sorry for him and said, 'Adam, live! Get up from the ground!' At once her word became an accomplished deed.*

While all this is quite amusing - soulless Adam perhaps getting up off the sofa because there was no football on the telly - various other events take place which are not so funny. As a result, more Adams are born.

> *The first Adam of light is spiritual and appeared on the first day. The second Adam is psychical and appeared on the sixth day, called Aphrodite. The third Adam is earthly, a person of law, who appeared on the eighth (sic) day, called Sunday after the Day of Rest. The offspring of earthly Adam multiplied and filled the earth.*

As in *Genesis 2:17*, Adam and Eve are told:

> *You may eat the fruit of every tree created for you in paradise, but be careful not to eat from the tree of knowledge. If you eat, you will die.*

---

[1] A name said to mean something like *child come here* or *child of chaos*.

[2] A word that means *hosts* as in *lord of hosts*.

[3] The name *Eve* was translated as *Zoe* by Hellenic Jews.

However, the beast, the wisest of all creatures,[1] urges them to eat.

> When they had eaten,
> The light of knowledge shone on them.
> When they clothed themselves with shame,
> They knew they were stripped of knowledge.
> When they became sober,
> They saw they were naked
> And they fell in love ...
> They understood a great deal.

The story goes on. I have cut out a large part of its cast of characters and indeed much of the plot. It derives a little of its content from *Genesis* but is a different, and immensely convoluted, story of creation. Near the end, it declares:

> Pistis Sophia will drive out the gods of chaos, whom she had created along with the chief creator, and she will cast them down to the abyss ... They will be like mountains of fire and they will consume one another until they are destroyed by their chief creator. When he destroys them, he will turn on himself and attack himself until he is no more.

Another Sophia story

Valentinius wrote about the same time as Marcion. His belief system was successful enough to be persecuted by orthodox Christians two hundred years later. As with many other gnostic structures, the Valentinian story has a first principle, the father, who is inconceivable and indescribable but wishes to be known. He produces a son who is *mind*. Now there are two. As the various aspects of the divine nature are seen, each aspect becomes a divine being, known as an *aeon*. Because so many beings now exist, there is tension. So this Sophia (*wisdom*), the last and youngest of the aeons, seeks to put things together by attempting to comprehend the father as one being instead of many aspects. She fails and is split into two, the part of her which is desire is divided away from everything else and matter originates.

Sophia prays for help and her repentance creates a psychical substance, soul. The other aeons respond to her appeal and create the saviour and the angels, which act unites the aeons once more. Sophia is overcome with joy and creates spiritual beings. Matter, soul and spirit all derive from her. The earth and the seven planets[2] are made of matter and soul and controlled by the aeons who are spirits. A demiurge, a sort of artisan god, then produces the rest of creation, unaware that he is controlled by Sophia.

The first human is created out of matter and soul by the demiurge but Sophia secretly puts in an element of spirit. Human beings are thus partly spiritual but are so tormented by their bodily passions that the saviour descends to earth as Jesus and teaches humans about the true father, overcoming matter and death.

---

[1] One of the characteristics of Ophism is the belief that the serpent, or here *beast*, was a benefactor to mankind. With the Sethites, the Ophites believed that the serpent gave wisdom, the knowledge of good and evil, to mankind.

[2] The sun and the moon, Mercury, Venus, Mars, Jupiter and Saturn.

You may see all this as nonsense but according to Einar Thomassen,[1] Valentinian communities were the most dangerous of gnostic heretics. We must assume that Valentinian beliefs had many followers who presumably did not see them as daft. Someone thought the text, *On the origin of the world*, worth protecting in the face of the somewhat Cromwellian orders from Athanasius, the Bishop of Alexandria, who in the 4th century CE ordered the destruction of all apocryphal writings. Rather than obey this command, someone buried forty-six different texts in a jar.

No monopoly

During the turning point, the Christian story did not have the monopoly that it does now. In the religious flux, competing myths abounded. Fowden writes:

> ... *all gnosticism tended to be anarchically speculative; and Christian gnosticism was worst of all, a many headed hydra ... likely to devour and regurgitate, often in a virtually unrecognizable form, any idea that came into view.*

Elaine Pagels writes:

> *Gnostic Christians ... expressed ideas that the orthodox abhorred. For example, some of these gnostic texts question whether all suffering, labour, and death derive from human sin ... Others speak of the feminine element in the divine, celebrating god as father and mother. Still others suggest that Christ's resurrection is to be understood symbolically, not literally.*

She points out that the,

> ... *writings discovered at Nag Hammadi offer only a glimpse of the complexity of the early Christian movement. We now begin to see that what we call Christianity - and what we identify as Christian tradition - actually represents only a small selection of specific sources, chosen from among dozens of others.*

As Oscar Wilde said:

> *For what is Truth? In matters of religion, it is simply the opinion that has survived.*

Science fiction

It has always been my view that the quality of a science fiction story depends to a large degree upon the number of logic jumps that are called for: the number of times we are asked to *suppose that* ... The best would have only one.

While I cannot find the actual source of this, I seem to remember a story in which people moved from one place to another by dialling up their destination and then stepping onto a disk. I seem to remember that people dialled up to the Amazon jungle to take a sauna and dialled up again for the North Pole to cool off. The part I liked best was that someone had to install the disks first in the relevant places. Clearly they could not use disk transportation to do this, even if they could use it to return home.[2] The story had a single logic jump which, once accepted, allowed the story to flow.

---

[1] Professor in Religious Studies at the University of Bergen, Norway.

[2] It may be that this story comes from Larry Niven's *Ringworld*.

I suppose that one might argue that faith is like this. It seems that the Greek word for *faith* (*pistis*) is better translated as *trust in* than *belief in*. Someone who has faith in a god is better described as having trust in that god rather than as believing in that god. You may have read the interlude at the end of Chapter 2. In this I wrote:

> In the 'Philosophical Investigations', Wittgenstein introduced the notion of a language game (sprachspiel). In the 'Tractatus', he had thought of language as having only one way of connecting with the world – essentially that of dividing of the world into facts. In the 'Investigations', he came to think of this as only one of several possible language games.

Perhaps we might put the two ideas together here. A logic jump made by author and reader together enables the *sprachspiel*[1] of the science fiction novel to flow. The acceptance of *pistis* may enable the *sprachspiel* of a religious belief to occur. This approach would fit St Augustine's answer to the problem of evil: *even though we cannot rationally understand, we must trust that god would not do evil things,* is his logic jump.

One might argue that any religious belief in the modern world depends on the acceptance of a logic jump. Armstrong says something like this:

> It is far more important for a particular idea of god to work than for it to be logically or scientifically sound. As soon as it ceases to be effective it will be changed - sometimes for something radically different. This did not disturb most monotheists before our own day because they were quite clear that their ideas about god were not sacrosanct but could only be provisional.[2] They were entirely man-made - they could be nothing else - and quite separate from the indescribable reality they symbolised ... One mediaeval mystic went so far as to say that this ultimate reality - mistakenly called god - was not even mentioned in the Bible.[3]

So, although the accounts given in the gnostic texts I have described may sound a bit weird, they may simply be different logic jumps, a different *pistis*, driven as much as anything by an attempt to resolve the problem of evil. Their eventual disappearance may be in part due to the number of jumps they call for. Perhaps their failure is one of narrative rather than religious belief. While it seems that people can believe almost anything, the complexity of many gnostic myths risks exasperation and rejection.

Onward

Gnostic stories are at the root of Constant's ideas, particularly one specific set of stories which we will now address. In this, we will find much of the weight that gives his ideas at least an appearance of credibility. So, as he says:

> Now the enchantments begin; now we can proclaim wonders and reveal the most secret things.

---

[1] The term *language game* may seem a little disparaging when talking about religion. It is not meant to be. The main purpose of the term in Wittgenstein's writing is to talk about meaning not religion. To avoid wrong connotations, I will use his German word, *sprachspiel*.

[2] Were *most monotheists* clear about this? Theologians might have been.

[3] We might note that *this ultimate reality - mistakenly called god - (that is) not even mentioned in the Bible* fits rather nicely with almost all the gnostic beliefs and with no traditional Christian or Jewish belief. Eusebius and his fellow apologists would have considered the words heretical.

Interlude: Q and the Jesus People

In her article on Q, Eta Linnemann argues against its existence:

> *The writings of the ancient church give not the slightest hint that such a source ever existed. Among the early church fathers there is not even a rumour of a lost canonical gospel.*

She goes on:

> *Paul never mentions Q although he could hardly have been ignorant of it if it had such virulent influence and championed a faith so contrary to his own. He could not have known the four gospels but there is no reason why he should not have known Q if it really existed in the decades prior to their appearance.*

Why does she refer to Q as championing a faith so contrary to that of Paul? It is because Q omits any mention of Mary or Joseph, the virgin birth, the choice of disciples, the last supper, crucifixion, atonement for sins or resurrection, all matters central to Christian belief; nor are there any miracles or mention of the messiah, salvation or a second coming. Q is a collection of sayings and, initially, an announcement of the imminent arrival of the kingdom of Yahweh here on earth, no mention of heaven. Yeshua tells his followers to work for this event, recognising that there is a cost to being a follower but warning that this is far outweighed by the cost of rejecting the message.

If Q represents the beliefs of the initial Christians, then they saw Yeshua as a human being, making predictions that would easily fit into the mouth of an *Old Testament* prophet. Linnemann is a Christian and is upset by what Burton Mack and other commentators deduce from Q. For example, Mack writes:

> *(The Yeshua people) did not imagine that he had been raised from the dead to rule over a transformed world. Instead, they thought of him as a teacher whose teaching made it possible to live with verve in troubled times. Thus they did not gather to worship in his name, honour him as god, or cultivate his memory through hymns, prayers, and rituals.*

Karen Armstrong writes that within the Yeshua movement:[1]

> *There was no general expectation that the Messiah would die and rise again; indeed the manner of (Yeshua's) death was a source of embarrassment. How could a man who died like a common criminal have been god's anointed? Many regarded the messianic claims for (Yeshua) as scandalous.*

The Gospel of Thomas

The *Gospel of Thomas* is first mentioned in early church writing around 200-230 CE and a copy was found in the *Nag Hammadi* codices. Meyer writes:

> *In contrast to the New Testament Gospels which focus upon the crucifixion and resurrection as they set forth a gospel of the cross, the Gospel of Thomas presents a figure of (Yeshua) who does not die for anyone's sins on the cross and does not rise*

---

[1] She also writes that *during the late second temple period, the Jesus movement had been just one of a multitude of fiercely competing sects.*

from the dead on the third day. Rather in the tradition of Jewish teachers of wisdom, the (Yeshua) of the Gospel of Thomas proclaims a gospel of wisdom.

The *Gospel of Thomas* appears to date from at least the time of the writing of the biblical gospels and is probably earlier. It is, even more than Q, a collection of sayings. Some appear deliberately contentious to the Jews of the time:

> *Jesus said to them, 'If you fast, you will bring sin upon yourselves, and if you pray, you will be condemned and if you give to charity, you will harm your spirits. When you go into any region and walk through the countryside, when people receive you, eat what they serve you and heal the sick among them. For what goes into your mouth will not defile you; rather it is what comes out of your mouth that will defile you.'*

Some are similar to sayings elsewhere:

> *Jesus said, 'You see the speck that is in your sibling's eye but you do not see the beam that is in your own eye. When you take the beam out of your own eye, then you will see clearly to take the speck out of your sibling's eye.'*

Some seem just a little weird:

> *Jesus said, 'Do not worry from morning to evening and from evening to morning, about what you will wear.'*

> *His disciples said, 'When will you appear to us and when will we see you?'*

> *Jesus said, 'When you strip without being ashamed and take your clothes and put them under your feet like little children and trample them, then you will see the child of the living one and you will not be afraid.'*

The *Gospel of Thomas* is quite different from the four official ones but is not so very different from Q. Both present a teacher whose method is to challenge his listeners to think and to interpret. As Meyer says, many of the sayings are like riddles, obviously designed to motivate creative interpretation.

Q and the development of the myth

New Testament scholars divide Q into three parts: $Q^{(1)}$ the earliest, which is a set of teachings and sayings, $Q^{(2)}$ which is more apocalyptic about the imminence of god's kingdom arriving on earth and the fragmentary $Q^{(3)}$, written after the destruction of the temple, perhaps around 75 CE. Burton Mack welcomes $Q^{(3)}$ as evidence of the survival of the people of Q through this dramatic period. $Q^{(3)}$ introduces the ideas of Jesus as the son of god and has given up on imminence of god's kingdom, seeing it as an event in a distant and unknown future.

The three parts of Q display a development of the myth. The sayings of $Q^{(1)}$ remind scholars of the Greek and Roman Cynics who believed that virtue was a life of reason and self-sufficiency as opposed to a life governed by social convention. The Cynics were known for their voluntary poverty and outspoken critiques of society which took the form of witty and competitive argument in public. They used put-downs to get people to see their points. Mack writes:

> *The marketplace was the Cynics' platform, the place to display a living example of freedom from social and cultural constraints, and a place from which to address*

townspeople about the current state of affairs.

Many of their sayings were apparently absurd. Diogenes, the most famous of the Cynics, when asked why he was begging from a statue, replied that he was getting practice in being refused. He was also asked why he begged. He replied that he did so to teach people. When the questioner scornfully asked what he taught, he replied, *Generosity*. The humour arising from the apparent absurdity was a means of getting people to think. Mack again:

> *Their task was not to pose as teachers of truths people did not know, but to challenge people to live in accordance with what they did know. They constantly called attention to the accidental nature of social status and the ephemeral rewards of material success. They criticised social structures of hierarchy, domination and inequity by poking fun at the superficial codes of honour and shame that supported them.*

The Jesus of $Q^{(1)}$ talks about voluntary poverty, lending money without expecting a return, the inadequacy of riches, etiquette for begging, avoidance of retaliation, rejoicing in the face of reproach, hypocrisy and not worrying about tomorrow, all of which would fit very neatly into the Cynics' way of life. However, while the Cynics had no religious purpose, the people of Q believed that they were teaching the rule of god.

$Q^{(2)}$ constitutes a change in atmosphere. The aphoristic style gives way to exhortation. Instead of teaching, $Q^{(2)}$ appears to be about justification as if, as a group, the people of Q had lost an argument and were being attacked from outside. To use a term from Pike's time, they were circling the wagons, giving each other solace by seeing the attacks as proof that they were right, assuring each other that the arrival of the kingdom would justify everything.

> *Whoever is not with me is against me and the one who does not gather with me scatters.*

The pain they were experiencing was to be expected.

> *Do you think that I have come to bring peace on Earth? No, not peace but a sword ... For I have come to create conflict between a man and his father, disagreement between a daughter and her mother and estrangement between a daughter-in-law and her mother-in-law. A person's enemies will be one's own kin.*

Mack's view of the change in note is that it reflects a change in circumstances. The people of Q had formed a group, had become a movement, but had been brought up short by the response of the Jewish establishment. They had been accused of being bad Jews and began to create myths to protect themselves. In place of a man who was a teacher, showing people the unworthiness of their lives, the people of Q started to see Jesus as someone who knew the future, particularly what would happen at the end of time. They believed that they would be justified at the end.

In $Q^{(3)}$ it is as if the community, or what remains of it, is saying, *You wait. You'll see!*

> *Jesus was no longer imagined as a sage $Q^{(1)}$ whose knowledge was divine $Q^{(2)}$. He was imagined as the otherworldly being, heir to the father's kingdom, in battle with the accuser* (perhaps Satan or perhaps the traditional Jews - or both) *for the authority to rule over the kingdoms of the earth, whose hour for full disclosure*

would come in the future, at which time he would turn the father's kingdom over to his followers (the people of Q) *so they can rule over the twelve tribes of Israel.*

We need not be surprised to see a myth developing. It is still developing. Take carols as an example. Many of the carols that we know well were written in the nineteenth century: *Silent Night* (1818), *The First Noel* (1823), *Away in a Manger* (1885) and *We Three Kings* (1857). The stories told in those carols are for the most part new and their setting, while apparently in the Holy Land, in reality is Europe or America. While it has snowed in Bethlehem, the average daytime temperature in December is 57°F (14°C.) During the night it may drop to 42°F (6°C.) If the three kings were Iranian magi, they had covered some 970 miles rather quickly. A camel train travels at a typical 15 miles per day, and so the journey would have taken more than two months, assuming ready availability of remounts.

Please understand that I hold no brief for Mack's view or for Linnemann's. I do not have sufficient knowledge of the background and texts to form an opinion but I do find the debate fascinating. It must be true that the early Jesus people had a different view from Paul and from the gospel authors if only because they had known Yeshua/Jesus as a person.

Dating the gospels

There is no complete agreement on the dates of composition of the gospels. Dr John Robinson has offered interesting evidence for his view that the Johannine gospel may be the earliest being written some time between 35 and 65 CE. He dates all the gospels to a period before the destruction of the temple in 70 CE because none of them mentions it.

The most common view is that *John* (possibly written in Ephesus) is the latest gospel and was written towards 100 CE, *Mark* (written in Rome) dating from about 70 CE, with *Matthew* (possibly written in Antioch) and *Luke* dated to about 85-90 CE. We do not know who wrote the gospels. The names they bear are those of significant figures in the early church but they are not the authors. Ian Wilson sums up the discussion:

> ... the canonical gospels are neither the second century tissue of fabrications argued by (some) nor quite the contemporary eyewitness descriptions that, given the nature of Christianity's claims, we might not unreasonably expect.

The split from Judaism

Paul, a Roman Jew, was converted to Christianity on the road to Damascus.

> And as he journeyed, it came to pass that he drew nigh unto Damascus: and suddenly there shone round about him a light out of heaven: and he fell upon the earth, and heard a voice saying unto him, Saul, Saul, why persecutest thou me?[1]

The *Catholic Encyclopædia* fixes 35 CE as the most likely date for his conversion. Paul's first mission is about ten years later. Jesus died between 30 and 36 CE so Paul's conversion and Jesus's death occur about the same time.

---

[1] *Acts* 9.

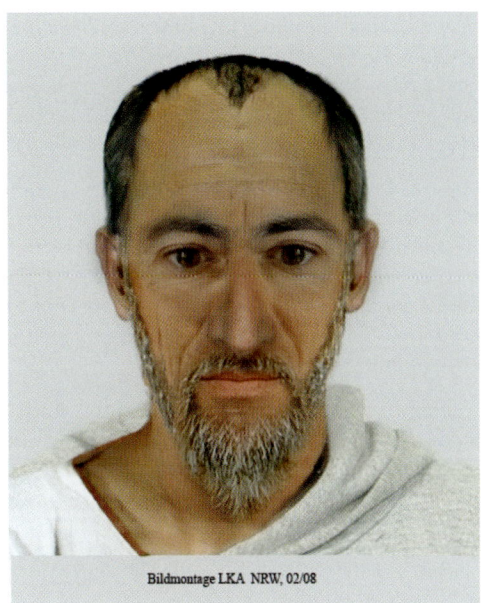

Bildmontage LKA NRW, 02/08

Modern facial composite of St Paul, created by specialists on the German police.

The one fact that I have always known about Paul was that he changed his name from Saul on conversion. Disappointingly, this turns out to be false. As one of the tribe of Benjamin,[1] he was named Saul at his circumcision. As a Roman citizen he was known as Paul. Just as many people in Hong Kong have a Chinese name and a western one so, as the *Catholic Encyclopædia* says:

It was quite usual for the Jews of that time to have two names, one Hebrew, the other Latin or Greek, between which there was often a certain assonance.

The Gentile question

Paul effectively took a Jewish sect and created a Gentile religion but this required a political battle with the sect's leaders. After the death of Jesus, it was not Peter who became the leader of the sect but James, the brother of Jesus (known also as James the Just.) He had to deal with the *Gentile Question* which ultimately caused the separation of the sect from its Jewish roots. The question was whether gentile converts had to become Jews first. Since it was a Jewish sect, the answer appeared to be *Yes*, but this implied circumcision and the adoption of the full panoply of Jewish laws and rituals, something that few gentiles would be prepared or even able to undertake.

Paul took it as his mission to convert gentiles but needed a better answer to the gentile question. He seems to have thought of it as a matter of marketing. If Christianity was to grow, it had to do so outside Judaism; by this time, there was already Jewish antipathy towards the sect.[2] The debate is reported in *Acts 15* which reads like the minutes of a management meeting. James, as head of the sect, sought a compromise. Here is an abbreviated version:

People in Antioch, a Greek city, were teaching would-be converts, 'Unless you are circumcised, you cannot be saved.' This brought Paul and Barnabas into sharp dispute with them and Paul and Barnabas were appointed to go to Jerusalem to see the apostles and elders about the question. In Jerusalem, they were welcomed by the church and reported everything god had done through them but some of the members stood up and said, 'The gentiles must be circumcised and required to keep the law of Moses.'

---

[1] Whose land was traditionally immediately south of the masonically famous Ephraimites.

[2] Paul himself had been employed to root out followers of Jesus and was responsible for the mob stoning Stephen to death.

> *After much discussion, Peter got up and said, 'Brothers, you know that some time ago god made a choice that the gentiles might hear the message of the gospel and believe. God showed that he accepted them by giving the holy spirit to them, just as he did to us. Now then, why do you try to test god by putting on the necks of gentiles such a yoke? No! We believe it is through the grace of our lord Jesus that we are saved, just as they are.'*

> *The whole assembly became silent as they listened to Barnabas and Paul telling about the wonders god had done among the gentiles through them. When they finished, James spoke up. 'Brothers,' he said, 'listen to me. It is my judgement that we should not make it difficult for the gentiles who are turning to god. Instead we should tell them to abstain from food polluted by idols, from sexual immorality, from the meat of strangled animals and from blood.'*

Circumcision was out and the gentile churches grew in number while the Jewish sect declined. Having won the battle over circumcision, Paul later rejected the dietary rules that James, of whom virtually nothing is heard again, had insisted upon in his compromise agreement. Paul then began the process of creating Christianity, perhaps without realising quite what he was doing.

Paul took as his authority that his revelation was from Jesus himself. He maintained that faith in Jesus alone was the route to salvation, that Christianity was now independent of the original Jerusalem sect and that the Mosaic Laws had become irrelevant. The gospels build upon Paul's work and Christianity happens.

What happened to the Jewish Christians?

Henry Chadwick, the Cambridge historian and theologian, writes:

> *The Jewish Christians, excluded by their fellow countrymen, continued to observe sabbaths, circumcision, and other Jewish feasts. As this distressed many gentile Christians, they became lonely, unsupported groups.*

Observing the Mosaic laws and regarding Paul as an apostate, such small Jewish Christian churches lasted in Syria into the fourth century but ...

> *The orthodox Jews could not forgive them for being Christians and the gentile majority in the church could not comprehend their continued observance of the traditional customs and rites of Judaism. Slowly the communities lost importance ...*

These Jewish Christians, who became known as the *Ebionites*, were not seen for what they almost certainly were, the true descendants of the original Jesus people. Giving substance to the Q theory, they were seen as an heretical sect who denied the pre-existence, divinity and virginal birth of Jesus.

Hasidim

In contrast to Mack's view of Yeshua as a Cynic, Vermes writes:

> *The representation of Jesus in the gospels as a man whose supernatural abilities derived, not from secret powers, but from immediate contact with god, proves him to be a genuine charismatic, the true heir of an age-old prophetic religious line.*

Vermes instances Honi the Circle Drawer and Hanina ben Dosa as first century BCE charismatics and *Hasidim* (devout holy men) preceding Yeshua. From the time of Elijah, such Hasidim were seen as miracle workers. Honi gained his title of *Circle Drawer* from an event reported in the Mishnah:[1]

> It once happened that Honi Hama'gel was asked by the people to pray for them, that rain might descend. Said he to them, 'Go and bring in the Passover ovens, that they may not be spoiled by the rain.' He prayed, but the rain did not descend ... He drew a circle around him, and placing himself within it, prayed as follows, 'Creator of the Universe! Thy children have always looked up to me as being like a son of thy house before thee. I swear, therefore, by thy great name, that I will not move from this place until thou wilt have compassion on thy children.'

> Whereupon the rain commenced to drop down gently. Said he, 'It was not for this I prayed, but for rain sufficient to fill the wells, cisterns, and caves.' The rain then fell in torrents, and he said, 'Not for such rain have I prayed, but for mild, felicitous, and liberal showers.' The rain then descended in the usual manner, until the Israelites of Jerusalem were obliged to seek refuge from the city on the Temple Mount, on account of the rain. They came and said to Honi: 'Even as thou didst pray that the rain might descend, so pray now that it may cease.'[2]

Honi's death came in an unusual manner. One day, he met a man who was planting a carob tree in a copse and, on asking how long it would take for the tree to bear fruit, was told seventy years. Honi asked him whether he was sure he would live seventy years and the man replied:

> I found carob trees in existence when I came into the world, so my ancestors must have planted them. Why should I not also plant them for my children?

After lunch by the new tree, Honi fell fast asleep, out of sight in the copse.

> When he awoke, he observed a man gathering the fruit from the carob tree; and he asked the man: 'Didst thou plant this tree?' The man replied: 'Nay, I am the grandson of the man that planted it.' Honi then realized that he must have slept for seventy years.

He went home and asked after his son. He was told his son had died but that his grandson was there. He announced who he was but no one believed him even in the synagogue where his name was revered.

> He went in and said to them, 'I am that Honi,' but they would not believe him, nor would they accord him due respect. This caused him to become downcast and despondent, and he prayed to God that he might die, and so he died.

---

[1] The Mishnah is the primary book of Jewish law and provides case law and interpretations of the commandments of the *Torah*, the five books of Moses. It is said that Yahweh gave law to Moses orally in addition to the written commandments. In 220 CE Rabbi Judah 'the Prince' undertook the massive task of collating into written form this hitherto orally communicated knowledge which was in danger of being lost following the destruction of the second temple.

[2] Honi's descendants also had the power to bring rain. Elijah did also. 1 *Kings* 18.

In the same section of the Talmud,[1] the story of Hanina ben Dosa appears:

> *Rabbi Hanina ben Dosa was going on his way when it began to rain. He said, 'Lord of the world! The whole world is at rest, but Hanina is in trouble!' The rain stopped. Likewise, when he reached his home, he said, 'Lord of the world! The whole world is in trouble, but Hanina is at rest!' Rain began to fall:*

Hanina was legendarily poor.

> *The wife of Hanina would make a fire in her oven on the eve of every Sabbath in order not to be ashamed before her neighbours. She had, however, one bad neighbour who said: 'I know that Hanina and his wife have nothing to cook for the Sabbath; why does she make fire in her oven? I shall go and see.' She went and knocked at the threshold, and Hanina's wife became ashamed and went into another room. In the meantime a miracle happened, and the oven became filled with bread. The neighbour, noticing the bread in the oven, called to Hanina's wife: 'Bring the bread-shovel, or the bread will be burned!' And she replied: 'I just went in for that purpose.' ... Hanina's wife really did go into the next room for a shovel, because she was accustomed to have miracles happen to her.*

He was also a man of great probity.

> *Rabbi Hanina ben Dosa had a few goats, and he was told that his goats caused damage to others. Said he, 'If my goats do damage, may wolves devour them; but if they do not, may they each bring a bear impaled upon their horns.' That same evening, each goat really brought in a bear mounted on its horns.*

> *How did Hanina happen to have goats? Was he not a poor man? Said Rabbi Pinchas, 'It once happened that a man left a few chickens at the house of Hanina, and the latter said to his wife, 'Do not use the eggs, for the chickens do not belong to us.' Accordingly the eggs were left untouched, and in the course of time quite a number of chickens were produced, so that they became too troublesome, and Hanina sold them and with the proceeds purchased goats.*

> *Subsequently the man who left the chickens returned to claim them. He was asked for a description of his property, which he gave correctly, whereupon Hanina turned over the goats to him, and these are the goats that brought bears upon their horns.*

Reading in the Talmud, something which I had never done before, made me realise that the sayings in the Bible, the sometimes gnomic instructions of Q and the Gospel of Thomas are not unique but part of a tradition. Here are a few examples from the Talmud, chosen to be suitable for freemasons:

> *He who has earned man's esteem and love, will also receive the favour of heaven; but he who is not worthy of such esteem, cannot expect to find favour with god.*

> *Seek not greatness for thyself, and desire not honour. Practise more than thou learnest, and lust not for the table of kings, for thy table is greater than theirs, and thy crown greater than their crown, and faithful is thy taskmaster, who will pay thee the wage of thy work.*

---

[1] *Seder Moed, Tract Taanith,* Chapter III.

There are four things which bear good fruit in this world, and yield greater benefits for the world to come ... honouring of parents, conferring favours, reconciliation of adversaries, and, above all, the study of the law. There are four things for which one who is guilty of them is punished both in this and in the world to come; namely, idolatry, incest, shedding of blood, and, above all, slander.

And a few brief lessons:

The place honours not the man, 'tis the man who gives honour to the place.

There are three crowns: of the law, the priesthood, and the kingship; but the crown of a good name is greater than them all.

Rabbi Ashi said, 'Charity is greater than all.' Rabbi Eliazar said, 'Who gives charity in secret is greater than Moses.'

If a word spoken in its time is worth one piece of money, silence in its time is worth two.

and perhaps one for over-indulgence at the festive board:

He who increaseth his flesh but multiplieth food for the worms.

There may be ten commandments carved in stone and 613 commandments in all but the Talmud contains 6,200 pages of sayings, case law and interpretations.

Cynic or charismatic?

Vermes, in describing Jesus as a charismatic and one of the Hasidim, is speaking of the Jesus of the New Testament. The Yeshua of $Q^{(1)}$ and of the Gospel of Thomas does not seem to be such a figure and is, according to Mack, more of a Greek Cynic. Both might be true if we see the difference as part of the development of a myth. In $Q^{(1)}$, Yeshua is a teacher and prophet. By $Q^{(3)}$, he has become an otherworldly being predicting a future event. As the gospels take up the story, he becomes one of the Hasidim, a miracle worker, exorcist and teacher. From there, he becomes the messiah and finally god himself come to earth, a figure unique to Christianity. Yeshua has completely disappeared and Christ has taken his place.

Chapter nine: Hermes Trismegistus

Advancement in science and technology looks forward, proceeding by hypothesis and experiment; it is about trying things out and seeking new knowledge. Constant's science is very different. It looks backward to discover what was known before by the ancients; it is about decoding old texts, looking for old knowledge, supposed to have been kept secret.

The ancient whose name is most used to conjure with is Hermes Trismegistus, Thrice-great Hermes. Said to have written 36,525 books, the few of his works that remain are known as the Corpus Hermeticum. The works form a set of gnostic texts which had attractions for St Augustine and other early Christian writers who believed that they ante-dated and foresaw the arrival of Jesus. It is here that we find the source of Pike's totally incorrect views on masonic beliefs about creation.

I could never see why anyone would believe that the location of the stars has any effect on our behaviour or fortunes on earth but the Corpus Hermeticum provides at least a rationale for astrology. Hermes Trismegistus puts forward a creation myth and an analysis of creation that combines divine energy and magic. It is this that forms the basis of Constant's science and in turn gives the goat of the sabbath much of its (spurious) profundity.

All this was lost in the paradigm shift to experimental science and to understand this, we will go into the nature of paradigms, look at the mechanical marvels of Salomon de Caus, give a nod in passing to the Emerald Tablet with a mention of Isaac Newton and learn how to become divine.

Finally, we will examine the magic of Cornelius Agrippa, his apparent irresponsibility and his view that man has 'elevated himself above the angels to the archetype itself.'

Power

Somewhat endearingly, Constant writes of a force in nature, *immeasurably more powerful than steam*. He is not referring to nuclear energy but a power,

> *... known to the ancients, a Universal Agent having equilibrium for its supreme law and directed by the Great Arcanum of Transcendental Magic.*

By which,

> *... it is possible to modify the very order of the seasons; to produce at night the phenomena of day; to correspond instantaneously between the ends of the earth; to see, like Apollonius, what is happening on the other side of the world; to heal or injure at a distance.*

He is not thinking of air conditioning, street lighting, email, TV or webcams, missiles or remote surgical procedures, but of a secret by means of which,

> *... the adept is invested with a species of relative omnipotence and can operate superhumanly ... Thereby many illustrious interpreters of sacred mysteries, such as Mercurius Trismegistus, Osiris, Orpheus, Apollonius of Tyana, and others whom it might be dangerous or unwise to name, came after their death to be adored and invoked as gods.*

Here then is the difference between today's science and that sought by Constant. The difference is not only that today's science works but in the direction of the search for knowledge. Constant is looking backwards, invoking the names of those who possessed knowledge but kept it secret. The knowledge he seeks is old.

Thrice-great Hermes

Of all the gnostic texts, the most important are those attributed to Hermes Trismegistu*s*. Referring to him sometimes as Mercurius Trismegistus, Mercury being the Roman equivalent of the Greek Hermes, Constant saw him as a figure deep in antiquity and as a pre-eminent Magus of the *science of the secrets of nature*. Clement of Alexandria[1] wrote in about 200 CE that Trismegistus had written forty-two books on magic, astrology, the significance of thunder, earthquakes, botany, mineralogy, alchemy, healing and most importantly, on the nature of creation, the gods, prayer and the way to heaven. Manetho, writing at the same time, put the number at three myriads, six thousand, five hundred and twenty five volumes,[2] more in line with the number used by Longfellow.

> *But where are the old Egyptian*
> *Demi-gods and kings?*
> *Nothing left but an inscription*
> *Graven on stones and rings.*
> *Where are Helios and Hephaestus,*
> *Gods of eldest eld?*

---

[1] Clement famously travelled in search of learning, to Ionia, Magna Graecia, Syria, Egypt, Assyria, Palestine and Alexandria. One of his pupils was Origen.

[2] A myriad is a classical Greek unit of 10,000. On this basis, Hermes wrote 36,525 books.

Where is Hermes Trismegistus,
Who their secrets held?
Where are now the many hundred
Thousand books he wrote?
By the Thaumaturgists plundered,
Lost in lands remote;
In oblivion sunk forever,
As when o'er the land
Blows a storm-wind, in the river
Sinks the scattered sand. [1]

Copenhaver writes that the number of surviving works now taken to be part of the *Corpus Hermeticum* (the body of work by Hermes) number no more than twenty-four.

Thoth, Hermes and Mercury

Thrice-great Hermes, the title having several interpretations,[2] was thought in antiquity to be the Egyptian god Thoth, here depicted as having the head of an ibis, a sacred bird. You will recall that Herodotus thought that the Egyptians were *religious far beyond all other men*, that many of the Greek gods were Egyptian under a different name. Just as Banebdjedet was identified as Pan, so Thoth was identified with the Greek god Hermes.

As with many of the popular Egyptian gods, Thoth's remit grew over time. He was initially a sort of secretary to the major gods but rose to preside over all religious and civil procedures, becoming like a Cabinet Secretary (or a Director of Ceremonies in a masonic lodge.) He became lord of all sacred literature and eventually all wisdom. As Fowden writes:

Esoteric wisdom was his special preserve and he was called the 'mysterious' and the 'unknown'. His magical powers made him a doctor too; and when the body finally succumbed to mortality, Thoth participated in the judgment of the soul.

---

[1] Henry Wadsworth Longfellow, *Hermes Trismegistus*, from *In the Harbour*.

[2] As Copenhaver tells us, an Egyptian named Hor, who was born during the reign of the fourth Ptolemy in about 200 BCE and grew up to be a clerk in the service of Thoth, wrote the minutes of a meeting of the ibis cult, held June 1, 172 BCE. He refers to Thoth as *megistou kaimegistou theou megalou Hermou* a phrase containing two superlative forms of *great* followed by the word *great* itself: thus more or less *three times great* or *thrice great*.

In a similar manner, the Greek Hermes was first known as the messenger of the gods, eloquent and skilled in public speaking. He too gained a reputation for wisdom, for example inventing the alphabet. Like Thoth, he took on duties in the afterlife, escorting the shades of the dead into the lower world.

Thus one can readily see how Thoth and Hermes became identified with each other, both absorbed into the figure of Hermes Trismegistus although, as Fowden writes, these two streams in the ancestry of Trismegistus never quite became one. The Thoth stream - *the adept of the temple cults, the law-giver, authority on astronomy, astrology, botany, mathematics and geometry ... (who) cut irrigation canals and established the exchange of contracts* - was very much a god. The Hermes stream sees him as originally human, a mortal who achieves immortality by means of great acts and through this bifurcation, Trismegistus became seen as at least partly human. It is in this guise that he is credited with the works collectively called the *Corpus Hermeticum* which, as Dame Frances Yates wrote, were believed even up to the Renaissance to be of profound antiquity. That belief faded after 1614 when Isaac Casaubon cast doubt on the origin of the writings. The great philologist wrote of the *Corpus Hermeticum* in a letter to his close friend Joseph Scaliger:

> *I will believe that they come from that very ancient Egyptian on the day when I begin divorce proceedings from the art of criticism.*

Anthony Grafton delightfully writes of him that:

> *Casaubon worked frenetically, 'I rose at five: alas, how late!' begins one characteristic journal entry. More important, he was consistently creative, in a wide range of fields. Casaubon produced seventeen children as well as a vast stream of learned works, some of which he wrote while using one foot to rock the current infant's cradle.*

Frances Yates writes that there were many who refused to believe Casaubon, but the truth is that there was no Hermes Trismegistus and the works are by several different, if unknown, authors. Far from being written in deep antiquity, it is generally accepted today that the *Corpus Hermeticum* dates from 100 to 300 CE. Most commentators place it more towards 100, thus in the second half of the turning point, squarely in the period of the other gnostic writings.

The science of magic

It has been usual to divide the *Corpus Hermeticum* into two, the *Philosophical Hermetica* and the *Technical Hermetica*. The former, also referred to as the *Theological*, is a collection of works on the nature of creation, gods and becoming divine, while the latter is a set of texts on practical magic and astrology. One can see immediately the attraction for Constant.

While the bridge engineer uses the principles of gravity, compression, tension, torsion and shear, the hermetic magician uses the principles of cosmic sympathy, dæmonology,[1] cosmology, astrology and psychology of the divine. The fact that we

---

[1] Dæmons and demons are not the same. The former appear in gnostic writings and are personifications of powers or forces which may be good or bad depending upon circumstance. They are a bit like boring versions of Greek gods. Demons exist within Christianity (and other religions) and are the baddies: fallen angels, devils and so on.

would not cross a bridge constructed according to the principles of dæmonology should not blind us to the fact that the ancient mind did not make as much of a distinction between magic and engineering as we do.

At the court of the Elector Palatine in Heidelberg in the early 1600s, the garden of the palace above the town was talked of as a new wonder of the world with its pneumatic and water driven marvels. Here Salomon de Caus created a statue which gave out strange sounds when the sun's rays struck it. Such mechanical marvels were not built by uttering magical incantations but what Salomon de Caus did was seen as the same kind of activity as the creation of gold from base metals, the divination of the identity of a guilty party by means of a key and book[1] or the accomplishment of the pleasures of the flesh by means of a love charm. Thus, when Constant writes that,

> ... there is one sole, universal and imperishable dogma, strong as supreme reason; simple, like all that is great; intelligible, like all that is universally and absolutely true; and this dogma is the parent of all others. A science which confers on man powers apparently superhuman ...

he is referring to the hermetic view of how the world works. Of course, Constant was writing in the 19th century when the principles of science were well-known and when bridge building was certainly not a matter of magic. Nonetheless, it is the hermetic world view that his ideas stem from.

Paradigms

The language of experimental science was not available before the 17th century and there was no way of expressing a difference between technology and magic. The thought world of the ancients was not divided, as today, into science and superstition.

In his book, *The Structure of Scientific Revolutions*, Thomas Kuhn speaks of a *paradigm*: the accepted way of understanding things within a community. All communities work with some set of received beliefs which derive from what people are taught and how they learn to see and explain the world as they grow up. Such received beliefs are called *paradigms*. A paradigm shift occurs when the accepted way of seeing things changes; when the old way no longer accounts for new discoveries and when explanation breaks down.

Kuhn wrote of all scientific research that it is *a strenuous and devoted attempt to force nature into the conceptual boxes supplied by professional education.* When facts start to rebel and refuse to be forced into existing boxes, a paradigm shift occurs. Such a shift is what Kuhn describes as a scientific revolution. We are forced to think of things in a different way.

Perhaps the best example of this is the break down of the Ptolemaic model of the universe: the view that the sun, moon and planets revolve around the earth. It became increasingly difficult to use this model as more phenomena were observed and the model was forced to become increasingly more complex to cope with them.

---

[1] In 1551, the Vicar of St Owen's in Gloucester inserted a key into a Bible and then tied the book up with string. Having invoked the Trinity, he read the names of the suspects. When he read the name of Margaret Greenhill, the key turned.

Its death blow came when Galileo observed that Jupiter had moons, objects that did not revolve around the earth. The recognition dawned that Copernicus was right and the sun was the centre of the solar system. The new solarcentric model was simple and accounted for all then known phenomena.

There are other examples of paradigm shifts:

- The model of a designed and created world giving way to one that is the result of happenstance and natural selection.

- The shift from Newtonian physics to relativity.

- The shift from one universe to the acceptance, mathematically at least, of parallel universes.

One cannot work with two paradigms at once; the new drives out the old:

> ... because it is a transition between incommensurables, the transition between competing paradigms cannot be made a step at a time ...

as Kuhn writes, but paradigms switch for individuals and for some the switch may be a long time coming. Max Planck (Nobel Prize winner 1918, initiator of quantum theory) said:

> A new scientific truth does not triumph by convincing its opponents and making them see the light, but rather because its opponents eventually die, and a new generation grows up that is familiar with it.

Prayer and the old paradigm

It is true that even in earlier times, there were thinkers who decried magic. Fowden points to Pliny the elder (23-79 CE) and Plotinus (204-270 CE) as such renegades. He quotes Pliny on the hold that magic has on people:

> Nobody should be surprised by the greatness of its influence, since alone of the arts it has embraced three others that hold supreme dominion of the human mind and makes them subject to itself alone. Nobody will doubt that it first arose from medicine ... that to those most seductive and welcome promises, it added the powers of religion, about which even today the human race is quite in the dark; that again meeting with success, it made a further addition of astrology because there is nobody who is not eager to learn his destiny ...

Plotinus was dismissive of the magical incantations used to manipulate the gods:

> They say that these powers obey and are led by a mere word, by whoever among us is better skilled in the art of saying just the right things in the right way, songs and cries and aspirated hissing sounds ...

and indeed, many people today are puzzled by claims that gods will respond to special pleadings made in special ways. Certainly to the outsider prayers of petition seem odd. Do we seriously believe that a deity would intervene to set aside the laws of physics because someone asked him to? Can we really accept that the sun stood still while Joshua overcame his enemies, because Moses prayed that it should?[1] Goodness only knows what that would have done to gravity!

Nevertheless, in the ancient world, prayer was focused on getting things done and, as we have seen, gods were worshipped only if they were useful. Thus the worshipper had to have a means of letting the gods know what was required. The methods often involved that hissing and popping that Plotinus disliked so much. They also included bribery (sacrifice), flattery, abuse and even threats.[2] Fowden writes:

> It is perhaps difficult for us to see how feelings of reverence and awe could be generated by divinities who were to such an extent the victims of their worshippers, unless the Egyptians' view of the relationship that should prevail between man and his gods was quite different from that which has been propagated by the higher forms of (say) Judaeo-Christianity. And it is essential to recognize that this was indeed the case.

The magician was deemed to have almost unlimited powers once he had command of the spells, the formulae, the incantations and other techniques necessary to bend supernatural beings to his will.

> Once a god's favour had been secured, it was up to the individual magician to pursue a limited, easily-definable objective, or to ask as Solomon had for a less tangible benefit.[3]

There was a concern beyond satisfying one's earthly needs, even in basic magic, and the *Philosophical Hermetica* demonstrate this. It is as if the preparation for worldly magic demonstrated the possibility of something more. It is important to note that the *Technical Hermetica* are part of the world view espoused by the *Philosophical Hermetica*. All metals were thought of as being of the same base substance. The difference between metals lay in the *invigorating principle* and by manipulating this, iron would become gold. In a religious or moral sense, the body is the base substance and the aim becomes the purification of the soul, the invigorating principle.

---

[1] A reference to the masonic ritual which conflates *Joshua* 10: *Then spake Joshua to the Lord in the day when the Lord delivered up the Amorites before the children of Israel, and he said in the sight of Israel, Sun, stand thou still upon Gibeon* ... and *Exodus* 17: *As long as Moses held up the staff in his hand, the Israelites had the advantage. But whenever he dropped his hand, the Amalekites gained the advantage* ...

[2] While all this may sound very different from monotheistic religious relationships, it might be said that the difference was more in the frankness with which it was expressed; a difference in degree rather than kind, one might think.

[3] *God appeared to Solomon and said to him, 'Ask for whatever you want me to give you.' Solomon answered, 'You have shown great kindness to David my father and have made me king in his place. Now, Lord God, ... give me wisdom and knowledge, that I may lead this people ...' God said to Solomon, 'Since this is your heart's desire and you have not asked for wealth, riches or honour, nor for the death of your enemies, and since you have not asked for a long life but for wisdom and knowledge to govern my people ... therefore wisdom and knowledge will be given you. And I will also give you wealth, riches and honour ...' Chronicles 7-11 New International Version.*

Creation

The *Corpus* has a typically complex account of creation. I will restrict this account to highlights because much of it is standard gnostic stuff and anyway it is the essence that matters.[1] So, in the beginning there was god-as-mind (*nous*). This god-as-mind makes contact with Trismegistus in his human embodiment and provides him with a vision that explains the rest of creation. To ensure there is no doubt about the message, he translates the vision:

> *'I am the light you saw, mind, your god,' he said, 'who existed before the watery nature that appeared out of darkness. The light-giving word who comes from mind is the son of god.'*[2]

Trismegistus asks how the elements of nature came about and is told:

> *The mind who is god, being androgyne, ... by speaking gave birth to a second mind, a craftsman ... (who) crafted seven governors.*

It is not altogether clear how many gods we have here. There would seem to be three: god-as-mind (*nous*), god-as-word (*logos*) and craftsman-god (*demiurge*). However, the second two are usually taken to be the same under different names, referred to by some commentators, notably Frances Yates, as the *demiurge*; a typical gnostic second god who actually creates the world and who may be good or evil. Note also the androgynous nature of god-as-mind. This theme appears in many gnostic accounts and is part of Constant's description of *le bouc de sabbat*.

> *One arm is feminine and the other masculine, as in Khunrath's androgynous figure; and indeed our goat and his figure are one and the same symbol.*[3]

The craftsman-god is the creator of the seven governors, the seven heavenly bodies that we meet in the Valentinian myth and most gnostic accounts - the sun, the moon, Mercury, Venus, Mars, Jupiter and Saturn. Here we have the root of astrology. The seven governors,

> *... encompass the sensible world in circles, and their government is called fate.*

The circles are the orbits around the earth. The sun, moon, etc. were not seen as the inanimate objects we know them to be but as divine beings, another example of the *bricolage* we met when discussing Lévi-Strauss and modes of thought. Next the craftsman-god creates the elements and these in turn enable the creation of living beings appropriate to each. Thus:

> *Air brought forth winged things, the water things that swim, the earth bought forth from herself the living things that she held within, four-footed beasts and crawling things, wild animals and tame.*

Then the god-as-mind himself gives birth to man *whom he loved as his own child* and so man is both mortal and immortal: mortal in body as part of nature and immortal in spirit as part of god-as-mind. Since man has been his personal

---

[1] That is probably a very bad gnostic pun!

[2] All translations from Copenhaver.

[3] Constant is referring to Heinrich Khunrath and his immensely complex 1595 engraving in *Amphitheatrum sapientiae aeternae* of a figure with one male breast and one female.

creation, god-as-mind wants man to return to him, mind to mind and so man, having been given,

> ... *a portion of the powers of each of the seven governors, ... wished to break through the circumference of the circles to observe the rule of the one.*

This he did and enabled nature to see the face of god-as-mind and *nature smiled for love*. At the same time, immortal-man saw his own image reflected in nature and wished to inhabit such a form. No sooner said than done,

> ... *and he inhabited the unreasoning form. Nature took hold of her beloved, hugged him all about and embraced him, for they were lovers.*

Even though immortal-man was still androgyne, the result of this union was that nature gave birth to seven men, also androgyne, whose natures reflected those of the seven governors. At that moment, everything was,

> ... *sundered by the counsel of god. All living things, which had been androgyne, were sundered into two parts - humans among them - and part of them became male, part likewise female.*

And then god gave a warning:

> *Increase in increasing and multiply in multitude all you creatures and craftsworks but let him who is mindful recognize that he is immortal, that desire is the cause of death and let him recognize all that exists.*

And so the world was populated. Man, however, still had a choice.

> ... *the one who recognized himself* (as an immortal soul) *attained the chosen good, but one who loved the body that came from the error of desire goes on in darkness, errant, suffering ... the effects of death.*[1]

Thus the aim of man becomes the re-assimilation with god-as-mind and the return to immortality and this is what Trismegistus sets out to teach - to Tat, his student, and the rest of the cast of the *Corpus Hermeticum*.

The attraction for the apologists

I have said that one can see the attraction for Constant and one can also see the attraction for the early Christian apologists. Passages in the *Corpus,* especially the bit about god-as-word or *logos,* seemed to presage a belief in one god and the birth of a saviour many years before Christ. Fowden writes that Lactantius, thinking the works were very old, seized upon Trismegistus as a prophet, pointing out his teaching of,

> ... *the majesty of the supreme and only god who is lord and father but himself motherless and fatherless. The hermetic god is the one without a name since on account of his unity he has no need of qualification. No mortal mind comprehends him nor does mortal tongue suffice to describe him.*

St Augustine, too, seemed to think that Trismegistus was on to something. He writes, in the *City of God*:

---

[1] The usual choice between sex and immortality, it seems.

> *Hermes makes many such statements agreeable to the truth concerning the one true god who fashioned this world.*

but he was disturbed by a passage in the *Asclepius*, a part of the *Philosophical Hermetica*, about man's ability to create gods:

> *Just as the master and father - or god to use his most august name - is maker of the heavenly gods so it is mankind who fashions the temple gods who are content to be near humans ... Not only is mankind glorified; he glorifies as well. He not only advances towards god; he also makes gods strong.*

While Augustine wanted to see a prediction of Christianity in the *Corpus Hermeticum*, he found it difficult to accept from a polytheist who believed,

> *... that men should always continue in subjection to those gods which he confesses to be made by men, and to bewail their future removal.*

He is also disturbed by the description of Egypt as heaven. Trismegistus shares the common Greek view that Egypt is the centre of religion:

> *Do you not know, Asclepius, that Egypt is an image of heaven or to be more precise that everything governed and moved in heaven came down to Egypt and was transferred there? If truth were told, our land is the temple of the whole world.*

Augustine was thus left with an approach/avoidance relationship with the *Corpus Hermeticum*. In the end he comes down on the negative side. Had Augustine known that it was all written at least one hundred years after the birth of Jesus, he would have been saved a great deal of anxiety.

How to become divine

Later in the *Philosophical Hermetica*, Trismegistus, now in his divine form, explains the nature of creation and the nature of the good. This teaching is not for academic interest but as a precursor to the attempt to return to god-as-mind, to become divine. One achieves this not by understanding alone; it is necessary also to achieve purity.

> *Leave the senses of the body idle and the birth of divinity will begin. Cleanse yourself of the irrational torments of matter.*

Trismegistus lists the twelve torments that must be expelled: ignorance, grief, incontinence, lust, injustice, greed, deceit, envy, treachery, anger, recklessness and malice. Only when these have been expelled is the mind/soul free from bodily sensation. In this tranquil state, the mind/soul becomes capable of seeing beyond the earthly world. Under the guidance of Trismegistus, Tat begins the process:

> *Since god has made me tranquil, father, I no longer picture things with the sight of my eyes but with the mental energy that comes through the powers. I am in heaven, in earth, in water, in air. I am in animals and in plants ...*

Tat is then guided to *sing the secret hymn*, part of which runs:

> *This is what the powers within me shout; they hymn the universe; they accomplish what you wish; your counsel goes forth from you, and to you the universe returns. Accept a speech offering from all good things. Life, preserve the*

> *universe within us; light, enlighten it; god, spiritualize it.*

and he experiences rebirth and comes face to face with god-as-mind.

> *You are god! Your man shouts this through fire, through air, through earth, through water, through spirit, through your creatures. From your eternity I have won praise, and in your counsel I have found the rest I seek; I have seen, as you wished it.*

Tat completes the return journey. Just as man was made during the descent from god-as-mind, so Tat goes back the other way. Tat was born from god and has become divine again by understanding that he is immortal and overcoming all desires that are the cause of death. Another hymn, from the *Discourse on the Eighth and the Ninth*, part of the Nag Hammadi find, runs:

> *I give thanks by singing a hymn to you. For I have received life from you, when you made me wise. I praise your name that is hidden from me: a ō ee ō ēēē ōōō iii ōōōō ooooo ōōōō uuuuuu ōōōōōōōōōōōōōōōōōōōōōō.*[1] *You are the one who exists with the spirit. I sing a hymn to you reverently.*

Here we see the gnostic experience, the attainment of divinity and immortality through understanding, purity and highly personal experience. The gnostic route to heaven is thus very different from that offered by the mainstream church: a reward for obedience to the church's rules. This was one reason why the early church was so opposed to gnosticism. It had no way to control it.

Pessimism and optimism

The question of duality, of supreme importance in understanding the narratives of *gnosticism*, is about mind (or soul) and matter and whether they are separate - matter being evil and mind good - or one. Frances Yates speaks about *pessimistic gnosis* (that the world is evil and we must escape from it) and *optimistic gnosis* (that matter is impregnated with the divine and there is no division.)

The pessimistic view is that taken by the Cathars, that the material world is inherently evil, being created by and under the control of evil powers[2] and one could understand Pike's American slaves accepting this view. For the Cathars, the demiurge (or craftsman-god) is the devil and the aim of life is to have as little as possible to do with the devil's world. You may remember that the logic jump of the Cathars was reincarnation and we quoted O'Shea as saying:

> *To be saved, then, meant becoming a saint. To be damned was to live again, on this corrupt Earth.*

The optimistic gnosis is that the material world, as Yates puts it,

---

[1] Glossalia, language-like strings of vowels which also occur in *speaking with tongues*. In the latter, the string of vowels is random. In this hymn, the sequence seems scripted.

[2] Hume argues against the argument-from-design proof of the existence of god, by saying that the world's imperfection could well be the result of it being *the first rude essay of some infant deity who afterwards abandoned it, ashamed of his lame performance.* Trekkies will remember the apparently omnipotent Q and his immature son who is given the choice of becoming a responsible member of the Continuum or spending eternity as an ameoba.

> *... is impregnated with the divine, the earth lives, moves, with a divine life, the stars are living divine animals, the sun burns with a divine power, there is no part of nature which is not good for all are parts of god.*

Here is god-as-mind talking to Trismegistus:

> *So you must think of god in this way, as having everything - the cosmos, himself the universe - like thoughts within himself. Thus, unless you make yourself equal to god, you cannot understand god; like is understood by like. Make yourself grow to immeasurable immensity, outleap all body, outstrip all time, become eternity and you will understand god.*

This being so, all man has to do is believe and he can do what he will. He will become at one with god and will become god.

> *Command your soul to travel to India, and it will be there faster than your command. Command it to cross over the ocean, and again it will quickly be there, not as having passed from place to place but simply as being there. Command it even to fly up to heaven, and it will not lack wings. Nothing will hinder it ...*

The *Corpus Hermeticum* is not consistently optimistic or pessimistic. After all, it was written by several authors each with his or her own ideas. Nevertheless, in both cases we are urged to become at one with god. Just as in creation, things descended through the spheres, so we have to return, ascend, and go back the way we came.

Divine energies and magic

This movement, from god-as-mind downwards during creation and return upwards by the rejection of earthly experience, is through three spheres of being: the sphere of the divine, the sphere of reason and the sphere of sensation.

The three spheres or levels are bound together by divine energies or daemons, which are sometimes spoken of as light,[1] deriving from the seven governors and the stars and affecting everything in sequence. Each sphere is said to be *in sympathy* with the others, up and down, and these sympathies can be used by one who understands them. As Fowden writes:

> *By establishing sets of sympathetic correspondences or 'chains', they maintain affinities between the most disparate areas of the natural realm so that each animal, plant, mineral or even part of the human or animal body corresponds to a particular planet or god whom (or which) they can be used to influence, providing the right procedures and formulae are known ... And just as the elements of one chain are mutually sympathetic, so those of different chains maybe antipathetic - a principle with obvious applications in the sphere of medicine,*

... or indeed magic which is nothing more than a matter of operating on the energies and the sympathies involved to create the result desired. In this sense, magic could be called a science.

---

[1] Astral light, perhaps?

Astrology

Astrology too is part and parcel of the deal. To know one's destiny is to know what the dæmons (personification of the energies) planets (the governors) and stars dictate. Astrological divination, in this way, is not simply superstition but a logical derivation from the nature of being. Constant's views on the Tarot can also be thought of as part of his science. For Constant, here is the hidden truth; hidden because it has been wrongly rejected by the church:

> Science is the basis of magic in the same way that love is at the root of Christianity ... but human ignorance has always feared the unknown and the science was driven into hiding. It clothed itself in new symbols, falsified its intentions, denied its hopes. Then the language of alchemy was created, an impenetrable illusion for the vulgar's greed of gold, a living language only for the true disciple of Hermes.

To step back to science fiction, the logic jumps are not that many and once made there does seem to be some continuity and consistency within the story. We can grant Constant and the *Corpus Hermeticum* that much. The magic derives from and is explained by way of the world view and it is thus that the *Technical Hermetica* and the *Philosophical Hermetica* fit together.

Constant's view

Did Constant think there really was a Hermes? One can rarely tell what he does believe as he always hedges his bets but in the *L'Histoire de la Magie*, he writes:

> The Emerald Tablet contains all magic in a single page. The other works attributed to Hermes ... are taken by critics to stem from the School of Alexandria.

Constant attributes the emerald tablet to Hermes but the rest to other writers from Alexandria, the centre of Hellenism in Egypt. The (no doubt mythical) emerald tablet has never been found although the content attributed to it appears in many documents, the earliest dated between 650 and 830 CE.[1] It has been transcribed and translated by many people, including Isaac Newton whose version starts:

> Tis true without lying, certain & most true, that wch is below is like that wch is above & that wch is above is like yt wch is below.

> What is certainly true is that what is below resembles that which is above and what is above resembles that which is below.

... which can be taken as a summary of the gnostic view of the sensible world as a copy of the divine. The phrase, *as above so below*, is a basic tenet of alchemy.

Agrippa

The *Corpus Hermeticum* inspired philosophy and medicine right up to the time of the Elizabethan mathematician, navigator and astrologer John Dee (1527-1608) who has been taken to be the instigation of Rosicrucianism (more later). One of those inspired was Henry Cornelius Agrippa (1486-1535),[2] he of the *Venomous Magic* that

---

[1] And thus some five to seven hundred years after the *Corpus* was written.

[2] Whose major work was *De occulta philosophia*.

Constant mentions. Agrippa sees creation as made up of the same three spheres; in his terms the intellectual, celestial and elemental worlds, connected by the power of sympathy. Again, as Yates writes:

> *Each world receives influences from the one above it so that the virtue of the creator descends through the angels in the intellectual world, to the stars in the celestial world and thence to the elements and all things composed of them in the elemental world, animals, plants, metals, stones and so on.*

And just as we saw in hermeticism, Agrippa explains that the effective use of elemental objects (plants, animals, stones, etc.) in medicine and magic, comes from the intellectual and celestial virtues drawn down to them by the power of sympathy. Thus by manipulating the sympathies, the Magus can use the elements to gain magical effects - but hereby hangs a tale.

You will recall that the energies which account for the sympathies are personified as dæmons and any attempt to draw down the power of the celestial realm risks their involvement. While Trismegistus holds that any dæmon may appear good or evil according to its disposition at that point in time, Agrippa, in common with most later Christian magicians, thinks of them as good or evil beings; that is, of angels and demons. The trick is, therefore, to ensure that one draws down only angels and not demons; easier said than done perhaps, though one has no personal experience.

Yates calls Agrippa *an irresponsible magician*, because he takes insufficient care with this, giving instructions on how to summon superior powers with no prophylactic. Get it wrong and it is trouble. One is immediately put in mind of those apparently beautiful courtesans in Marlowe's *Dr Faustus* which turn out to be demons in disguise. Like Constant, Agrippa thinks of the Magus as all-powerful:

> *He who has cohabited with the elements, vanquished nature, mounted higher than the heavens, elevated himself above the angels to the archetype itself, with whom he then can do all things.*

Again like Constant, Agrippa represented his work as religious magic, but his views rested upon the basis of hermeticism and St Augustine had already banned Trismegistus. Worse, Agrippa spoke of man as being active in creation in the same way that the Corpus Hermeticum spoke of making gods. As Yates puts it, Agrippa sees man as,

> *... no longer only the pious spectator of god's wonders in the creation and the worshipper of god himself above the creation, but man the operator, man who seeks to draw upon the power of the divine.*

Agrippa, and indeed the hermetic authors, saw the purpose of knowledge as the discovery of the power which would enable man to move between the three spheres of being and to create what he wished. Yates calls Milton's *Il Penseroso* to our attention.

But let my lamp at midnight hour
Be seen in some high lonely tower,
Where I may oft outwatch the Bear,
With thrice great Hermes, or unsphere
The spirit of Plato, to unfold
What worlds or what vast regions hold
The immortal mind that hath forsook
Her mansion in this fleshly nook;
And of those dæmons that are found
In fire, air, flood or under ground,
Whose power have a true consent
With planet, or with element.

These lines, as Yates says, brilliantly suggest the state of the hermetic adept who separates his mind from his body and journeys upward, consorting with the dæmons, those personifications of the energies, on a dangerous route towards union with god-as-mind. It was this power that Constant promised, a magical power based on his science of magic.

Now, the magic of the kind that Agrippa and Constant promise could be very easily mistaken as consorting with devils. So this is where we must go next, to see the devil ride out. Watch your step!

Chapter ten: The Devil Rides Out

We first revisit the idea of a mytheme, a building block of myth. There is nothing mysterious about mythemes and I seek to demonstrate this by looking at research into the way that our minds work. I go on to refer to the standard list of crimes (including devil worship) which 'other people' are accused of and point out that Jesus was himself accused of being a devil worshipper. Since consorting with the devil would seem to be an almost universal pastime, I think it is very important to get clear what it is that people are accused of. We will find that devil worship is another mytheme.

We then look at the strange idea of worshipping the devil, a phrase which seems to be a contradiction in terms, partly due to the meaning of the word 'worship' and partly due to the word 'devil'. The idea of a devil turns out to be very odd. After all since the devil can never do anything right, not even repent, we should investigate whether 'the devil is evil' is a tautology; something not a matter of fact but a matter of meaning. I then take us into the idea of causation and compare the word 'devil' with the word 'luck'. Both words seem to explain the occurrence of events but neither really do. In this context, I look at statements such as, 'If we obey god, the volcano will not erupt.'

Looking at evil and what turns out to be the banality of its occurrence, we may conclude that the concept of a devil neither has utility nor sense but, in all this, we must recognise that theology and philosophy on the one hand and popular belief on the other, so rarely connect. I show some survey data on religious beliefs.

In the interlude I go into more detail about the sprachspiel of religion and look at the notion of worship, the metaphor of seeing as and the nature of truth.

Mythemes and schema

Earlier I spoke of horns representing male virility as being an example of what Lévi-Strauss calls a *mytheme*, a building block of myths. When horns are introduced into a tale, male virility is also introduced. If you remember, I speculated on the changed appearance of satyrs: that they took on the aspect of the faun and its horns to be the more satisfactorily seen as sexy beasts. There is nothing mysterious about the process of mythemes. One can see them as social forms of *schema* - part of the way our minds work. Let me explain.

We see and do many things during the day, only a few of which are new to us. Most of the time we operate on what one might call automatic pilot. From tying a shoelace to walking into work, we are operating in an unconscious mode. We don't have to think about how to do these things; we just do them. Even driving the car becomes automatic. How many times have you driven from A to B with no recollection of doing it?

In general, we do not consciously analyse and decide how to react to events, people or sounds, etc. which we have experienced before. There are so many that we would not have the time. So our mind stores experiences away in a filing system together with a package of reactions - words, opinions, actions and emotions - to go with them. Normally lying dormant, the relevant package is triggered by the appropriate stimulus. This explains stereotypes.[1] We are normally unconscious of the existence of these packages, which psychologists call *schema*, but much of what we think, do, say and feel is caused by them. They can be triggered by the most subtle cues in our surroundings. I recommend the book, *A Mind of its own*, by Dr Cordelia Fine.

> *The truth of the matter ... is that your unscrupulous brain is entirely undeserving of your confidence. It has some shifty habits that leave the truth distorted and disguised. Your brain is vainglorious. It deludes you. It is emotional, pigheaded and secretive. Oh, and it is also a bigot.*

Mythemes are rather like social schema; ones that a group of people unconsciously share so that for a given stimulus, every member of that group has the same understanding and reaction. Again there is nothing complicated about socially shared responses; just think of catch phrases. When Eric Morecambe asked the audience, *What do you think of it so far?* everyone gleefully responded, *Rubbish!* When Brucie on *Strictly Come Dancing*, exclaims *Nice to see you*, the audience responds as one, *To see you, nice.*

Horns as male virility is a mytheme and the devil as goat is also a mytheme. A web search for images of the devil will display a host of horned figures. The associations triggered by the phrase *devil worship* form yet another.

What is devil worship?

Worshipping the devil is one item on the standard list of crimes of which other people - *people who hold views contrary to our own* - are accused.

---

[1] Sometimes what is triggered can be very surprising, for example, a sexist or racist remark made by someone who would never consciously be sexist or racist.

The standard list includes witchcraft, rape, incest and other forms of non-marital sex, secrecy, fomenting rebellion and child murder with a few optional extras such as cannibalism, cutting off the hands of teenage boys, bayoneting babies, giving children hand grenades to play with and causing floods, pestilence and famine. Such crimes have been laid at the door of Christians, Jews, Catholics, Protestants, Muslims and Atheists as well as Vikings, American Indians, soldiers of all nations, and supporters of opposing football teams, with exactly the same amount of evidence in each case.

Even Jesus was accused of being a devil worshipper. Celsus, the Greek philosopher, claimed that miracles were produced by demons and that the Jesus of the gospels was a sorcerer, consorting with the devil.[1] Celsus made his accusations just a little before Clement of Alexander became the first Christian apologist to claim that the gods of other religions were demons. All of which goes to support the *Catholic Encyclopædia's* opinion that a source of accusations of devil worship lies in,

> ... *racial rivalry and hatred sometimes (leading) one nation to regard the protecting divinities of its enemies as evil demons. In this way many who merely worshipped gods whom they themselves regarded as good beings would be called devil worshippers by men of other nations.*

Since consorting with the devil would seem to be an almost universal pastime, we ought to get clear what it consists of. What was it that Jesus and so many others were accused of doing? Well, what usually comes to mind is the stuff that Dennis Wheatley used to write about.

> *Mocata raised the Talisman and set it on the forehead of the Beast, laying it lengthwise upon the flat, bald bony skull where it blazed like some magnificent jewel ... Then he stooped, seized the child and, tearing off her clothes, flung her naked body full-length upon the altar beneath the raised fore-hooves of the Goat. Sick with apprehension and frantic with distress, the prisoners in the circle heard the sorcerer begin to intone the terrible lines of the Black Mass.*
>
> *Horrified but powerless they watched the swinging of the censer, the chanting of the blasphemous prayers and the blessing of the dagger by the Goat, knowing that at the conclusion of the awful ceremony, the perverted maniac playing the part the devil's priest would rip the child open from throat to groin while offering her soul to hell. Half crazy with fear, they saw Mocata pick up the knife and raise his arm above the little body ...*[2]

His explanation of this is based upon *Hebrews* 9:22:

> *And according to the law almost all things are purified with blood, and without shedding of blood there is no remission.*

Wheatley writes:

> *The blood is the life. When it is shed, energy - animal or human as the case may be - is released into the atmosphere. It if is shed within a specially prepared circle, that energy can be caught and stored or redirected in precisely the same way as*

---

[1] Celsus wrote in about 175 CE.

[2] *The Devil Rides Out.*

electric energy is caught and utilised by our modern scientists.

To be technical, what happens in a Black Mass, Wheatley's *Duke De Richleau* tells us,

> *... depends on the form of evil they wish to bring upon the world. If it is war they will seek to propitiate Mars with a virgin ram; if they desire the spread of unbridled lust - a goat, and so on.*

Note that the goat/sex mytheme is working well. Of course, Wheatley is writing a novel but, even so, this somewhat pornographic make believe is not a million miles away from Constant's *science which confers on man powers apparently superhuman.* Mocata's or Wheatley's *Energy* and Constant's *Astral Light* have similarities (and not only that both are imaginary.) It is through them that the adept makes things happen in the world. Gaining control of them is the study of the Magus.

Nevertheless, there is a difference, and an important one between Constant's *Astral Light* and Mocata's *energy*. The former does not depend upon the participation of evil supernatural powers, although we know them to be a danger in all forms of high magic. You will remember that Frances Yates castigates Agrippa for not being careful enough to avoid such beings. In Mocata's case it is by the very involvement of such evil powers that he seeks to gain his ends. In the *Devil Rides Out*, Mocata's motivation seems to centre on control.[1] He seeks to summon evil powers as the Egyptians sought to entice gods into their statues and as the practitioners of the *Technical Hermetica* sought to control such powers by various incantations.

This is a high risk strategy. If things go wrong, the results would seem to be terminal. In Mocata's case, things do go wrong because he has reckoned without the mother's recollection of the *Red Book of Appin* (well, you would, wouldn't you?) and the words on the *stained vellum*:

> *They only who love without desire shall have the power granted to them in the darkest hour.*

and so,

> *... with no knowledge of its meaning and a certainty she had never seen it written or heard it pronounced before, she spoke a strange word having five syllables ...*

and everything goes haywire. The crypt spins around; the altar candles sway and dance and then:

> *Mocata staggered back. The Goat reared up on its hind legs above him. A terrible neighing sound came from his nostrils and the slanting eyes swivelled in their sockets; their baleful light flashing around the chamber. The Beast seemed to grow and expand until it was towering above them all as they crouched, petrified with fear. The stench of its fœtid breath poured from between the bared teeth until they were retching with nausea. Mocata's knife clattered upon the stones as he raised his arms in frantic terror to defend himself. The awful thing which he had called up out of the Pit gave a final screaming neigh and struck out with one of its great fore-hooves. He was thrown with frightful force to the floor where he lay sprawled head downmost on the chapel steps.*

---

[1] And sex; if you look on the web for images of the black mass and devil worship, a very high percentage of the results feature young ladies reclining naked on altars.

Cue thunderous crashes, satanic figures dissolving into thin air, veils of smoke, black candles snuffed out and *an utter silence beyond the human understanding* closing in *from the shadows that were all about them.* A Lord of Light announces that the adversary has been driven back to the halls of *Shaitan.*[1]

The accusation

People accused of devil worship - such as the New York Jets quarterback Tim Tebow, Procter & Gamble, Pokemon, people enjoying Hallowe'en, Nick Clegg, Lady Gaga, Jay-Z and a host of people in the music business - are very unlikely to have been involved in such night time revels. Nevertheless, a mytheme has been created. The accusation triggers the associations. When someone is accused of being a devil worshipper, up comes the mental image of them dressed in a rather sad outfit, leaping round fires with scantily clad members of the opposite sex while someone intones imprecations and spells.

One can be accused of devil worship for all sorts of reasons. At jesus-is-savior.com, we find that all members of all religions are worshipping Satan, without knowing it:

> *Over one billion foolish people around the world have bowed their knee to Satan unknowingly by bowing to a statue of Mary or the Pope. The second of the Ten Commandments strictly forbids us from bowing to the likeness of ANYTHING.*

In case you think this is just a case of the crazies, Peter Stanford writes:

> *When the Reformation shattered the hope of one holy apostolic Europe under the papacy, both sides were quick to see the devil's hand manipulating their rivals. Luther had only to think of Rome to see a hellish city full of demons parading around in the scarlet robes of cardinals, while one of the most popular depictions of the Protestant reformer among Catholics had him listening attentively as the devil whispered in his ear.*

Indeed, the most common activity of the devil was always the creation of heresies, the greatest evil being to seduce a believer away from the true faith and thus endanger his or her immortal soul. The devil's work was seen as anything contrary to the teachings of the church or anything which it thinks will damage belief in the true faith. Holding such beliefs would be evidence of devil worship even if the believer thought he or she was on the side of the angels. Thus people can very easily end up worshipping the devil by mistake.

Even what you buy can damn you. According to jesus-is-savior.com, there are several companies to be wary of: *Lucent*, which has software with the brand name *Inferno*; *Reebok*, which has a type of running shoe named *Incubus*; *Honeywell*, whose employees attend diversity training which praises the gay lifestyle; *Apple*, whose logo has a bite taken out of it; and *Procter & Gamble* which steadfastly refuses to,

> *... toss out its logo of an old man in the moon surrounded by 13 stars. Some people*

---

[1] The word *satan* means adversary, as we know, and Shaitan is the Islamic version of Satan. Of course, the risks depend not only upon the possibility of mistakes but upon the nature of the consorting. In the tales of Faust, there is no getting away from the fact that, at the end of the entertainment, Faust's soul belongs to the devil. The tale is based, of course, on *Matthew* 16:26-27: *For what profit is it to a man if he gains the whole world, and loses his own soul? Or what will a man give in exchange for his soul?*

suspect that the stars represent the occultic number 13, and the belief is that they were arranged to roughly appear as a 6, the number of the beast of Revelation 13.

Perhaps the website is indeed just an enormous joke as some have claimed but an example of the devil's work can also be seen, less amusingly, in the development of science. In 1530, Copernicus wrote that the sun, and not the earth, was the centre of the universe, contrary to church teaching.[1] Eighty years later, Galileo invented a telescope with which he sort-of-proved[2] the theory of Copernicus, the result of which was that he was placed under house arrest for the rest of his life. If the earth revolved around the sun, how could heaven be above and hell below, as the church taught? Thus Galileo, and those who accepted his views, were leading people astray from the true faith and must be inspired by the devil. In something of a dualist vein, Paul himself spoke of Satan as the god of this world[3] and those unfortunates,

> *... that are lost: in whom the god of this world hath blinded the minds of them which believe not, lest the light of the glorious gospel of Christ, who is the image of god, should shine unto them.*

Though this seems a lot less exciting than stories of the black mass, its consequences were unpleasant for Galileo.

Worship and meaning

You may remember that even after the publication in 1542 of Pedro Mexia's book, *Silra di Varia Leccion,* which brought the image of the devil-as-goat back into use, it was not the only image and in many ways has seemed to be the least powerful. It has had currency mainly in the limited world of the occult and I have argued that the foundations of the image, in the forms of Banebdjedet and Pan, are not strong enough to support a superstructure of evil; but then no image of the devil seems to fare much better. Indeed, the only one that works at all well is the devil as a human figure. So is there a problem with the very idea of the devil and of worshipping him? As the *Catholic Encyclopædia* says;

> *There is such a strange, startling incompatibility between the notion of devil and that of an object of worship.*

This incompatibility seems to be one of logic. Words have rules for their use, necessary if we are to use them for communication. If you say to me, *Pass the hammer,* and I do but you then say, *That is not what I want,* we have a communication problem. What you mean by *hammer* is not what I mean by it. The rules you are using are not mine and this makes communication impossible. (There are ways around it. Occasionally, my wife or I have a right/left problem and the other will exclaim, *Oh, you mean the other right!* - meaning left, of course.)

---

[1] Interestingly, from a masonic point of view, Copernicus's heliocentric theory was attacked because it seemed to contradict Joshua 10:12-13, about the sun being made to stand still.

[2] Copernicus showed that the sun was the centre of our solar system but that, of course, is far from being the universe.

[3] A title which would not be out of place in the heresy of Catharism in which the devil is indeed taken to be the creator of this world.

The word *worship* is not a word whose meaning is easy to grasp. Perhaps it cannot be satisfactorily translated into other words; any more, for example, than the word *love* but it seems to connect with such concepts as:

> *showing respect*
> *giving service*
> *bowing down*
> *expressing love*
> *being devoted*
> *holding in reverence*
> *praising*
> *having high regard for*

and so on. These words are part of the language of the religious life but also of the moral life and expectations arise from their use. For example:

> *If you say you are proud of someone, I would expect that someone to be related to you in some way and to have achieved something meritorious.*
>
> *If you say that you feel disgusted with yourself, I would expect that you have done something (morally) wrong.*
>
> *If you say that you respect someone, I would assume that person to be a role model.*
>
> *If you hold someone in high regard, I would expect that person to stand out because of his or her meritorious conduct.*

These expectations are part of the rules for using the words and the rules seem to preclude them being used of the devil - but perhaps that depends on the devil.

If the devil is just god's executioner, as he appears in Job, one might describe what he does as *dreadful but someone's got do it*. One might even feel sorry for him: that alone among all the angels he gets all the dirty jobs. We might hold him in regard for that very reason. It might be going a bit far to express love for the devil because he does god's dirty work but there is no reason to think that doing all the dirty work precludes someone from being loved. We could certainly respect him for his loyalty and willingness to do whatever job he was assigned. We can understand the psychology of a devil of this kind and we can understand how moral words can be applied to him.

On the other hand, if the devil is an independent being, the case is different. We are faced with a being who chooses only to do evil things. While the concept of an independent being devoted completely to evil is somewhat difficult to grasp, having respect or high regard for such a being makes no sense at all. The notion of worshipping this devil translates as evaluating as morally praiseworthy, someone who is always morally bad. This is a misuse of language; a nonsense.

So of course the incompatibility that the *Catholic Encyclopædia* refers to is startling. It is a contradiction in terms; not a psychological difficulty but a logical one. You can use the words but they have no meaning.

> *When I say that the orders 'Bring me sugar' and 'Bring me milk' make sense, but not the combination 'milk me sugar', that does not mean that the utterance of this*

> *combination of words has no effect. And if its effect is that the other person stares at me and gapes, I don't on that account call it the order to stare and gape, even if that was precisely the effect I wanted to produce.*[1]

An accusation of devil worship can cause an effect, just as *milk me sugar* can. It doesn't thereby become meaningful. Even if the words *worship* and *devil* have meaning, the phrase *worshipping the devil*, it seems, does not.

Does the *devil* make sense?

Perhaps at least part of the problem is the word *devil*. What exactly are the rules for the use of this word? Could the rules allow the following sentences?

> *The devil is a loving person at heart.*
> *The devil does his best.*
> *The devil doesn't do bad things all the time.*
> *I expect the devil will apologise at the end.*

It seems not. The rules for the use of the word *devil* appear to forbid him being described other than as evil. If this is so, then to say that the devil is bad is not really a description. The devil is defined as evil. He is not allowed any redeeming features because if he had them, he would not be the devil. Whatever he does is evil, not because he might do something good but doesn't, but because if a good act did occur, it could not have been done by him.

There is an argument in the Christian religion about whether the devil will be redeemed at the end of things. Origen wrote that the goodness of god will surely bring all creatures to one and the same end. This view is called *apokatastasis* or universal restoration and it is officially *in error* as the church says. According to the Catholic Encyclopædia, Origen should be censured for his suggestion. St Augustine also attacked Origen and,

> *... those tender-hearted Christians who decline to believe that any ... whom the infallibly just judge may pronounce worthy of the punishment of hell, shall suffer eternally, and who suppose that they shall be delivered after a fixed term of punishment, longer or shorter according to the amount of each man's sin.*[2]

Neither, in his view, can those doomed to eternal punishment have any remission for good conduct. So it would appear that the devil can never do anything right, not even repent and one cannot help coming to the conclusion that this is a matter of logical necessity, not of fact. The equation $2+2=4$ is a logical necessity, a tautology: $2+2$ does not $= 5$ and never can do. There is nothing that can happen in the world which would mean that $2+2 =$ anything but 4. The proposition, *The devil is evil*, is another tautology. There is nothing that can happen in the world which would mean that the devil is or can become good.

The startling thought then occurs that perhaps the statement *God is good* is a tautology as well. Certainly St Augustine says that god can never do anything

---

[1] Wittgenstein, *Philosophical Investigations* 498.

[2] *City of God* 17.

which is not good and the Cathar argument we followed earlier would seem to support this.

> *... because there exists in god no potency for evil by which he might bring evil things into existence ...*

Thanking, blaming and causing

Suppose at the end of a battle between two religious armies, one side thanks god for its deliverance while the other side blames the devil for helping the enemy escape. How do we account for that? Thanking god and blaming the devil here seem to add no more content than the words *Goody!* and *Blast!* At best they are emotional outbursts.

Honi the Circle Drawer appears in the Talmud as we have seen but he also appears in the *Antiquities* of Josephus, under the name of *Onias*. Josephus has a different account of Honi's death from the one we discussed earlier and it is relevant here. During a civil war in Judæa around 64 BCE, Hyrcanus had fortified himself in the citadel of Jerusalem which was then besieged by the forces of his brother Aristobulus. Honi had recently distinguished himself by relieving a drought and Hyrcanus demanded that,

> *... as by his prayers he had once put an end to the drought, so he would in like manner make imprecations on Aristobulus and those of his faction.*

Honi, being compelled to speak, prayed that god would listen to neither side.

> *Whereupon such wicked Jews as stood about him, as soon as he had made this prayer, stoned him to death.*

Honi was a man of peace. It was just his bad luck, one might say, that his fame as a miracle worker placed him in this position; but consider the word *luck*. Its use also can be very odd.

> *I missed the jackpot by one number; just one figure. I had 22 and the last winning number was 26. I had all the rest! How unlucky was that!*

What about people who have all the right numbers? They never say:

> *I won the jackpot by one number; just one figure. I had 26 and the last winning number was 26. I had all the rest! How lucky was that!*

The fact that the explanation operates only one way should alert us to the dodginess of the concept. Some events turn out to benefit us; others benefit other people and not us. The word *luck* is unnecessary. It adds no semantic content. Belief in luck is as daft as Terry Pratchett's wonderful riff on probability:

> *Scientists have calculated that the chances of something so patently absurd actually existing are millions to one. But magicians have calculated that million-to-one chances crop up nine times out of ten.*[1]

So perhaps thanking god and blaming the devil do not add very much except another concept, that of a *cause*, and perhaps this *cause* adds no more to our

---

[1] *Mort.*

understanding than the word *luck*. Both may well be instances of primitive thinking; of *bricolage*. Remember:

> The people of ancient Egypt had little or no understanding of the science of the flooding Nile and, in an attempt to explain it, had recourse to the repertoire of thought at their disposal. If sometimes the flood was good and sometimes it was bad, someone was making it so.

Luck gives us an apparent explanation of why an event happened. The idea of supernatural intervention provides another. Some such explanations are obviously primitive:

> If we obey god, the volcano will not erupt.

We no longer see as meaningful, statements to the effect that obedience to a god's commands has an effect on natural events. That does not prevent them being made. (*Milk me sugar.*) The evangelist Pat Robertson suggested that Hurricane Katrina was god's punishment for abortion, while Pastor John Hagee said:

> All hurricanes are acts of god because god controls the heavens. I believe that New Orleans had a level of sin that was offensive to god and they were recipients of the judgment of god for that.

There is no evidence to support such statements although perhaps an experiment might be imagined to test Robertson's claim. Suppose somehow that all abortions could be prevented for a defined period of time, say two years. We could test the claim by examining whether the number of hurricanes decreased during those two years but returned to normal after. I know that sounds silly and it is - and so were Robertson's and Hagee's statements. As we said earlier, religious statements no longer make sense when they make reference to the world of things that exist. Crossing the *sprachspiel* barrier results in nonsense.

The banality of evil

The historian, Christopher R. Browning, carried out a study of *Reserve Police Battalion 101* which, during the holocaust, captured and shot one hundred thousand Jews.[1] The battalion was composed of ordinary middle-aged, lower-middle-class family men. They were not soldiers, let alone SS. Browning asks:

> If the men of the Reserve Police Battalion 101 could become killers under such circumstances, what group of men cannot?

His answer was that bureaucratisation through official policy reduces personal responsibility and that peer groups exert tremendous pressure on norms. Browning's question is rhetorical and Battalion 101 is far from a unique case. Philip Zimbardo is Professor Emeritus of Psychology at Stanford University. In 2004 he acted as an expert witness in the court martial of Sergeant Ivan Frederick who was accused, with others, of abuse and torture of prisoners and detainees in Abu Ghraib prison in Iraq. The sickening crimes of which Sergeant Frederick was accused, and subsequently found guilty, were made infamous by the publication in the international press of photographs showing prisoners being abused by several guards at Abu Ghraib.

---

[1] Reported by Luther Link.

Zimbardo speaks of the *banality* of evil. We may wish to believe that evil can be contained; that it is the result of a bad apple; that those who do wrong are in some way different from us and that we would never act in any such way ourselves. We'd like to believe that there is some unworldly and certainly non-human cause; that it is the work of the devil; but Zimbardo shows that evil is so often the result of the actions of very ordinary people.

> *I believe that deindividuation is involved. The anonymity of person and place ... can create an altered state of mind, which, when combined with diffused responsibility for one's actions, induces deindividuation ... It is the 'Mardi Gras effect' of living for the moment behind a mask that conceals one's identity and gives rise to libidinous, violent and selfish impulses that are ordinarily contained.*

His evidence was a powerful condemnation of interrogation techniques that were used at Abu Ghraib causing guards, he argued, to lose touch with sanity and reality. Like Browning in his study, Zimbardo argues that the rules of Abu Ghraib caused the behaviour and the rules came from the culture and the climate. Only a hero would have resisted them. Frederick was a normal human being, an experienced prison guard in civilian life but not a saint. He was not evil either.[1]

No need for a devil

The explanation of these horrible, but sadly not unique, events requires no devil. The same can be said to obtain for more day to day events. Do we need a devil to account for sexual abuse of children, PPI mis-selling, dishonest advertising, abuse of financial systems, altering exam results to make the school look good, cheating in prescription drugs research, lying about expenses, covering up sexual misconduct, cartel behaviour, PR statements, guaranteed bonus systems, political half-truths, selling horse meat as beef or failure being rewarded while the innocent are blamed?

Tragically, today none of these events are anything out of the ordinary. Rather than invent a devil to explain how they happen, we would do better to accept that the regulations we create (and enforce), the way people are managed, the norms that we allow society to accept and the presence or absence of genuine role models are all more likely explanations - and ones that we might be able to do something about. We may wish to believe that human beings would do evil things only if the devil made them do it but sadly the evidence is otherwise. The devil is merely an inadequate excuse. As Darren Oldridge writes:

> *The concept of Satan provides a potent psychological resource; it permits the comfort of believing in a benevolent and all-powerful creator while conceding that an evil power is at work in the suffering of the world.*

The concept of worshipping the devil makes no sense. The concept of a devil makes no sense. The idea that divine causes explain evil makes no sense. This use of language is like a cogwheel spinning freely, unconnected with reality.

---

[1] A fictional version of this tale is to be found in the film *A Few Good Men.*

The man and woman in the street

Such talk is only for philosophers and theologians. The average man or woman in the street has little patience for such speculations. After all, remember that:

> *Christ our saviour was born on Christmas Day to save us all from Satan's power when we were gone astray.*

Oldridge draws our attention to the 15th century poet, Francois Villon, and in particular the poem, *Ballade que Villon feit à la requeste de sa mère pour prier Nostre-Dame:*[1]

> *Femme je suis povrette et ancienne,*
> *Ne riens ne sçay; oncques lettre ne leuz;*
> *Au monstier voy dont suis parroissienne*
> *Paradis painct, où sont harpes et luz,*
> *Et ung enfer où damnez sont boulluz:*
> *L'ung me faict paour, l'autre joye et liesse.*
> *La joye avoir fais-moy, haulte Deesse,*
> *A qui pecheurs doivent tous recourir,*
> *Comblez de foy, sans faincte ne paresse.*
> *En ceste foy je vueil vivre et mourir.*

> *I am just a poor old woman. I know nothing; I cannot read or write. In my parish church there is a painting of paradise where there are harps and lutes, and one of hell where the damned are boiled. The one strikes fear into me; the other gives joy and bliss. Let me have joy, Our Lady, to whom all sinners must return; immerse me in joy without pretence. It is in that faith I would live and die.*[2]

Heaven and hell may provide fairness where none seems evident. The spirituals, sung by American slaves, bear witness to this. Many express the expectation of eternal comfort at the end of this life in which only the free and rich gain.

> *Steal away, steal away, steal away to Jesus!*
> *Steal away, steal away home, I ain't got long to stay here.*
>
> ....
>
> *Swing low, sweet chariot,*
> *Coming for to carry me home.*
> *Swing low, sweet chariot,*
> *Coming for to carry me home.*
> *I looked over Jordan, and what did I see,*
> *Coming for to carry me home?*
> *A band of angels coming after me,*
> *Coming for to carry me home.*

---

[1] *A ballad that Villon made at his mother's request, to pray to Our Lady.* The 15thC French is interestingly different from the modern form; in some ways closer to English.

[2] My translation. As Oldridge points out, the fear of hell did not hold Villon back from a criminal career. Arrested and imprisoned many times, he was banished from Paris in 1463 aged 33 and never heard of again.

Home is not here on earth but in the heaven that awaits:

> *Hurry on, my weary soul,*
> *And I heard from heaven today.*
> *Hurry on, my weary soul,*
> *And I heard from heaven today.*
> *My sin is forgiven and my soul set free,*
> *And I heard from heaven today.*
> *My sin is forgiven and my soul set free,*
> *And I heard from heaven today.*
> *My name is called and I must go.*
> *And I heard from heaven today.*
> *My name is called and I must go.*
> *And I heard from heaven today.*

Theological questions seem irrelevant in the face of such emotion. It is a really powerful example of how theology and popular belief are unable to connect. Nietzsche saw such emotions as the source of the idea of the afterlife:

> *It was suffering and incapacity that created all afterworlds - this and that brief madness of bliss which is experienced only by those who suffer most deeply.*

True but one would not want to take that solace away from sufferers. The phrase, *worshipping the devil,* has no meaning but the people who use it are not aware of this.

> *The trouble was that he was talking in philosophy, but they were listening in gibberish.*[1]

Anyway the devil is quite a story:

> *As he knelt his foot caught one of the cups of holy water set in the vales of the pentacle. It toppled over. The water spilled around waste upon the floor. Instantly a roar of savage triumph filled the room, coming from beneath their feet. The ab-human monster from the outer circle - that obscene sack-like Thing - appeared again. Its body vibrated with tremendous rapidity. It screamed at them with positively frantic glee.*

> *With incredible speed, the stallion was swung by its invisible rider at the gap in the protective barrier. The beast plunged, scattering the gutted candles and the dried mandrake, then reared above them, its great, dark belly on a level with their heads, its enormous hoofs poised in mid-air about to batter out their brains.*

> *For one awful second, it hovered there while Richard crouched gazing upward, his arms locked tight around the unconscious Mary Lou. De Richleau stood his ground above them both, the sweat pouring in great rivulets down his lean face.*

> *Almost, it seemed the end had come. Then the Duke used his final resources, and did a thing which shall never be done except in the direst emergency when the very soul is in peril of destruction. In a clear sharp voice he pronounced the last two lines of the dread Sussamma Ritual.*

---

[1] Terry Pratchett, *Small Gods.*

Beliefs to the effect that the devil and/or goat are worshipped in freemasonry are not the beliefs of sophisticated people. They are as much a nonsense as the beliefs of the Romans about the early Christians:

> *As for the initiation of new members, the details are as disgusting as they are well-known. A child, covered in dough to deceive the unwary, is set before a would-be novice who stabs the child to death with invisible blows. Deceived by the covering of dough, he thinks his stabs harmless. Then, horribly, they greedily drink the child's blood and compete with each other as they divide the limbs.[1]*

Belief may linger if only because:

> *La plus belle des ruses du diable est de vous persuader qu'il n'existe pas.[2]*

Does anyone believe in a devil?

Theology is not the arbiter of popular religion. As Jennifer Robinson wrote, introducing Gallup studies of religious belief:[3]

> *Science has been able to explain many phenomena that once seemed supernatural ... With the advent of evolutionary theory and modern psychology, these days we're more likely to think of people who do terrible things as broken human beings, rather than agents of the netherworld ... So we might expect belief in the devil to have ... evaporated. It hasn't. Regardless of political belief, religious inclination, education, or region, most Americans believe that the devil exists.*

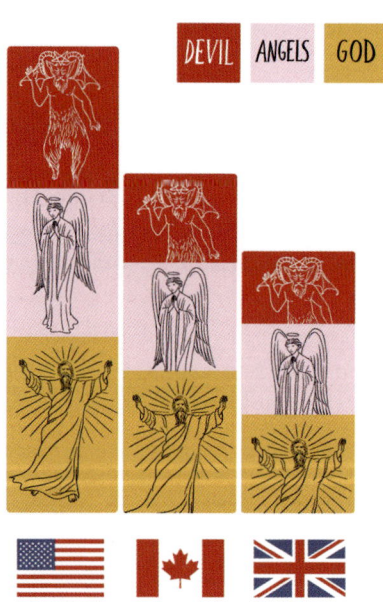

Beliefs in god and the devil differ by country. The USA is given much more to belief in supernatural beings country than the UK with Canada positioned between the two.

According to Gallup, in 1990 55% of Americans said they believed in a devil. By 2003 that had increased to 70%. Perhaps unsurprisingly, belief in the devil has been highest among protestant, republican voters in the southern states of the USA.

One does have to be careful with the data. A 2009 Barna Group survey, with a rather different research format, showed that only 35% of American Christians thought of Satan as a living being while

---

[1] Minicus Felix, a Christian apologist of about 150 CE, reporting what *they* say about *us*.

[2] Baudelaire, *Le Jouer Généreux*.

[3] Gallup.com, February 25, 2003

nearly 59% saw him more as a symbol of evil. Even so:

> About half of the Christians who believed that Satan is merely a symbol of evil nevertheless agreed that a person can be under the influence of spiritual forces such as demons.[1]

We have made much play of logic, philosophy and theology in this book, but people do not think deeply about their religion.[2] It is not difficult to recognise that statements about devil worship are not the result of mature and sophisticated judgement. A 2009 Harris Poll[3] showed that 76% of Americans believed in miracles; but it also showed that 42% believed in ghosts, 32% in UFOs, 26% in astrology and 23% believed in witches; this in a country with a 99% literacy rate.

Many are inconsistent in their beliefs. The Barna report again:

> Although a core teaching of the Christian faith is the divinity and perfection of Jesus Christ, tens of millions of Christians do not accept that teaching. More than one-fifth (22%) strongly agreed that Jesus Christ sinned when he lived on earth, with an additional 17% agreeing somewhat ... Six percent did not have an opinion on this matter.

As many as 70% of born-again Christians believe that Satan is a real being and it is generally among fundamentalists we find beliefs about freemasonry and the devil. The heresy of dualism that their belief represents does not appear to bother them - and they might well dismiss talk about the logical impossibility of a devil as the devil's own work.[4]

---

[1] barna.org, April 10, 2009

[2] In a 2006 survey by *Le Monde*, 51% of the population said they were Catholics. Only half of these said they believed in god and less than half ever attend church for more than the traditional *hatches, matches and dispatches*. Only 8% of French Catholics attend mass weekly.

[3] Harris Interactive Inc.

[4] 68% of born-again Christians accept creationism.

Interlude: The *Sprachspiel* of Religion

The word *worship* is related to words that are positive within the moral universe and it is impossible to apply these words to a devil, defined as evil. The word *worship* seems on the surface to be easy enough to understand but it turns out to be rather a tricky one which leads to further thoughts about religious language and *sprachspiele*. To illustrate this, let us take a look at three of the main theories on reasons for worshipping a god.

Worship as thanks

The most commonly given reason is *gratitude*: that we should be grateful to god for creation. This seems a little odd. The concept of gratitude implies that a benefactor has done something in a spirit of kindness, with the implication that s/he could have chosen not to do it and to have done something else.

Could s/he have done anything else? We are expected to be grateful for a god who created everything there is. *Creating everything* seems to count out - or perhaps count in - any other possible action. There are no alternative actions he could have taken. Augustine, who can sound extraordinarily like a modern linguistic philosopher, argues that the question of what god did before the creation of the world is a nonsense question anyway. Since god created everything, what he created included time. As Augustine expresses it:

> For there was no 'then' when time was not ... At no time, therefore, had thou not made anything, because you had made time itself.[1]

One might argue that god might have done nothing. But could he? And if so when? Following Augustine's argument, there was no *when* before creation and thus no time when god might have been doing nothing at all.[2]

Constant says that god is always creating; that it is his nature to create. In *La Clef des Grands Mystères* he writes:

> God creates himself eternally, and the infinite which he fills with his works is an incessant and infinite creation.[3]

Constant is not alone in this belief. We saw earlier that this view is originally from Philo (20BCE - 50CE.) If god is just being him or herself in creating the world, the concept of gratitude does not arise. It is a bit like being grateful to the sun for coming up each morning. Paul Tillich,[4] one of the greatest of modern theologians, viewed god not as a being but as being itself, the ground or possibility of anything existing at all. Again, the idea of gratitude for creation makes little logical sense.

---

[1] Confessions Book 11.

[2] Any in any case, there seems little point in being god if you do nothing at all.

[3] This translation is by Aleister Crowley who was very rude about AE Waite's skills as a translator: *He not only mutilates and distorts his authors, but ... he is totally incapable of understanding their simplest phrases and even their commonest words.*

[4] 1886-1965

Worship as obedience

Another common view is that worship is necessary because god commands it. Pope Leo XIII, an unwitting participant in Léo Taxil's follies, wrote:

> *But assuredly of all the duties which man has to fulfil, that without doubt is the chiefest and holiest which commands him to worship god with devotion and piety.*[1]

The command theory of worship certainly makes sense in early polytheistic Judaism when Yahweh is demanding exclusive terms. The demand for worship was backed up by a threat. The destruction of Jerusalem by Nebuchadnezzar was the implementation of the threat:

> *Thus saith ... the god of Israel; Behold, I will turn back the weapons of war ... wherewith ye fight against the king of Babylon and ... I myself will fight against you with an outstretched hand and with a strong arm, even in anger, and in fury, and in great wrath ... And I will smite the inhabitants of this city, both man and beast: they shall die of a great pestilence ... I will deliver ... such as are left ... into the hand of Nebuchadnezzar ... and he shall smite them with the edge of the sword; he shall not spare them, neither have pity, nor have mercy.*[2]

The explanation is less happy in monotheism. For example, the careless thinking of the leader of the unusual *Church of the Great God*,[3] John W. Ritenbaugh, leads us directly into dualism:

> *He must command us to worship him because it is possible to worship others and things besides god. Satan was clearly attempting to get Christ to worship him - a being besides god - and Jesus replies, referring to the father, 'Him only you shall serve.' Not only does he command us to worship him, he also forbids us to worship any others.*

In such a spirit, we encountered in the *Zohar* what we might call Moses de Leon's *supporter theory*; that prayer, ritual acts, and even the rejection of sinful thoughts, give strength to the divine in its battle against the evil powers. In god's war with the devil, prayer has value similar to cheering at a football game to encourage your team. (Of course, worshipping the devil is tantamount to cheering for the opposition and, if doing this, it pays to choose carefully in which grandstand to sit.)

It may be useful to remind ourselves that dualism is held to be the worst of all heresies because it sets a limit on god's powers.[4] It implies that god is either not omnipotent or not omniscient and the notion of worship often seems to imply polytheism. Take the puzzling question of why a god wants or needs worship. Polytheistically, it makes some sort of sense. If each god is competing with other

---

[1] Encyclical *Libertas Praestantissimum* (On human liberty), 1888.

[2] King James Version, *Jeremiah* 21 4-7 exerpted.

[3] Related, it turns out, to Garner Ted Armstrong who gave us great joy in student days with his fulminations against science. I can still hear him proclaiming, *Science proves that a bumble bee can't fly.*

[4] It is disconcerting that Benedict XVI, *pontiff emeritus*, several times referred to the existence of the devil.

gods, worship could be seen as a way of gaining power or keeping score. As Terry Pratchett writes, *It's a god-eat-god world.*[1]

Worship for reward

Let us try another track. Perhaps worship is explained by the reward that it brings, the reward of heaven. That is not true of the Greek or Roman polytheistic gods who had little impact upon what happened to humans after death. Then again, the sacrifices made to them were not exactly what one might think of as worship but, as we have seen, more a form of insurance or protection: to placate or make a deal with a god concerning matters in this life.

However, if the reward for worship of a monotheistic god is eternal life, then one might think it very odd to believe in such a god but not worship him. Belief seems to imply worship - but does it? We have seen that the word *worship* is connected with such words as *respect, love, devotion, reverence, praise* and *regard* - but what if the monotheistic god was unworthy of *respect, love, devotion, reverence, praise* or *regard*? I suppose one might still obey his commands but draw the line at worship. For example, Richard Dawkins describes the Old Testament Yahweh as:

> ... arguably the most unpleasant character in all fiction: jealous and proud of it; a petty, unjust, unforgiving control-freak; a vindictive, bloodthirsty ethnic cleanser; a misogynistic, homophobic, racist, infanticidal, genocidal, filicidal, pestilential, megalomaniacal, sadomasochistic, capriciously malevolent bully.

One might (just about) justify obedience to such a god on the grounds that although the actions commanded were vile, obedience would benefit one's children and one's children's children. Remember that Yahweh was not promising eternal life; the deal was that if the Israelites obeyed his commands, he would look after Israel but, even if one might (or might not) obey, it doesn't sound a meaningful basis for worship. Obedience to certain dietary regulations or specific religious observances is one thing but worship - *respect, love, devotion, reverence, praise* and *regard* - is another. To worship as opposed to obey a god seems primarily to require that such a god is good.

Of course, the New Testament god is different, if only because very little is known about him. Dawkins has said that,

> ... from a moral point of view, Jesus is a huge improvement over the cruel ogre of the Old Testament. Indeed Jesus, if he existed (or whoever wrote his script if he didn't) was surely one of the great ethical innovators of history. The Sermon on the Mount is way ahead of its time.

Nevertheless, while it is fine to say that loving god and loving your neighbour as yourself is all you need to know, what loving god or indeed loving one's neighbour consists of, is not defined. This would not matter if the wages of sin were not death. Since they are, what god counts as sin seems to be of enormous importance. For example, there is powerful disagreement among Christians about whether the ten

---

[1] *Small Gods.* The god, *Om*, in the shape of a tortoise, discovers that he has only one believer left, which explains why he is but a tortoise. The more believers, the more power a god has and the more impressive his shape. A tortoise is not the most powerful of animals, although as Om repeatedly and worryingly discovers, people think *there is good eating on one of them.*

commandments still apply and indeed whether the Mosaic law is still current, despite St Paul's rejection of it all those years ago.

Of course, whatever they might be, the New Testament rules are still open to ethical debate: what god orders, we may find immoral. While the nature of god may have changed, the debate has not. You can only worship a god you think of as morally good. You can obey any god, especially if that gets you into heaven.

Sprachspiele

None of these attempts to give a reason for worship seem to help and all seem to miss the point. In so far as they have any meaning at all, they reduce the act of worship to an empty formula, an action performed to get something out of it. It seems as difficult to give a reason for worship as it does to argue that a god exists. In both cases, the difficulty arises because they are attempts to explain something from one language game, one *sprachspiel*, in the terms of another. Wittgenstein wrote:

> For a large class of cases - though not for all - in which we employ the word 'meaning' it can be defined thus: the meaning of a word is its use in the language.[1]

and

> To imagine a language is to imagine a form of life.[2]

This comment is quoted by PF Strawson who says that it may serve,

> ... to remind us of a general prescription for doing philosophy: to understand a concept, a word, put the word in its linguistic context and the whole utterance in its social context and then describe, without preconceptions, what you find: remembering that each word, each utterance, may figure in many contexts.

Worship is a word that belongs within the form of life of religious belief. It has no meaning outside of that form of life. Within it, perhaps, worship is simply what one does with, to or for god. (If this is so, then the concept of worshipping the devil makes even less sense.)

The Cambridge philosopher, John Wisdom, in his famous article *Gods*, gives the example of two people returning to a long neglected garden in which they find some of the garden plants surprisingly healthy among the weeds.

> One says to the other, 'It must be that a gardener has been coming and doing something about these plants.' Upon enquiry they find that no neighbour has ever seen anyone at work in their garden. The first man says to the other, 'He must have worked while people slept.' The other says, 'No, someone would have heard him and besides, anybody who cared about plants would have kept down those weeds.' The first man says, 'Look at the way these are arranged. There is a purpose and a feeling for beauty here. I believe that the more carefully we look the more we shall find confirmation of this.'

> They examine the garden ever so carefully and sometimes they come on new things suggesting that a gardener comes and sometimes they come on new things

---

[1] *Philosophical Investigations*, 43.

[2] *Op. cit.*, 19

suggesting the contrary and even that a malicious person has been at work. Besides examining the garden carefully they also study what happens to gardens left without attention. Each learns all the other learns about this and about the garden. Consequently, when after all this, one says, 'I still believe a gardener comes,' while the other says, 'I don't,' their different words now reflect no difference as to what they have found in the garden, no difference to what they would find in the garden if they looked further and no difference about how fast untended gardens fall into disorder.

Wisdom makes the point that neither expects anything to happen to the garden which the other does not. The story works on many levels. One person may be seeing beauty remaining in the middle of decay while the other sees just the remnants of design overtaken by randomness. One may delight in what he sees while the other may be disappointed but the discussion at this point is no longer about empirical facts but about how the facts are interpreted.

Seeing as

Of course, the story is really a parable. In reality, few people would continue to argue the existence of a gardener when no independent evidence of his presence could ever be found. The parable is about creation and about *seeing as*.

In double aspect pictures, we can see one of two images but not both at the same time. In this example, we can see the picture *as* a candlestick or *as* two female faces looking towards each other.

Someone may have a difficulty in seeing the picture one way. We explain it by showing it.

Look, here is her nose, here her lips and this is her chin.

Ah! Now I've got it!

Wittgenstein gives the example of someone faced with a formula, perhaps $x^2+1=y$. Understanding the formula is knowing how to continue it.

> *We can also imagine the case that nothing at all occurred in B's mind except that he suddenly said, 'Now I know how to go on.'*

If $x = 2$, then $y = 5$; if $x = 3$, then $y = 10$, if $x = 4$, then $y = ?$

Wisdom's parable shows that no discussion of facts can resolve a difference between two people who work with different *sprachspiele*. Whether there is a gardener is not a matter of argument but of how we see the garden. In a like manner, we might see the difference between deism and atheism as a matter of *seeing as*. One person sees the world as god-created; the other as a random event. We could see the gaining or losing of faith as a case of changing language games, of seeing things differently. *Now I've got it! Now I know how to go on.*

A difficulty with religious discussion arises when we try to reduce the religious *sprachspiel* to the rules of what one might call a scientific one - and we find we cannot. This is why the attempt to give a reason for worship fails. Religious statements make sense only within religion. Messages posted outside churches are good examples of this and many are rather witty. They make assumptions that stem from the religious *form of life*.

> *The fear of the lord is the beginning of knowledge.*
> *Would you believe god if he showed himself? He did!*
> *God seems so far away? Guess who moved!*
> *Let us help you study for your final exams.*
> *God answers knee mail.*

Many an atheist would understand these statements but only because s/he was brought up in a society in which religious language was often used. While that provides a context, there is no way that a statement such as, *Would you believe god if he showed himself? He did!* can be debated by an atheist and a believer. The claim that Jesus was/is god is not one like the claim that John Cairncross was the fifth man. [1]

Coherence and correspondence

Philosophers sometimes talk of the difference between a *coherence* and a *correspondence* theory of truth. The coherence theory holds that a statement can be said to be true if it coheres with, or is consistent with, other statements. Think of the pathologist on the TV who speaks of a mark on the body being *consistent* with a blow from a blunt instrument. The correspondence theory holds that a statement can only be true if it can be checked against, or corresponds with, a fact in the world. For example, when the pathologist demonstrates that the mark was caused by that specific blunt instrument which the detective has found.

A religious belief, it might be held, does not have to correspond to facts in the world. That would be to measure one *sprachspiel* using the terms of another. It has only to be internally coherent, hence the discussion over whether the idea of a devil coheres with, or is consistent with, the idea of an all-powerful and all-knowing god. Of course, without any reference to any external decision criteria, a claim that one religion is more true, does not make sense. There is nothing against which to measure the word *more*. In arguments over which religion is better, the most that any religion can claim is that it is more internally coherent.

For as long as a religion makes no claims about the world external to its *sprachspiel*, criticism is limited to any internal incoherence, but many religions do make claims about the world outside: creation, miracles, faith cures and so on. As we have seen, the 17th century church refused to accept the discoveries of Copernicus and Galileo because they did not cohere with its established beliefs of heaven and hell. [2] Galileo's statements could be and were proven by observation. The earth does circle the sun and eventually the church accepted this, retreating from its views on

---

[1] Alongside the spies Kim Philby, Donald Mclean, Guy Burgess and Anthony Blunt.

[2] Today, the church would of course accept scientific discoveries about the universe although Benedict XVI, as Cardinal Ratzinger, is said to have argued that the Church had acted reasonably given the knowledge of the time.

the geography of heaven and hell and each time the church retreats from statements about the world, its set of beliefs become smaller and less about day to day life.

Just as the people of Q retreated from an expectation of an immediate implementation of god's kingdom on earth and in Q[3] came to view it as an event which they would experience only after death, so the creation stories of all religions, the gnostics included, are now seen to be poetic myths.

List of things that exist

> *For every expression of a common language, there must exist, in the common practice of the use of the expression, criteria for determining whether a given use of it is correct or not.*[1]

Historically the problem that theologians have faced is that there is what we might call the *sprachspiel* of listing the things that exist. Some of these things are easy to list: tables, chairs, dentists, velodromes and fashion parades. Some things are less easy to list. It is not always easy to tell if they are really there or not: the yeti, the Loch Ness monster and the sasquatch. While there is no evidence for these creatures, many people are willing to go on looking for them.

We accept that unicorns do not exist. We have never found one nor is anyone willing to keep looking because we know the unicorn to be an invention of medieval romance; a beast that can only be commanded by a virgin. Others have been in debate, notably the Higgs boson, which at the time of writing seems to have been discovered but until now has been a theoretical construct. Some, such as dark matter, will never be seen. As the Guardian reported:[2]

> *The label 'dark' refers to the fact that the substance neither emits nor reflects light. The only way dark matter has revealed itself so far is through the pull it exerts on galaxies. Studies of spinning galaxies show they rotate with such speed that they would tear themselves apart were there not some invisible form of matter holding them together through gravity.*

The point is that all the contents of our list exist in a way that can be described and can be tested for. This is the rule of the list and the way the language game is played. It is not always easy.

> *This is one of the frontiers of knowledge. Either dark matter is about 80% of the matter in the universe and we don't know what it is, or our theory of gravity is wrong. One way or another, we want to know.*

Thus, experiments are being designed using the Large Hadron Collider at Cern in Switzerland. The LHC might be able to make dark matter particles which:

> *While they would zip through the collider's detectors unseen ... would carry energy and momentum with them. Scientists could then infer their creation by totting up the energy and momentum of all the particles produced in a collision, and looking for signs of the missing energy and momentum.*

---

[1] Strawson.

[2] 1 January 2013.

God does not get into the list. We have never been able to find a way of deciding whether there is a thing or a being referred to by the word nor do we have any expectation that we will. We cannot design an experiment to test for god, even by inference. The LHC is no help here.

Of course, a belief in god does not work this way, anymore than does a belief in Wisdom's gardener. The statement that there is such a gardener or a god does not obey the rules for the language game of listing things. Statements can fool us. Some look like statements within the same language game but on closer inspection, we find that they are not. Wittgenstein again:

> *What am I believing in when I believe that men have souls? What am I believing in, when I believe that this substance contains two carbon[1] rings? In both cases there is a picture in the foreground, but the sense lies far in the background; that is, the application of the picture is not easy to survey.*

Existence and theology

Julian Huxley said:

> *The god hypothesis is no longer of any pragmatic value for the interpretation or comprehension of nature, and indeed often stands in the way of better and truer interpretation.[2]*

This is atheism; that the idea of god is unnecessary and dysfunctional. Nietzsche famously hailed the *death of god*. He saw this as the single most significant event in the history of human development, one which left man seeking his own sense of meaning in life rather than depending on an external agent to tell him what to be. Nietzsche saw religion as denigrating human life by restricting it to the creation of a passport to the next. Charles Taliaferro writes:

> *Some philosophers have charged that the very idea that god should command or desire praise reflects a crude anthropomorphism.*

This is not atheism as such but a comment on primitive or unsophisticated understanding of the idea of god. Much of modern theology accepts that *god exists* no longer means that there is a thing or a being called god. Tillich viewed the idea of a god who kept tinkering with the universe as absurd and a god who interfered with human freedom and creativity as a tyrant.

> *An omnipotent, all-knowing tyrant is not so different from earthly dictators who made everything and everybody mere cogs in the machine which they controlled. An atheism that rejects such a god is amply justified.[3]*

Writing in 1963, the then Bishop of Woolwich, John Robinson, was not convinced that there is a god-shaped hole in everyone's minds. After all, man had learned to cope with many questions of importance without recourse to god. The Bishop

---

[1] *Hydrocarbons are a class of chemicals that contain only hydrogen and carbon atoms. Some have hydrogen with rings of carbon atoms, called polycyclic aromatic hydrocarbons ... Typical substances include automotive gasoline, benzene, butadiene, fuel oils, jet fuels.* Agency for Toxic Substances and Disease Registry.

[2] In his 1957 book, *Religion Without Revelation*.

[3] Armstrong.

quoted Bonhoeffer who argues that *god is teaching us that we must live as men who can get along very well without him.* In place of the old man in the sky, he proposed that:

> *Belief in god is the trust, the well-nigh incredible trust, that to give ourselves to the uttermost love is not to be confounded but to be accepted, that Love is the ground of our being, to which we ultimately come home.*[1]

and that theological statements are not descriptions of a supreme being but an analysis of the depths of personal relationships. He wrote:

> *To assert that 'God is love' is to believe that in love one comes into touch with the fundamental reality in the universe, that being itself has this character.*[2]

He quoted Tillich meditating on Psalm 139, which begins:

> *You have searched me, lord, and you know me.*
> *You know when I sit and when I rise; you perceive my thoughts from afar.*

Tillich himself wrote:

> *Does anyone believe that his most secret thoughts and desires are not manifest in the whole of being, or that the events within the darkness of his subconscious or in the isolation of his consciousness do not produce eternal repercussions?*

Tillich was writing long before revelations about the behaviour of those in whom we had hitherto placed trust. One can, unfortunately, readily believe that market traders in derivatives can get along very well without their subconscious troubling them and that their banking masters would happily acquiesce without worrying about any *eternal repercussions.* All the same, modern theology seeks to dissuade us from treating god as a being like others and sees the word *god* as a logical marker for something else, not as a name. Tillich wrote:

> *Faith consists in being vitally concerned with that ultimate reality to which I give the symbolical name of 'god'. Whoever reflects earnestly on the meaning of life is on the verge of an act of faith.*

This sounds very much like St Augustine. It would clearly be impossible to fit a devil into the theology of Tillich or Robinson and had St Augustine pushed his theology to its logical conclusion, it would have been so for him as well. If there is no room for a being-that-is-god, there is no room for a being-that-is-the-devil.

Philosophy and theology

Philosophy is the study of meaning. It seeks to understand what is said, to make clear whether what is said has meaning or not, to show the dependencies of one

---

[1] The resistance of modern theologians towards the use of the word *god*, is not that new. The sixth century theologian known as *Pseudo-Denys* (because his name is a pseudonym) strove to avoid the word *god* because he too saw it as having anthropomorphic connotations. He said *He is not one of the things that are.* He said that reading the Bible was a way to ascend to god himself and a way to stop us thinking too much. We should read, listen and accept.

[2] I do not quote what Robinson says here just because it is similar to Constant but the similarity is certainly there. You may remember Constant's words from *La Mère de dieu: The present generation is dying of ice in the soul because it lacks love. Without love, all belief is extinguished and without religion social order becomes impossible.*

concept on another and the logical implications of statements. The philosophy of religion is a study of the meaning of religious statements. One statement it would question is *God exists*.

Theology is the study of the nature of god and religious belief. It seeks to understand the implications of god's existence, to investigate religious comments, to show the dependencies of one religious concept on another and the logical implications of religious statements. One statement it does not question is *God exists*. Theology starts from the acceptance of this belief and works within the *sprachspiel* of religion.

Chapter eleven: Loose Ends

Templar church.
The remains of the Commanderie Saint-Martin-des-Champs, La Ferté-Gaucher, France.

In this, the final chapter, we will wrap up some loose ends, notably the question of secrecy, the Templars, the Kabbalah, and the Rosicrucians. The last three are fairly massive loose ends, agreed, but we will deal with them only in so far as Constant does. We will look at the Baphomet, the ideal of the Christian Knight and how the admission of defeat by the Knights Templar in 1291 was seen as Christ's defeat by Satan, discussing the trial and torture of the Templars during which they were accused of worshipping the devil.

We will move on to Kabbalah, the centre of Jewish theology for a thousand years. We will be looking for Chesed and Geburah, words which appear in Constant's engraving, coming across Ezekiel, his chariot and those dry bones commanded to hear the word of the lord, as well as a surprising explanation of the problem of evil which will lead us to the tree of life. We will then look at the Rosicrucians and the mythical Christian Rozenkreutz, discussing the three manifestos, the Fama, the Confessio and the Chymical Wedding. We will hear the sad tale of the Winter King and Queen, discuss an early French poem and meet yet another impressive woman, Christine de Pizan. Through all of this, we will be seeking the hidden knowledge that Constant believes will yield to him the secrets of power.

I will then reflect back on our start point and where we have been since to pull together the main elements of the story. As I said right at the beginning, ideas do not spring anew from one mind and the legends behind the goat, the devil and the freemason go back a very long way. During their descent through time, they have gathered the credibility of innumerable associations, gaining mass rather like a snowball rolling downhill.

During the postlude that closes the book, I will reveal the real secrets and powers of freemasonry but first let us deal with that question of secrecy.

Secrecy - why?

> *They recognize each other by secret marks and signs, and they love one another almost before they become acquainted. Everywhere they mingle together in a kind of religion of lust, indiscriminately calling each other brothers and sisters, with the result that ordinary debauchery, by means of a sacred name, is converted into incest.*

Here is Minicus Felix again, talking about Christianity, not about freemasonry. Secrecy is an item on the standard list of crimes we have come to know so well, but it is still incumbent upon me to deal with it, because freemasonry does have secrets.

Is freemasonry secret? Its existence certainly is not. The George Washington Masonic National Memorial in Washington, DC. The first President of the USA, George Washington was a freemason, initiated in the Fredericksburg Lodge No. 4 in 1752.

While they are nothing more sinister than formal words and signs of recognition, the masonic secrets are not revealed to non-masons, even though most of them are known to dogs taken for walks. Why do we retain them? There are many reasons.

There is that old reason, tradition. The masonic secrets go back many centuries. They once may have had a practical use, as proof of holding a qualification in the masons' trade or as passwords to fool spies, as I said earlier. Having held these secrets for at least 360 years and being committed to continuity with the past and future, masons understandably do not wish to give them up.

The ability to keep a secret is also a virtue and masonry is primarily about the inculcation of morality. Its motto is *Aude, Vide, Tace* which means hear, see and be silent. Such advice might well be heeded at a time when instant revelations on social networks get so many people into trouble.

In addition, the secrets control access to the various steps or stages in freemasonry, making each just that little bit more exciting. Knowing the secrets before completing the next step would be a bit like opening your presents before your birthday or before Christmas morning. What you get is the same but it does not feel the same and it must be acknowledged that the secrecy and mystery are a major part of the attraction, part of the thrill in joining. Knowing the secrets produces a feeling of belonging. It satisfies what some psychologists call a need for affiliation.

So mystery may attract or repel but the secrets we have remain central to freemasonry. Were we to give them up, we would lose members and attract fewer initiates, becoming indistinguishable from the Lions Club or the Round Table. Now there is absolutely nothing wrong with the Lions or the Round Table. They are very worthy organisations, dedicated to charity, full of decent men. However, they are not the same as freemasonry which, despite its enormous charitable giving, sets out firstly to inculcate virtue and brotherly love and only secondly to raise money for charity.

Freemasonry is described as a system of morality, veiled in allegory and illustrated by symbols. In our meetings, we practise age old ritual: a matter of learning and performing stories, entirely from memory. (Hence my comment about dogs taken for walks knowing the secrets. Masons spend a lot of time muttering to themselves as they seek to imprint the script in their memory!) The stories in the ritual are based upon the allegory of the building of the Temple(s) at Jerusalem. Our ceremonies use symbols to teach and remind us of important truths about our relationship to each other and to the world at large. It is a form of teaching that pre-dates books and which has been going on in masonry for many centuries and is enjoyed by freemasons throughout the world.

If you asked the brethren of my mother lodge what they get out of membership, I doubt whether the secrets would get a mention. My brethren might say many things but most would point to that sense of continuity I have mentioned, close fellowship and mutual support, a feeling of doing what is right, the satisfaction of ritual well performed, perhaps an enjoyment of the theatrical aspects, a great deal of laughter, a few drinks,[1] a good meal and something not easy to put into words. While many of the brethren might be a little embarrassed to say it out loud, what we really gain is a feeling of something beyond ourselves, something that lifts us onto a higher plane, something that makes us want to live up to the ideals of freemasonry.

The Knights Templar

You may recall that in Chapter 15, *Le Sabbat des Sorciers*, Constant announces:

> *We now arrive at that terrible number fifteen which the tarot pictures as a monster perched on an altar, wearing a mitre and horns, having female breasts and male sexual organs; a chimera,[2] a misshapen sphinx, a synthesis of monstrosities; and underneath this figure we find, artlessly and openly, the title THE DEVIL.*

---

[1] In the USA, freemasonry is dry. In the UK and many other constitutions, wine is served with dinner.

[2] A monster created from parts of several animals, typically a lioness, a snake and a goat.

He goes on:

> *Yes, we must now approach that phantasm of all fears, the dragon of all theogonies, the Ahriman of the Persians, the Typhon of the Egyptians, the Python of the Greeks, the ancient serpent of the Hebrews, the Wyvern, the dragon of Metz and of Provence, the Gargoyle, the great beast of the Middle Ages and, worse than all these, the Baphomet of the Templars, ...*

So here is the second of our loose ends, *the Baphomet of the Templars.*

Knightly ideals

The ideal of the Christian knight is an essential element of the middle ages. The knightly code of chivalry develops within such poems as *La Chanson de Roland,* dating from the time of the first crusade; an idealised perfection of bravery, courtesy towards friends and foes, honour, self-deprecation and loyalty, combined with such courtly behaviour as good manners, urbanity and gallantry towards ladies. In its Christian aspect it fought holy wars.

> *Constantly seek after wonders*
> *Prize nothing more than honour*
> *Praise god*
> *Never break faith*
> *Never wrong another knight*
> *Never lay down arms in defeat*
> *Defend your country to the death*
> *Defend the rights of the weak*
> *Injure no one without just cause*
> *Tell the truth*
> *Be hospitable*

Courtly and chivalric literature is centred on the stories of King Arthur and the knights of the Round Table: Lancelot, the most formidable; Tristan and his tragic love of Isolde; Perceval, whose purity initiates the grail quest; Galahad, the perfect knight who finds the grail; Sir Gwain of the mysterious Green Knight tale and Sir Bedivere who, when Arthur dies, returns Excalibur to the Lady of the Lake in Dozmary Pool high, it is said, on Bodmin Moor.

As Alan Young tells us, the knightly tournament flourished well into the Tudor period, reaching its peak as a theatrical spectacle at the court of Queen Elizabeth I. It lasted even into Jacobean times and a tournament took place in 1625 to celebrate the marriage of King Charles I. Money lavished on tournaments exceeded the spend on pageants, masques and plays. They were,

> *... a vehicle for the expression of royal magnificence, the ideals of courtly virtue and the unity of the body politic.*

The reality of the tournament in its earliest days was different, as Young writes:

> *In its most straightforward, but to us perhaps least attractive, form the tournament consisted of a single event involving two large opposing groups of knights who fought each other at some agreed upon place and time (usually*

midway between two towns or villages) in response to a formal challenge. There was frequently no predetermined boundary to the combat area and fighting might range across considerable tracts of country and even through the streets of nearby towns and villages ... The fighting in a tournament could be fierce, bloody without judges to see fair play and virtually without rules ...[1]

All too easily the tournament could become a disguise for a feudal war in which case the death of an opponent would be no great cause for regret. However the tournament seems principally valued for the financial profit to be derived from ransoms and booty.

The internal contradictions of the tournament, money and death on the one hand and honour and virtue on the other, might very well stand as descriptions of the historical Knights Templar. As Peter Partner writes:

It is well known that the taking of Jerusalem by the Crusaders in 1099 occasioned a terrible massacre of its inhabitants, in which the Crusaders walked in blood. It is not only the well-lit and rational part of our minds which is stirred by the crusading idea; we may also find it evokes Gothic fantasies of conflict and slaughter.

The idea of a knight vowed to the accomplishment of crusading ideals seems noble and praiseworthy, yet those ideals were dictated by a medieval church which now seems to us to have been bigoted and obscurantist, and were put into practice in a manner which now seems barbarous and cruel.

Failure

The Knights Templar were formed around 1120, just after the first crusade. They amassed extraordinary wealth all over Europe, becoming the first bankers, but largely failed in their military aims. They were finally dissolved in 1314, following persecution and torture by King Philip the Fair of France, when the Grand Master, Jaques de Molay, was burned at the stake.

The failure of the Templars to defend the Holy Land may seem to us to be unsurprising and excusable since the forces opposing them were much greater, based in their own land with shorter supply lines and a constant source of reinforcements. However, to the medieval mind, it did not appear simply as a military conflict. Peter Partner quotes words contemporary with the crusades:

God has ordained a tournament between Heaven and Hell, and sends to all his friends who wish to defend him, that they fail him not.

In this tournament, the crusaders, and particularly the Knights Templar who had taken holy vows, were the champions of Christ in the lists, ready to fight for his name and defend his honour. Their defeat was seen as Christ's defeat by Satan. As Jonathan Riley-Smith writes:

All Christian justifications of positive violence are based partly on the belief that a particular religious or political system or course of political events is one in which Christ is intimately involved. His intentions for mankind are therefore bound up

---

[1] All of which sounds like the hooligans of the *Inter-City Firm* of West Ham United who once arranged pitched battles with the gangs of other clubs such as the *Chelsea Headhunters*.

with its success or failure ... If the only way to preserve the integrity of his intentions from those who stand in their way is to use force, then this is in accordance with his desires ... and participation in Christ's own violence is demanded of those qualified as a moral duty.

The Knights Templar answered the call, taking the cross and making war against the infidel. Very much like WWI recruitment campaigns, answering the call involved making a vow, as Riley-Smith says:

... at emotional public gatherings under the influence of preachers whose business was to whip their audiences into a frenzy.

Pope Urban II quoted Matthew's gospel, somewhat out of context, to make it clear that taking the cross was following Christ:

And every one that hath forsaken houses, or brethren, or sisters, or father, or mother, or wife, or children, or lands, for my name's sake, shall receive an hundredfold, and shall inherit everlasting life. (Matthew 19:29)

and in particular:

Then said Jesus unto his disciples, If any man will come after me, let him deny himself, and take up his cross, and follow me. (Matthew 16:24)

Uban's motivation may have been partly religious but was probably more political, seeking to stop the civil wars between the forces of the Holy Roman Emperor Henry IV and the amazing Matilda of Tuscany.[1] Urban proclaimed:

Let them turn their weapons dripping with the blood of their brothers against the enemy of the Christian faith. Let them - oppressors of orphans and widows, murderers and violators of churches, robbers of the property of others, vultures drawn by the scent of battle - let them hasten, if they love their souls, under their captain Christ to the rescue of Sion.

The crusaders took Jerusalem in 1099 and Tyre in 1124, by when they occupied almost all the coastline. In 1187, having recaptured every Templar city except Tyre, Saladin (1137-1193) retook Jerusalem for Islam but maintained a chivalric relationship with Richard I, allowing Christian pilgrims to enter the city. Jerusalem was retaken in 1229, but was finally overwhelmed by Khwarezmian mercenaries in 1244, essentially as a by-product of Arab-Egyptian civil wars. After the siege of Acre and the fall of Tyre in 1291, the Knights Templar were forced to retreat to Cyprus. In 1307, all members of the Templar Order in France were arrested.

The Baphomet

As we saw earlier, defeat of religious belief needs rationalisation. The initial impetus for the destruction of the Knights Templar may well have been financial jealousy. It has been argued that the King of France was in need of money and that he could not tolerate a wealthy, independent, military and aristocratic institution

---

[1] Warrior and collector of manuscripts, supporter of the legitimate papacy and patron of the arts, needlewoman and linguist, she battled against Henry who crowned an antipope in Rome and defeated him at the battle of Sobara. After Henry's death she made her peace with his successor. Her tomb is in St Peter's, Rome with a monument by Bernini.

within the borders of his kingdom but Alan Forey discounts these as Philip's main reasons, arguing that:

> *It is possible ... that Philip actually believed rumours which had been circulating about the Templars. He seems to have become increasingly preoccupied with matters of religion after the death of his wife in 1305, and may have doubted that the Pope would take what he would have regarded as adequate action.*

So what were these rumours? Presumably they were similar to the charges finally brought against the Templars, and so yet again we welcome back our standard list of crimes that *people we really don't like* are accused of: sexual deviance and devil worship. It is amazing how uncreative those who deliver false accusations can be. Partner reports that in the papal decree of 1308:

> *The vital points were denial of Christ, spitting on the cross, a ritual kiss on the back and navel of the brother receiving the postulant, promise to commit sodomy with the brothers or else to obtain sexual relief only from such sodomy, worship of an idol (and) of weird women or female demons.* (Try not to yawn.)

The idol referred to was named *Baphomet* by the prosecution, although no such idol was ever found and most scholars take the word to be a corruption of *Mohamet.[1]* One of the accusations made against the Templars was that they had gone native and started to worship Islamic idols; a nonsense, since the very idea of creating idols is anathema to Islam. The decoration of Islamic buildings avoids any representational art.

There was never any evidence at all produced to support any of the accusations against the Templars. For example, as Alan Forey writes,

> *... it is noteworthy that during the trial no witness who had heard Templar confessions before 1307 claimed to have encountered error.*

The Templars were convicted solely by confessions obtained through deprivation and torture, in many

The Friday Mosque in Herat.

---

[1] Abū al-Qāsim Muḥammad ibn ʿAbd Allāh ibn ʿAbd al-Muṭṭalib ibn Hāshim was born in Mecca in 570 and died in Medina in 632 and thus preceded the crusades by about 500 years. His revelations and teachings form the Qurʾan. A man of undoubted courage, generalship and patriotism, most modern scholars agree on the purity of his motives, personal qualities and sincerity.

cases rescinded later. So why were the Templars exterminated? The main reason was surely that a scapegoat was needed to explain why Christ had been overcome by Satan. By showing that the Knights Templars had worshipped heathen idols and consorted with the devil, the failure of the attempt to hold Jerusalem could be explained away. Christ had not been defeated; he had been betrayed and so the *Baphomet* has become one of the enduring images of evil; an idol worshipped by those who abandoned Christ.

In discussing all this, the fact that the *Baphomet* didn't exist and that the Templars betrayed no one, should be kept in mind. Constant's engraving is in no way the *Baphomet of the Templars*. He made it up.

Despite romantic stories in books and films, the modern masonic order of the Knights Templar has no historical connection with the medieval order.[1] The Knights Templar ceased to exist as an organisation in 1314 and such of its wealth that remained after Philip the Fair took his cut, was given to the Knights Hospitaller. The masonic order of Knights Templar in England originated in the late 18th century[2] and its only link with its medieval namesake lies in the religious ideals and chivalric virtues. The masonic order is a Christian one, unlike craft masonry which is open to men of all religions and none. Its full title is *The United Religious, Military and Masonic Orders of the Temple and of St John of Jerusalem, Palestine, Rhodes and Malta.*

Kabbalah

In his description of his *Baphomet*, Constant writes:

> *It forms an occult sign with its hands, one pointing upward towards the white moon of Chesed, and the other downwards to the black moon of Geburah, expressing the perfect equality of mercy and justice.*

The words, *Chesed* and *Geburah* come from Kabbalah, in particular from the Tree of Life, and I enter upon this subject with a great deal of trepidation. It is not really right to refer to it as *the* Kabbalah. For example, it is not a book. The word works rather like the word *poetry*. It is a massive area of study: a school of thought, an approach to religious teaching and the centre of Jewish theology for at least a thousand years. Its understanding requires something more than part of a chapter devoted to loose ends. The proper study of Kabbalah is a lifetime's work, but as the immortal Schnozzle Durante sang, *I can't wait that long. I've got only one change of clothes.*[3] What gives me sufficient heart to talk about it at all is something Joseph Dan writes in his introduction to the subject:

> *A common denominator, I believe, of answers to the question, 'What is Kabbalah?' is that Kabbalah is something that I have a vague notion of, but somebody, somewhere, knows exactly what it means.*

---

[1] By far the best novel about the so-called connection between the medieval Templars and the modern occult is *Foucault's Pendulum* by Umberto Eco.

[2] The first Grand Conclave was held in 1791.

[3] *I'm the guy who found the lost chord.* The B side is just as good: *A little bit this, a little bit that.*

Moreover, Constant's actual use of Kabbalah was fairly minimal, although he mentions it often. You may remember that AE Waite, in his introduction to his translation of *L'Histoire de la Magie*, said that Constant had,

> ... no extensive knowledge of those Kabbalistic texts on the importance of which he dwells so much and about which he claims to speak with full understanding.

Waite's summary of Constant was that:

> It remains to say that Éliphas Lévi represents the invention of a new and gratuitous phase in the study of the Kabbalah.

The word *gratuitous* means *unjustified* or *unwarranted*. It is not a compliment.

Kabbalah and magic

Part of Constant's interest in Judaic mysticism may have been that, as did the *Corpus Hermeticum*, Kabbalah produced its own science of magic. The ancient book, *The Sword of Moses*, is said to contain incantations and other magical processes for curing illnesses, creating love potions, even walking on water and Constant seems to use the word *Kabbalah* as a synonym for magic which he traces back to antiquity.

> The transcendental science ... is assuredly magic (which) was the science of Abraham and Orpheus, of Confucius and Zoroaster, and it was magical doctrines that were graven on tables of stone by Enoch and by Trismegistus. Moses purified and re-veiled them ... The new disguise which he gave them was that of the Holy Kabbalah - that exclusive heritage of Israel and inviolable secret of its priests.

He goes on to say that while Ancient Greece preserved some knowledge of Kabbalah, albeit in a debased form, Jerusalem lost them, being,

> ...the murderer of its prophets and prostituted over and over again to false Assyrian and Babylonian gods.

until,

> ... a Saviour, declared to the magi by the holy star of initiation, came to rend the threadbare veil of the old temple, to endow the Church with a new network of legends and symbols - ever concealing from the profane, and always preserving for the elect, that truth which is the same for ever.[1]

This elect seems to include in his mind the *Rosicrucians* (who never really existed but of whom more later), the *Illuminati* (who certainly never existed[2]) and *Freemasons* (who do exist but few of whom know anything about Kabbalah.)

---

[1] From Waite's translation of *L'Histoire de la Magie*. Constant may be making use of a legend that the true pronunciation of the tetragrammaton, revealed to Enoch, Jacob and Moses, was lost during the Assyrian invasion of the northern kingdom of Israel and only recovered when Moses and Elijah appeared with Jesus to Peter, James and John on Mount Tabor. In *The Royal Arch Journey*, Neville Barker Cryer discusses this legend as used in *Le Rite de Bouillon*, worked by at least two lodges in about 1740.

[2] Unless one refers to the Bavarian society of freethinkers that had a brief existence in 1776.

The spiritual dimension in Judaism

There is a legend that a form of esoteric knowledge existed around 1000 BCE, later being hidden by the Sanhedrin, particularly around the time of the exile, to prevent it being misused. This legend stems from a tale that Moses received a great deal more than was written down when he received the tablets on Mount Sinai. This extra knowledge was transmitted orally from then on until it was codified in the Mishnah in the second century CE.

Dan tells us that the word *kabbalah* has many uses in Hebrew but all are connected with the idea of *being received*. As a prophylactic against taking the word *kabbalah* to be always mystical, he points out that the sign reading *Kabbalah* in a hotel means *Reception* and that on a piece of paper in a restaurant, it means *receipt*.

Dan supports the view we have taken that *au fond*, the Jewish religion is straightforward. Yahweh sets out in apparent detail what he wants and if the people obey his commands, the nation of Israel prospers. The 613 commandments (*mitzvot*) call for or prohibit action, spiritual demands being largely absent:

> *Even prayer was not regarded as properly performed unless one's lips moved during recitation.*

Nevertheless, Jewish theologians from the early middle ages onward sought to provide a spiritual dimension to Judaism and this Kabbalah has provided. *Pace* Constant, Kabbalah as we see it today is a medieval creation but Dan sees its beginnings in the Talmud itself. It is held that elements of esoteric knowledge can be found in *Genesis, Isaiah* and *Ezekiel*; for example in the stories of the garden of Eden, the tree of life, Jacob's ladder, and the chariot. I found it fascinating to discover that young scholars were forbidden to study these texts because they were regarded as spiritually and even physically dangerous. For example, in the Talmud, *Tractate Hagiga*, Chapter II, we find the advice that one should not discuss,

> *... the creation unless there were two besides him, nor the divine chariot with one individual, unless he was a wise man and had much knowledge of his own. Everyone who tries to know the following four things, it were better for him if he had never come into the world, viz: What is above and what is beneath, what was before creation, and what will be after all will be destroyed.*

This is exemplified by stories in the Mishna such as:

> *Four men went up into the heavenly garden ... Ben Azzai and Ben Zoma, A'her and R. Aqiba. Ben Azzai gazed and died ... Ben Zoma gazed and went mad ... A'her cut the plants (destroyed the garden). R. Aqiba departed in peace.*

Only Rebbe Aqiba was capable of handling the esoteric texts.

Ezekiel

At first sight, Ezekiel seems to be yet another smiting story. As we saw earlier, in the story of the man with the inkhorn, some of it is very unpleasant. It is an odd work, and rather repetitive with its threats and judgements against the disobedient and demands for sacrifice. The events in the book take place before, during and after the destruction of the temple in Jerusalem and it contains an account of Egypt and Nebuchanezzar:

Therefore thus saith the lord god; Behold, I will give the land of Egypt unto Nebuchadrezzar king of Babylon; and he shall take her multitude, and take her spoil, and take her prey; and it shall be the wages for his army.

The Delta Rhythm Boys

It contains two famous passages: the allocation of land to the tribes of Israel and the story of the dry bones as in the 1947 hit by the Delta Rhythm Boys.[1]

The hand of the lord came upon me ... and set me down in the midst of the valley; and it was full of bones ... He said to me, 'Son of man, can these bones live?' So I answered, 'O lord god, you know.'

Again he said to me, 'Prophesy to these bones, and say to them, O dry bones, hear the word of the lord!' ... 'Say to the breath: Come from the four winds ... and breathe on these slain, that they may live.' So I prophesied as he commanded me, and breath came into them, and they lived, and stood upon their feet, an exceedingly great army.[2]

The book opens with a dazzling description of a vision. Ezekiel sees a violent storm, surrounded by brilliant light, coming out of the north, flashing with lightning. The centre of the storm is ablaze with fire and in it are four beings: winged and man-shaped but with four faces each - of a man, a lion, an ox and an eagle.[3] The creatures appear in burning coals or torches of fire and beside each is a wheel sparkling with topaz, a precious stone whose colour alters with heat.

The wheels are complex, as if each is inside another so that they can move in any direction without turning and the rims have eyes all round. Above the storm hangs a vault, sparkling like crystal, from which booms a voice belonging to a figure with the appearance of a man seated on a throne of the intense blue stone *lapis lazuli*. From his waist up he is glowing metal and from waist down he is fire. Yet more brilliant light surrounds him. Ezekiel prostrates himself before what he takes to be the face of god, but the voice says:

Son of man, stand up on your feet and I will speak to you. I am sending you to the Israelites, to a rebellious nation that has rebelled against me. Do not be afraid of them or their words. Do not be afraid, though briers and thorns are all around you and you live among scorpions. You must speak my words to them, but do not rebel

---

[1] *Dem bones, dem bones, dem dry bones. Now hear the word of the Lord.* Written by James Weldon Johnson (1871-1938), author, politician, diplomat, teacher, lawyer and civil rights activist.

[2] The seventh volume of Anthony Powell's *A Dance to the Music of Time* is entitled *The Valley of Bones. An exceedingly great army* is the theme of a sermon preached to the battalion to which Nick Jenkins, the narrator, is attached for basic training during the early days of WWII.

[3] Familiar to members of the Royal Arch.

like that rebellious people; open your mouth and eat what I give you.

An outstretched hand unrolls a scroll, on both sides of which are written words of *lament, mourning and woe*. Ezekiel eats as he has been ordered and the scroll tastes as sweet as honey. Then Ezekiel hears the sound of wings and wheels as the glory of the lord rises up in a chariot. Later Ezekiel has another very similar vision and realises that the creatures he has seen are cherubim, angels who attend on god. The cherubim, with their wings and wheels, form the chariot in which god rides.

In Ezekiel, there is a description of god himself. An attempt to understand Ezekiel is thus an attempt to understand the appearance of god (the *ma'aseh merkavah* or *arrangement of the chariot*), a project fraught with danger for the uninitiated in a culture for which the use of the name of god was forbidden.

Genesis

Ezekiel reveals what god looks like while *Genesis*, just as dangerously perhaps, reveals how god works. To attempt to understand *Genesis* is dangerously close to considering *what was before creation*, one of the questions that the *Tractate Hagiga* forbids. It is to ask also why creation happened in this particular sequence rather than in another. For example, Isaac Luria (1534-1572) asked why creation occurred at all. He went back to the problem of evil, to ask how and why imperfection occurs when creation is the work of a prefect creator. As Dan writes:

> The most innovative concept that lies at the heart of Luria's teachings is the imperfection of beginning. Existence does not begin with a perfect creator bringing into being an imperfect universe; rather the existence of the universe is the result of an inherent flaw or crisis within the infinite godhead and the purpose of creation is to correct it.

The logic jump in Luria's narrative is the acceptance of an imperfect creator whose failure left a residue which is the cause of evil in the world. What we see around us is in effect the result of a second attempt at creation. Had all gone well the second time and good triumphed over evil, creation would have been purified but this also failed; first Adam transgressed; next the people of Israel went to the bad and so it will continue until goodness reaches critical mass and evil is finally defeated. This can only happen when enough people live in obedience to god's commands - a story thus similar to that in the *Zohar*.

On this thesis, the commandments are not much to do with us at all. It is irrelevant to ask why one must put tzitzit[1] on the corners of clothing (18), eat matzah[2] on the first night of Passover (120), not sell a Hebrew maid-servant to another person (197), nor wear garments made of wool and linen mixed together (367) but sound the trumpets at the offering of sacrifices (455). Obeying the mitvot helps the forces of good. Disobeying helps the forces of evil. As Dan puts it:

> God did not give human beings these commandments in order to achieve any earthly purpose. What god demands of man is participation in the past drama of the dynamic occurrences in the divine world.

---

[1] Knotted fringes.

[2] Unleavened bread.

Isaac Luria's ideas exemplify the danger for a believer trying to make sense of *Genesis*. One ends up with a view of god as imperfect.

Modern Kabbalah

The *Sefer Yezira* (Book of Creation), written sometime after the first and before the ninth century CE, is seen as a source for the modern Kabbalah although not kabbalistic itself.[1] It uses the letters of the Hebrew alphabet to give an explanation of the process of creation, arguing that since the world was created by god's words, the laws of language are the laws of creation.

The *Book Bahir*, written around 1185 is seen as the earliest manifestation of Kabbalah proper, describing the divine world as made up of ten divine powers. One hundred years later, the *Zohar* describes the emanation of these powers from a divinity which becomes known as *ein sof*, meaning *no end*, described as an infinite, perfect, supreme entity that cannot change. *Ein sof* is indescribable, being beyond language, but it may not be totally wrong to say that we have met this concept in god-as-mind in the *Corpus Hermeticum*. No description is possible, except in negatives. *Ein sof* is positively not anything - but from it stems everything. Dan writes:

> The most important aspect of ein sof in Kabbalistic thought is as the ultimate source of the flow of the purist divine light (shefa) that constantly provides the power to exist in both divine and earthly realms. Emanation is not a one-time event, but an ongoing vital process that maintains the existence of all beings.

We may be getting somewhat close to Constant's *Astral Light* here. Constant writes:[2]

> To become initiated into the Kabbalah ... it is necessary to study and understand the ... Sepher Yetzirah above all; it is essential in particular to master the great book Zohar.

Not that he did. The emanation and structure of the divine world is represented by the tree of life and the ten *sefirot* of the *Book Bahir* and it is here that we will find Constant's words *Chesed* and *Geburah*.

Dan refers to the arrangement of the *sefirot* (singular *sefirah*) as the core of envisioning and understanding the divine world. The tree itself is an arrangement in which (usually) ten *sefirot* are linked by twenty-two arms, each carrying one of the letters of the Hebrew alphabet. Everything starts with *ein sof*, which is not represented on the tree. The emanation starts, as traditionally conceived, when *god wishes to behold god*, indicating that *when* is not a useful word in this context. Time does not exist until creation and so there is no *when*.

The sefirot are, so to speak, the basis of everything and so the tree of life can be used to describe anything. Rather than attempt to explain someone else's use of the tree and risk misunderstanding, I have created my own, based on a somewhat old fashioned idea of consciousness.

---

[1] Constant says that it was compiled by Abraham on the basis of the teaching of Enoch who was also Hermes Trismegistus. It wasn't and he wasn't.

[2] *Introduction* to Volume II of *Dogme et Rituel*. In Waite's opinion, Constant had never studied the *Sefer* or the *Zohar*.

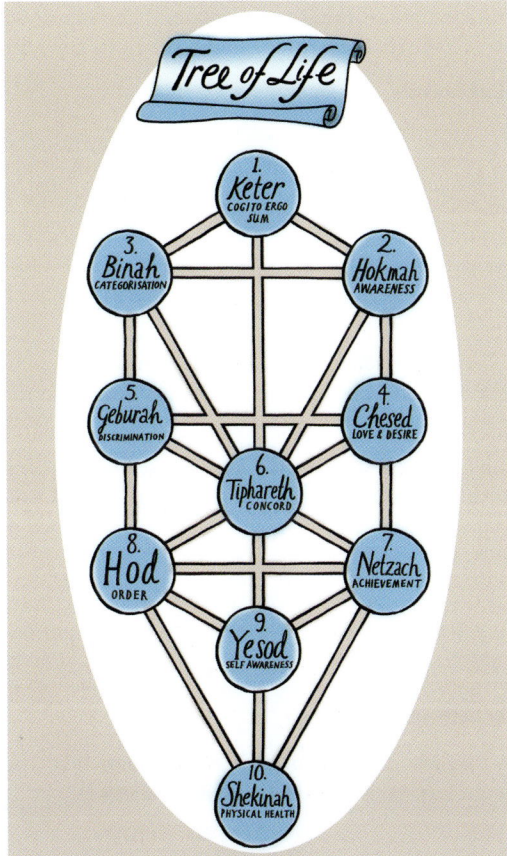

The first step in the emanation of consciousness is the creation at the edge of nothingness of being, *keter*. In Cartesian terms, this might be taken as the *cogito ergo sum* (I think therefore I am) the point from which the world is seen. The next step is *hokmah* (knowing) immediately given balance by *binah* (understanding.) Descartes deduced *sum res cogitans* (I am a thinking thing) from *cogito ergo sum* and *hokmah* might thus be seen as cognition or awareness of the external world. *Binah* may be thought of as categorisation, giving form to what is perceived.

Thought on its own is empty; without emotion, decision making seems to be impossible. Located in the temporal lobes of the brain, the amygdala manages and stores our emotional responses. Experiments on subjects with amygdala damage show that while they can create plans and strategies, they cannot initiate action. They know what to do but can't do it.

Thus motivation comes next: love and desire (*chesed*) being balanced and controlled by discipline and discrimination (*geburah*) and these are the two words found on the arms of the creature in Constant's engraving. As he puts it, the left arm points upward to the white moon of *chesed* while the right arm points downward to the black moon of *geburah*, expressing the beauty (*tiphareth*) of the concord between mercy and justice. This reinforces the fact that *le bouc de sabbat* is not the devil.

Decisions are decisions to act, and so from thought and feeling, we go to the sphere of action; to *netzach* which some psychologists might call a need for achievement, balanced by the cognitive *hod*, perhaps a need for order. Supporting all this are two foundations: *yesod* (the intellectual) by which we might mean consciousness and *shekinah* (the physical), perhaps the health necessary to sustain consciousness.

While one can follow the logic of the *sefirot*, their existential status is not so easy to grasp. Is the tree of life meant to be the structure of all things - the structure of reality - or a method of analysis? I applied the tree to a top down emanation of consciousness in human beings but few anthropologists would accept it as an historical account. Indeed, it might be argued that the process is bottom up; that in evolution, consciousness arises from bodily awareness via feeling and judgement;

that god, certainly a monotheistic god, is the last thing to be created. The top down account sounds like creationism but, of course, the tree of life is a religious concept.

A final note on Constant and Kabbalah

Robert Uzzel writes:

> One of Lévi's major contributions to esoteric thought was his claim of correspondences between Kabbalah and Tarot. He was the first writer to 'discover' a connection between the twenty-two Tarot trumps and the twenty-two paths of the Kabbalistic Tree of Life symbolised by the twenty-two Hebrew letters.

Uzzel is honest enough to add:

> As a result, critics such as Gershom Sholem[1] have charged him with 'supreme charlatanism' in mistaking a matter of coincidence for an organic and historical connection.

I think we know enough about Constant now to say that he would have had no evidence for any historical connection between Kabbalah and the Tarot. As I said earlier, Constant wants to see Kabbalah as the mystical knowledge of his science of magic that goes far back into antiquity. He wrote:

> The holy Kabbalah, or tradition of the children of Seth, was carried from Chaldea by Abraham, taught to the Egyptian priesthood by Joseph, recovered and purified by Moses, concealed under symbols in the Bible, revealed by the saviour to Saint John, and contained, entire, under hieratic figures analogous to those of all antiquity, in the Apocalypse of that Apostle.

or he would have, had he written in English. These words are from Albert Pike and are yet more plagiarism from Constant's *Histoire de la Magie*. The ancestry is wholly imaginary.

The Rosicrucians

One can take a narrow or a broad view of Rosicrucianism. The narrow view is that it is confined to a series of publications usually known by their abridged titles, the *Fama* and the *Confessio*[2] (authors unknown), which appeared in 1614 and 1615 and the *Chymical Wedding*,[3] written in 1616 by Johann Valentin Andreae[4] (1586-1654.) The *Fama* relates a story of one Christian Rozenkreutz, who travelled in Spain and Arabia seeking what is clearly hermetic knowledge:

> As in every several kernel is contained the whole good tree or fruit, so likewise is

---

[1] Gerhard (Gershom) Scholem (1897-1982), preeminent modern scholar of Jewish mysticism. Scholem was also convinced that Kabbalah is a medieval phenomenon.

[2] Thomas Vaughan translated the works into English in 1652 under the titles of *Fama Fraternitatis, or A Discovery of the Fraternity of the Most Noble Order of the Rosy Cross* and *Confessio Fraternitatis, or The Confession of the Laudable Fraternity of the Most Honourable Order of the Rosy Cross, written to all the Learned of Europe*.

[3] *Chymische Hochzeit Christiani Rosencreutz anno 1459*, translated as *The Chymical Wedding of Christian Rozenkreutz in the year 1459*; the word *chymical* being taken to mean *alchemical*.

[4] According to Frances Yates, whose 1972 book is still the most important (and beautiful) explanation of what she refers to as the Rosicrucian Enlightenment.

> *included in the little body of man the whole great world, whose religion, policy, health, members, nature, language, words and works are agreeing, sympathizing and in equal tune with god, heaven and earth.*

As above so below, the basic tenet of alchemy once again. Having completed his travels, Christian Rozenkreutz returned to Germany where he created the *Fraternity of the Rosy Cross* with four members at first, later expanded to eight, to receive revelation. Then, when the members were,

> *... sufficiently instructed and able perfectly to discourse of secret and manifest philosophy, they would not remain any longer together but ... separated themselves into several countries.*

... agreeing, among other things, that they would meet annually, seek successors to replace those who died, keep the fraternity secret for one hundred years and occupy their time in healing the sick. One hundred years passed, successor following successor, until a magical vault was discovered, into which no natural light could shine but which was lit by an inner sun. The vault contained the tomb of Christian Rozenkreutz. In it, the brethren found,

> *... a fair and worthy body, whole and unconsumed ... with all his ornaments and attires. In his hand he held a parchment book named 'I', the which next to the Bible is our greatest treasure ...*

The vault was closed again against the time when there would be *a general reformation of divine and human matters* and the brethren issued an invitation to others to join their Fraternity in order to,

> *... make a happy and wished for beginning of our Philosophical Canons, prescribed by our brother R.C. and be partakers with us of our treasures ... in all humility and love, to be eased of this world's labour and not walk so blindly in the knowledge of the wonderful works of the almighty.*[1]

The brethren gave no address at which to receive applications but said:

> *Nevertheless everyone's opinion shall assuredly come to our hands in what language so ever it be: nor anybody shall fail, who so gives his name, but to speak with some of us, either by word of mouth, or else, if there be some let, in writing.*

The *Fama* concludes with a promise and a warning:

> *And this we say for a truth that whosoever shall earnestly and from his heart bear affection unto us, it shall be beneficial to him in goods, body, and soul; but he that is false-hearted or only greedy of riches, the same first of all shall not be able in any manner or wise to hurt us, but bring himself to utter ruin and destruction.*

The *Confessio* repeats the message of the *Fama* and adds some new elements. It says that Brother R.C.'s learning is such that if all human knowledge were lost, Brother R.C.'s teachings would be sufficient to replace it. It is explicitly anti-papist, accusing the Pope (and *Mahomet*) of blasphemy against Jesus and it is more defensive than the

---

[1] I cheat just a little with the final phrase in order to echo the masonic ritual. The actual phrase is *wonderful works of god.*

Fama, predicting the end of all things before a government according to the principles of Brother R.C. can arise. It ends with a statement that,

> ... *although we (the brothers of the Rosy Cross) might enrich the whole world, and endue it with learning, and might release it from innumerable miseries, yet shall we never be manifested and made known to any man without the especial pleasure of god.*

The publications of these manifestos caused a spate of letters, pamphlets and other publications as the *litterati* of Europe clamoured to make contact and apply for membership. None ever received a reply but several people claimed, in a mysterious and indeed Constant-ian way, to know about them, for example the physician Michael Maier (1568-1622):

> *We cannot set down the places where they meet, nor the time. I have sometimes observed Olympick Houses not far from a river, and known a city which we think is called S. Spiritus - I mean Helicon or Parnassus, in which Pegasus opened a spring of overflowing water wherein Diana washed herself, to whom Venus was handmaid and Saturn gentlemen usher. This will sufficiently instruct any intelligent reader, but more confound the ignorant.*

You can see how like Constant this is, creating a mystery to cover the fact that the author is making it all up. Robert Fludd (1574-1637) the astrologer, mathematician and physician, takes another line and backs off from the claim that the Rosicrucians had any real knowledge, in the way that the church had progressively backed off claims that belief alters the world. He says that the Rosicrucians must be understood as giving simply spiritual advice. If so, then it was much fuss about nothing in particular.

The Chymical Wedding

The *Chymical Wedding* is a work very different from the first two. Frances Yates refers to it as a romance or an *alchemical fantasia*. I will summarise it following Yates:

> In the first of the seven chapters, Christian Rozenkreutz is seen preparing for communion when he receives a vision of an allegorical figure of Fame,[1] who gives him an invitation to a royal wedding, which he quickly accepts. He dresses himself in white linen with a bright red sash across his shoulder and sticks four red roses in his hat.

> On the next day, he travels to a royal castle on a hill. The porter demands to know who he is and he replies, *A brother of the Red Rosy Cross.* He dodges a roaring lion and follows a virgin who is lighting the lamps, just making it to the venue before the gates swing shut. Inside the wedding hall, some of the guests turn out to be bores claiming to be able to see Plato's Forms or able to count the Atoms of Democritus[2] but the wonderful and harmonious music silences everyone.

> On the third day, the guests assemble for the wedding proper and everyone gets weighed. When it is the turn of Christian Rozenkreutz, a

---

[1] A figure with a golden trumpet and wings covering her eyes.

[2] Plato's *Forms* are not visible to sight and Democritus's *Atoms* are infinite in number.

page boy announces, *That is he,* and he is given a high place at the banquet. The table is covered in red velvet and laid with gold and silver drinking cups. The guests each wear a golden fleece or a flying lion, being emblems of a knightly order to which they will be admitted later. The castle is full of wonderful objects: a lion fountain, a clockwork representation of the heavens and a great globe of the world.

As the fourth day dawns, Christian Rozenkreutz, refreshes himself at the lion fountain and finds that it now bears an inscription, *Hermes Princeps* (Hermes the Prince.) The guests attend a play with a plot a little like that of *The Tempest.*[1] They return to the castle where they find six coffins. Six people are beheaded and placed in the coffins and found alive next day.

The fifth day involves the discovery of a vault, like that of the *Fama,* and the sixth day sees the alchemists creating life in the form of a magical bird. On the last day, the wedding party prepares to depart in twelve ships, each bearing a sign of the zodiac and the guests are informed that they have been made Knights of the Golden Stone.

Very obviously the story is an allegory illustrated by symbols but an attempt to unpack it all would take far too much time now and indeed much of the necessary knowledge is lost but we can immediately see elements that we have met before. It is obvious that *Chymical Wedding* is written within the hermetic tradition of magic and secret knowledge, and given a Rosicrucian context represented by the vault.

The Rosicrucian Enlightenment

The mechanical marvels built by Salomon de Caus at Heidelberg were created as part of the celebrations of the marriage of Elizabeth Stuart, the daughter of King James I of England (VI of Scotland) to the Elector Palatine, Frederick V in 1613. Yates sees the marriage as the centrepiece of what she refers to as the Rosicrucian Enlightenment. One can see a reflection of this marriage in the *Chymical Wedding.*

The wedding itself took place in London but went on throughout a procession by the couple back to their home in Heidelberg. It was an extravagantly romantic affair, much more masque than the union of two lovers. It featured decorative arches, massive pageant cars, tournaments, representations of mythical deities, fireworks, costumes of great magnificence, poetry and song. Frederick was seen as a member of the Order of the Garter in London and as Jason of the Golden Fleece, a mystical Prince, in the Palatinate.[2]

The procession ended in the castle of Heidelberg, passing under a triumphal arch sixty-five feet high. The gardens of the castle were decorated with grottoes, mechanical marvels and water-organs, as full of noises, as Yates puts it, as Prospero's Island.

---

[1] Written 1610-1611.

[2] The masque form of courtly theatre was a spectacular and often open air event consisting of extravagant sets, costly costumes, moving models, dancing, poetry and music. In England, Edmund Spenser, Ben Jonson, Inigo Jones and John Milton were involved in creating masques. They flourished in the 16th and 17th centuries.

Modern view of Heidelberg across the Neckar with castle above it (left)

The couple were seen as a courtly ideal. Yates quotes Lord Doncaster, ambassador to Heidelberg, writing in a report that Frederick was,

> *... much beyond his years religious, wise, active and valiant,*

and Elizabeth was,

> *... that same devoute, good, sweet princess ... obliging all hearts come near her by her courtesy, and so dearly loving and beloved of the Prince her husband that it is a joy to all that behold them.*

John Donne wrote *An Epithalamion, or marriage song on the Lady Elizabeth and Count Palatine being married on St Valentine's Day.*[1] Addressed to St Valentine, the central image of the poem is the phoenix, which dies, is consumed by fire and arises anew from the flames, the conceit being that the two lovers die as individuals and then arise, immortal, as one being.[2]

> *Till now, thou warmd'st with multiplying loves*
> *Two larks, two sparrows, or two doves;*
> *All that is nothing unto this;*
> *For thou this day couplest two phoenixes;*
> *Thou makst a taper see*
> *What the sun never saw, and what the ark*
> *- Which was of fowls and beasts, the cage and park -*

---

[1] In his religious capacity, he also preached before them in Heidelberg.

[2] Donne uses this same image in his *Canonization* which I have already quoted.

Did not contain: one bed contains, through thee;
Two phoenixes, whose joined breasts
Are unto one another mutual nests,
Where motion kindles such fires as shall give
Young phoenixes, and yet the old shall live;
Whose love and courage never shall decline,
But make the whole year through, thy day, O Valentine.

...

And by this act these two phoenixes
Nature again restored is;
For since these two are two no more,
There's but one phoenix still, as was before.
Rest now at last, and we -
As satyrs watch the sun's uprise - will stay
Waiting when your eyes opened let out day,
Only desired because your face we see.
Others near you shall whispering speak,
And wagers lay, at which side day will break,
And win by observing, then, whose hand it is
That opens first a curtain, hers or his: no
This will be tried to-morrow after nine,
Till which hour, we thy day enlarge, O Valentine.

Here was a marriage, not only of two young people in love, not only of two Protestant royal families but a marriage of mysticism with mechanics, religion with science, art with politics, and all within an allegory of Rosicrucian thinking; the old paradigm reaching a climax. As Yates writes:

> *Though the production of masques, or the grottoes, singing fountains or pneumatically controlled speaking statues may not seem to us important applications of technology, it was in fact such ways as these that Renaissance science, still involved in a magical atmosphere, began to use technical skills on a large scale.*

Frances Yates sees the excitement generated by this wedding as the last flowering of the hermetic tradition; the last and failed attempt to combine religion with science in the explanation of the world. The attempt was made in the face of the new paradigm of scientific discovery presaged by Francis Bacon and his *Advancement of Learning*, published in 1605. Bacon did not create a paradigm change overnight, but from his time on, science develops independently of religion which, gradually but inexorably, ceases to be relevant to the explanation of the workings of nature; the latter increasingly seen as a matter of mechanics, culminating in Newton's *Philosophiæ Naturalis Principia Mathematica* published in 1687. Truth is often sad.

The Winter King

The phoenix in Donne's poem may be a symbol of immortality but, just as that flowering of the old paradigm was almost immediately swamped by the new one of science, so the romantic flowering of love, romance, beauty and the arts was swamped by the politics of the Holy Roman Empire.[1] Frederick, a Protestant, was invited to take the throne of Bohemia[2] as leader of the Protestant princes. He accepted, becoming King in August 1619, but in November 1620, Frederick was defeated at the Battle of the White Mountain by the Catholic forces led by Ferdinand II, the Holy Roman Emperor. Frederick and Elizabeth became known as the *Winter King and Queen*.

Any thought that Elizabeth's father might send English forces to assist was soon dispelled[3] and the couple spent the rest of their lives, exiled in the Netherlands, Frederick seeking the restoration of his lands and wasting donations from the English and Dutch court on foolish extravaganzas to bolster his self-image.

Le Roman de la Rose

The Templars and the Rosicrucians are part of a pathway that Constant wants to see conducting the secret knowledge of the ancients towards himself as the guardian of occult knowledge for the late 19th century. There is a gap in the transmission and to fill it he seizes upon the 13th century poem, *La Roman de la Rose*.

> *The Roman de la Rose is the epic of old France. It is a profound book, under the form of levity, a revelation as learned as that of Apuleius, of the mysteries of occultism ... The Rose was for the Initiates the living and blooming symbol of the revelation of the harmonies of being. It was the emblem of beauty, life, love, and pleasure ... Such is the key of the Roman de la Rose.* [4]

Frances Horgan describes the poem as a best seller in its day. It was:

> *... read, quarrelled over, printed and reprinted, moralised and admired until the 17th century, edited and re-edited from 1735 onwards and has in recent years been the subject of a vast and daunting body of critical study.*

The first 4,000 lines of the poem written in 1225-1230 are by Guillaume de Lorris of whom nothing is known. It was completed 40 years later by Jean de Meun, a graduate of Paris University, and a Latin translator and teacher who died in 1305.

It may best be described as a semi-pornographic manual of courtly love interposed with observations on such familiar topics as the seven planets and the twelve signs of the zodiac. While both authors use the same narrative and characters, they differ considerably in style.

The Guillaume de Lorris portion, by far the shorter of the two,[5] is a love allegory which tells of the *Lover's* quest for the *Rose*, aided and opposed in turn by a cast of characters including *Fair Welcome, Rebuff, Idleness* and *False Seeming*. The nature of allegory is to tell one story while appearing to tell another.

---

[1] At the time including Belgium, Germany, Czechoslavakia, Austria, Northern Italy and Switzerland.

[2] The Palatinate was a fragmented territory, bordering on Luxembourg in the west of modern day Germany. Bohemia occupied much of what is now the Czech Republic.

[3] Although English popular opinion and parliament would have supported it.

[4] From Constant via Pike.

[5] de Meun adds a further 17,000 odd lines.

Detail from Bruges edition, late 15th century

In *Le Roman de la Rose*, the underlying story is of sex and the different views taken of it by men and women. The rose, or rather the rosebud, which is hidden, initially in a walled garden and later by castle walls, is female virginity and the story is of an attack on that virginity which finally ends with intercourse. It begins with Guillaume de Lorris's ardour:

From among these buds I chose one so beautiful that when I had observed it carefully, all the others seemed worthless in comparison. It shone with colour, the purest vermillion that Nature could provide, and Nature's masterly hand had arranged its four pairs of leaves, one after the other. Its stem was as straight as a reed, and the bud was set on top in such a way that it neither bent nor drooped. The area around it was filled with its perfume ...

He goes on to provide the rules of courtly love: the avoidance of baseness, slander, pride, and the need for cleanliness, elegance, generosity and blitheness. He speaks of the pains of love, the inability to think of anything other than the loved one, the agony of absence, all richly rewarded by a single kiss.

A noble heart does not stop loving because it is beaten or mistreated.

Jean de Meun, by contrast, uses the story as a hook on which to hang his often crude opinions and he provides the pornography at the end:

I began, very gently and without pricking myself, to shake the bud for it would have been hard for me to obtain it without thus disturbing it. I had to move the branches and agitate them, but without destroying a single one, for I did not want to cause any injury. Even so, I was forced to break the bark a little for I knew no other way to obtain the thing I so desired.

I can tell you that at last, when I had shaken the bud, I scattered a little seed there. This was when I had touched the inside of the rosebud and explored its little leaves, for I longed, and it seemed good to me, to probe its very depths. I thus mingled the seeds in such a way that it would have been hard to disentangle them, with the result that rosebud swelled and expanded.

Although *Le Roman de la Rose* is neither, love poetry can be insightful as in the hands of John Donne and it can be funny as in the poems of John Suckling (1609-1642), one of the Cavalier poets.

Why so pale and wan, fond lover?
Prithee, why so pale?
Will, when looking well can't move her,
Looking ill prevail?
Prithee, why so pale?

Why so dull and mute, young sinner?
Prithee, why so mute?
Will, when speaking well can't win her,
Saying nothing do't?
Prithee, why so mute?

Quit, quit, for shame, this will not move:
This cannot take her.
If of herself she cannot love,
Nothing can make her:
The devil take her!

Christine de Pizan

Le Roman de la Rose was the cause of what commentators see as the first literary war. The poet Christine de Pizan (1364-1430) was provoked by the poem's treatment of women and by its justification of rape, especially its triumphal conclusion in which the *Lover* celebrates his victory. She also objects to its language. No prude herself, being the daughter of a doctor and a mother of three, she was, as Charity Canon Willard points out, undoubtedly well acquainted with the facts of life. She simply did not see why it was necessary to go into such detail over what comes naturally to most people. De Pizan says of de Meun:

> *If you wish to excuse him by saying that it pleases him to make a pretty story of a culmination of love using such images, I reply that by doing so he neither tells nor explains anything new. Doesn't everyone know how men and women copulate naturally?*

De Pizan's own major works, published in 1405, were *The Book of the City of Ladies* and *The Book of the Three Virtues*. Both enjoyed success well into the 16th century. Willard writes:

> *The first of these undertakes to show the importance of women's contributions to society in the past, whereas the second attempts to teach women of all estates how to cultivate useful qualities in the society in which they live and thus become worthy inhabitants of the City of Ladies described in the first book.*

Christine de Pizan was quite an amazing person. She would have been unusual at any time but writing as she did in the Middle Ages, when women were simply not thought of as independently capable beings, she was a phenomenon. Born in Venice but brought up in Paris at the court of King Charles V the Wise (her father was an academic favoured by the king), she was very well read, consulting books and manuscripts in the King's library (although her mother thought she should pay more attention to her spinning.) She was married off, at the age of fifteen to Etienne de Castel who became a royal secretary. The marriage turned out to be very happy.

The early death of Charles V in 1380 caused many problems in France, not the least of which was that his successor, Charles VI the Mad, suffered delusions and frequent bouts of insanity. Etienne died in 1390 during an epidemic and Christine was left with responsibility for her children, a niece and her widowed mother. As with most women of the time, and all too often of today as well, she had no idea of her husband's financial situation and she struggled with law suits, dishonest brokers and deliberate obstruction from civil servants. Willard writes:

> In 'The Mutation of Fortune', Christine explains how her change of fortune had obliged her to 'become a man' and take on a man's responsibilities in the world ... She admonishes widows to take on a man's heart and be constant, strong and wise in pursuing their own advantage, rather than crouching in tears like a poor woman or like a stray dog.

On the other hand, she also met with kindness, notably from Jean de Montaigu, of whom she said that he was a man generous in wealth and word, and from the Earl of Salisbury, who noticed her poetry and took her son into his household. She managed to support her family by copying manuscripts and book production and four years after Etienne's death, she started to write, becoming a major figure in the literary circles of the time.

Constant's history

So does the poem support Constant's contention that it is *a revelation ... of the mysteries of occultism?* The answer must be no. It demonstrates no connection with the Templars and has nothing to do with any hidden knowledge. It is a tedious and occasionally unpleasant work that has almost nothing to do with the occult. Written one hundred years before Chaucer's brilliantly witty *Canterbury Tales*, it is remembered more for the literary war it provoked than for any intrinsic worth.

Its presence in *L'Histoire de la Magie* reinforces a suspicion that I have tried to avoid. Constant lists a great number of authors and books, but how many he read and understood is not clear. After what seems only surface reading, sometimes restricted to the title, he all too often builds an amazing and inaccurate history. Having read *Le Roman de la Rose*, I am not at all sure that Constant did because the poem simply does not play the role that he wants it to.

Secret power

So where is that hidden power known to the ancients which invests the adept with omnipotence? The disappointing truth is that there is none; no secret power, no hidden knowledge. While many talk about it and give mysterious hints, none ever sets it out nor shows it at work; not Trismegistus, not Agrippa, not the Rosicrucians and certainly not Constant.

There is no evidence that the Templars had any esoteric knowledge. Kabbalah may help a believer add depth to his or her relationship with god but does not offer a power to do anything remarkable in this world, its learning being confined to the religious *sprachspiel*. The Rosicrucians certainly promised remarkable knowledge which would enrich the whole world, endue it with learning and release it from innumerable miseries but that knowledge existed no more than did the Rosicrucians themselves.

Indeed, the only mystery, looking back from today, is how so many apparently educated and intelligent people could not only believe that such knowledge existed but wrote reams of empty nonsense about it. The solution to this mystery, of course, lies in the word *educated*.

There was almost no technological advance from the end of the Roman Empire in the fifth century CE until the invention of cannons in the 14th century, if one can call that an advance. The paradigm of the search for knowledge in the Middle Ages was the study of ancient texts and the Bible. It was assumed that knowledge to create power was to be found there and many gained fame by pretending to have discovered it.

Consistent failure did not cause the paradigm to be questioned and education simply repeated the past. Theory was accepted uncritically and practice derived from it. Since the theory was wrong (Plato is not a good guide to mechanics), the practice was wrong but in a world dominated by static religion, there was no expectation of progress so no one noticed.

John Dee

The mechanical marvels of the Palatinate were not created until the 17th century and even as late as the time of Queen Elizabeth I, the world view espoused by the Corpus Hermeticum and Agrippa still dominated. John Dee, the Elizabethan mathematician, astronomer and navigator, owned a library of several thousand books, most of which were works on the occult. He was the Queen's navigator and gave practical training many of the sea captains who made the dramatic voyages of discovery but he devoted much of his own time to summoning angels. His associate, Edward Kelley, claimed to converse with angels in an angelic language he called *enochian*.

Dee saw his practical work as merely part of Agrippa's lower sphere, the elemental world; of interest only because by the power of sympathy it could affect the intellectual and celestial worlds. He saw his greatest discovery to be the *Monas Hieroglyphica*, a sign which he created to describe the whole of creation. It appears in the *Chymical Wedding* but no one today can make head nor tail of it.

Dee (1527-1608) and Bacon were almost contemporaries but to Dee mathematics was a matter of meaning and numbers held mystical content. To Bacon (1561-1626), mathematics was a tool. The new paradigm proved the efficacy of the *hypothetico-deductive* method; the creation of an hypothesis to account for phenomena and the testing of the implications of that hypothesis to see if it is true. As difficult as it is to believe, it was the step of testing that never occurred to earlier thinkers.

Retrospect

As I said at the very beginning, ideas do not spring anew from one mind. The legends and ideas of the goat and the devil go back a long way and, during their descent through time, they have gathered the credibility of innumerable associations, gaining weight rather in the manner of a snowball rolling downhill. In tracing the derivation of these ideas, we can see the power that they collected, strong enough to linger as mythemes at least in the minds of those who wish to see the occult as meaningful.

I began with Constant for many reasons but primarily because of his position in time, recent enough to be almost modern but so antiquated in perspective as to be a link to ancient ideas. His work is a source book of early thinking and this together with his pretended knowledge of modern freemasonry, his connection with Pike and Taxil and, above all, his engraving and marvellous use of language, make him an ideal fulcrum for our purposes.

Constant is a microcosm of the suspicion of freemasonry - and how he would have loved being referred to as a *microcosm*! He wrote without evidence; without much thought either if the stories about him are to be believed. It is said that he never went back to read what he had written, moving from one idea to another almost in a stream of consciousness - and this is the real story of the snowball and the hill. The ideas have built one on the other without critical analysis.

From Constant, it is easy to spin out into the sources of the ideas he uses, jogging back to him at intervals for a refill. I went next to Pike to show how freemasonry can be its own worst enemy. Pike gets it all wrong; he lifts great undigested chunks from Constant and makes *ex cathedra* statements about freemasonry which are false. Why did he do this? We can only speculate on his psychology but, like Constant, he clearly had a need to be noticed and to be taken as a superior mind, a Magus even. Disappointment early in life is a common denominator.

Few have read Pike right through but his reputation made his work a virtual bible of American freemasonry, even if it is unknown outside North America; and even if his major publication was one enormous plagiarism. I trust you enjoyed the excursion into Pike's journeys and the world of the fur trappers and mountain men. I find such historical overlaps quite fascinating but there was a specific reason for the excursion. I wanted to show that there was more to Pike than just his writing; that he was a man of courage and that he achieved much social good in the legislative world even if, in the end, it caused his financial and moral downfall. His racism, I fear, adds to the problem he presents for freemasonry, even though, as our small insight into the plight of the American Indians showed, casual racism was tragically normal in those days.

Freemasonry has long been a field in which it seems anyone can write rubbish and get it read.[1] Taxil is a case in point. His story offers much amusement value but it amazes me that people can still take him seriously, given that he admitted his hoax. His story is almost incredible, given how comparatively recently he lived. After all, he died only one hundred and five years ago in a year when many modern

---

[1] This is not helped, it has to be admitted, by much of the stuff written by freemasons.

sounding events occurred: women's suffrage began;[1] Baden-Powell held the first Scout Camp; Marconi started commercial transatlantic radio communications; Katherine Hepburn was born; and the Peking to Paris motor race took place.[2] To believe what Taxil wrote in such a period seems very odd indeed but then so does the encyclical of 1888.

I then took us off on a search for horns and the *Goat of Mendes*. The civilisation of ancient Egypt and its religious life was far more complex than I could possibly describe within the limits of this book, even if I had the ability. The ram-headed gods and the male fertility myths have a direct line to the goat-headed Pan and the shape changing satyrs. This enabled me to put forward the idea of the mytheme, an idea that travels in time.

Herodotus, the old gossip, was very helpful in establishing the link between Egypt and Greece and the death of Pan gave us an introduction to the early Christian apologists and the goat-headed figure of the devil, even if this had to wait for an obscure 16th century author to come to fruition.

I used the investigation into the various views on the afterlife to demonstrate that religion has many different forms. The monotheism we are used to in the West is only one of them. The relationship between religion and morality is much more complex than Christians and indeed freemasons think and most people get the relationship wrong. I am with Kant and the categorical imperative, that moral action is an end in itself and not a means to further ends. This fits with our psychological experience, that things are just right or wrong, as well as making it clear that virtue has no need of reward. To hark back to worship, Kant held that:

> *Apart from conducting a good life, anything which a man (or woman) supposes s/he can do to become more pleasing to god is mere religious delusion ...*

I found the status of gods among the Greeks and the Romans quite fascinating, reinforced by modern African beliefs. The idea of prayer and worship as a contract with a god certainly makes both explicable. I also found the notion of *henotheism*, and its application first to Cyrus and thence to the development of Judaism, very useful in understanding the development of religions. I have always felt that the distance from polytheism to monotheism is too big for one jump and so what may have seemed an excursion around the dating of the Bible had a point. It showed how ideas familiar to us developed from some fairly surprising beginnings and that monotheism arises from henotheism rather late in the story. It was the development of the promise of heaven which finally created monotheism.

I went back to our heroes, Pan and Banebdjedet, to develop the problem of evil and to look at some depictions of the devil. I distinguished between sin and evil. Banebdjedet was neither sinful nor evil and while Pan may have been sinful, it was largely the *naughty but nice* sin. However, the early church thought sex was really, really bad and I put forward the idea that, to the committed Christian, the worst action possible is to tempt someone into risking their immortal soul. Other events, no matter how dreadful they may seem to us, pale into insignificance by

---

[1] Finland: 19 women were elected to Parliament.

[2] Won, apparently, by the Italian Prince Scipione Borghese whose chauffeur did most of the driving.

comparison. That is what sin is about and so naughty-but-nice won't wash. Personally I think the problems most religions have with sex and women are both sexist and emotionally immature, but you may think otherwise and, if god is *agin* sex, then we must be *agin* it if we want to get to heaven.

Whatever the case, the problem of evil is a serious issue and not lightly overcome. It speaks to the nature of god, of course, and enabled me to introduce the heresy of dualism, on which you may think I harped a little too much. Nevertheless, just as the problem of evil has been seen as the major cause of loss of faith, so dualism has been seen as the very worst heresy because it sets limits on god. An independent devil means that god cannot be both all-knowing and all-powerful but a dependent devil means that god cannot be beneficent. Pope Francis, in March 2013, headed straight into this problem when he said, *He who does not pray to the lord, prays to the devil. When we don't proclaim Jesus Christ, we proclaim the worldliness of the devil.* He seemed also to be putting forward a version of the *supporter* theory of worship, stemming from Luria and Moses de Leon in the *Zohar*.

I was not sure when in the book I should deal with magic but since I had used the title of Constant's book, *Dogme et Rituel de la Haute Magie,* very early and you might be losing patience, I thought it best not to delay any longer. Today, it is obviously a nonsense and that may convince you of Constant's charlatanism but the point I sought to put over, reinforced by the later discussion of Agrippa, is that Constant seeks to present a whole *science*, not just a cook book of spells. Just as today the nature of engineering is predicated on our world view, the nature of magic was predicated on the ancient world view. This enabled me to introduce gnosticism and the turning point together with the *Corpus Hermeticum.*

I learned a lot about the Jewish sects, the beginnings of Christianity, the theory of Q and the early Jewish Christians, whose fate I had never considered before. The gnostics were a fascinating bunch with many wild ideas - and some perhaps less wild. All religious beliefs call for a certain amount of logic jumping.

I then dealt with the *Corpus Hermeticum* itself, the mistaken dating of which caused great excitement in early Christianity. This took us into the world of the sympathies, the celestial spheres and the logic of astrology, the latter also being entirely new to me. Agrippa was just one magician who exemplified that world even if by his time, orthodox belief was beginning to censor such thinking. I didn't mention the *weapon salve* in dealing with sympathies; the idea that by putting a salve on the blade that caused the wound, the wound itself would heal. I can't see how anyone could have maintained this belief in the face of what must have been constant evidence of its failure, but then even today, the oddest beliefs obtain regarding the treatment of ills.

I looked at what devil worship might entail which took us into the weird and wonderful world of Denis Wheatley. I then made an attempt to understand the nature of worship and consequently of worshipping the devil. I sought to show that the phrase, *worship the devil,* has no meaning but that has not prevented people from using it. It seems to mean something to some people, even if it wouldn't if they thought it through, which they won't and probably couldn't. That should make it clear! I think the concept of a devil is fatally flawed as well.

In passing, I should add that worship has been described as a means of attaining esoteric experience. This fits rather well with the purpose of worship and prayer in the *Corpus Hermeticum,* although becoming divine is rather more than just an esoteric experience. Such a view is ancient and modern, to coin a phrase. Some twentieth century theologians would find themselves in agreement thus far with Hermes Trismegistus.

No, there is no goat in freemasonry. There never was. No, freemasons do not worship the devil. No one can. There have been accusations of sexual frolics over the years but these are simply part of the standard list of crimes, sticks with which to beat those *people-different-from-us*, a list that was certainly used to beat Christians and which in turn Christians have used to beat pagans, gnostics and forms of Christianity they do not like.

Postlude: The Secrets of Freemasonry

So does the fact that there is no hidden knowledge in hermeticism *et al*, mean that there is none in freemasonry either? Yes it does. No alchemy, no lead into gold? I fear not. Except ...

It can produce such charitable funds that each year in the UK it is second in charitable giving only to the lottery, fully half going to non-masonic causes. It can take an ordinary chap and turn him into a Master of the Lodge: capable of running a meeting, making a speech, learning and delivering from memory a part in the ritual at least the same length as Hamlet, and handling with aplomb such tricky words as *acquiescence, corporeal, immemorial* and even *parallelopipedon*. It enables everyone to shine, to take a place in the sun, to be recognised and congratulated and to feel good about themselves.

It takes five million men (and several hundred thousand women) world wide, of *divers*[1] nations, creeds and cultures, and makes them the firmest of life-long friends. It enables a stranger to find a welcome in virtually any city in the world but most importantly, it creates goodness. Freemasons think the best of each other and seek to live up to the estimation of their brethren, setting high standards of behaviour, not by rules but by mutual expectation.

They live by three principles: brotherly love, relief and truth. The first is pictured above,[2] the second is charity and the third concerns honesty in word and deed. These are the secrets of freemasonry. Nothing occult but something of the very

---

[1] Another tricky word. You pronounce it almost like *diverse* without quite so much *ess* sound. It means *sundry, various* or *differing*.

[2] In more senses than one. In this picture, the new Master is accompanied by his brother, nephew and two brothers-in-law.

highest importance, especially in an ethically deprived world in which money is deemed to be the measure of success and morality increasingly subservient to it.

To finish with, here is a bit of English masonic ritual used when the lodge is closed at the end of a meeting. It is part of what we call the *Long Closing*; a suitable title, perhaps, on which to end the book.

> *Remember that at this pedestal, you have solemnly and voluntarily vowed to relieve and befriend with unhesitating cordiality every Brother who might need your assistance; that you have promised to remind him in the most gentle manner of his failings and to aid and vindicate his character whenever wrongfully traduced; to suggest the most candid, the most palliating and the most favourable circumstances, even when his conduct is justly liable to reprehension and blame. Thus shall the world see how dearly freemasons love each other.*

> *But, my Brethren, you are expected to extend these noble and generous sentiments still further. Let me impress upon your minds, and may it be instilled into your hearts, that every human creature has a just claim on your kind offices. I therefore trust that you will be good to all. More particularly do I recommend to your care the household of the faithful, so that by diligence and fidelity in the duties of your respective vocations, liberal beneficence and diffusive charity, by constancy and sincerity in your friendships, a uniformly kind, just, amiable and virtuous deportment, you may prove to the world the happy and beneficial effects of our ancient and honourable institution.*

> *Let it not be said that you laboured in vain nor wasted your strength for nought; for your work is before the lord and your recompense is with god. Finally Brethren, be of one mind, live in peace and may the god of love and mercy delight to dwell amongst you and bless you for evermore.*

❦ THE END ❦

Works referred to

Allsopp, Frederick W., *Albert Pike: a biography*, first published 1922, republished by Kessinger Legacy Reprints

Anderson, James, *CONSTITUTION, History, Laws, Charges, Orders, Regulations, and Usages of the Right Worshipful FRATERNITY of Accepted Free MASONS*, 1723, Facsimile edition 1976, Quatuor Coronati Lodge

Armstrong, Karen, *History of God*, William Heinemann, 1993

The Bible: the biography, Atlantic books, 2010

Atsma, Aaron J. (ed.) The Theoi Project: Greek Mythology, online at theoi.com

Augustine, *City of God*, online at newadvent.org
Confessions, online at gutenberg.org

Ayer, AJ, *Language Truth And Logic*, Gollancz, 1947

Bacon, Francis, *Novum Organum Scientiarum*, published 1620, online at archive.org; *The Advancement of Learning*, published 1605, online at gutenberg.org

Baker, Simon, *Ancient Rome: the Rise and Fall of an Empire*, Random House/BBC Books, 2006

Bate, Walter, *Frontier legend: Texas finale of Capt. William F. Drannan, pseudo frontier comrade of Kit Carson*, OG Dunn & Co., 1954, republished by Literacy Licensing LLC, 2011

Beckwourth, James P., *The life and adventures of James P. Beckwourth*, originally published by Harper and Brothers in 1856, republished by Elibron Classics; Boardman, John

Griffin, Jasper, and Murray, Oswyn (eds), *The Oxford History of the Classical World*, Oxford University Press, 1986

Borgeaud, Philippe, *The Death of the Great Pan: The Problem of Interpretation, in History of Religions*, February 1983, The University of Chicago Press; Bremmer, Jan N., 'The Rise and Fall of the Afterlife' : *1995 Read-Tuckwell Lectures at the University of Bristol*, Routledge, 2002

Brown, Walter Lee, *A life of Albert Pike*, The University of Arkansas Press, 1997

Browning, Christopher R, *Ordinary Men*, Penguin, 2001

Browning, Elizabeth Barrett, 'The Dead Pan', in *The Complete Poetical Works of Mrs E. B. Browning*, edited by Charlotte Porter and Helen A. Clarke, Riverdale Press, 1903

Carr, Harry, *The Freemason at Work*, Lewis Masonic, 1976

Catholic Encyclopaedia, online at catholic.org

Chadwick, Henry, *The Penguin History of the Church*, Penguin, 1967

Cleland, Robert G, *This Reckless Breed of Men: the trappers and fur traders of the Southwest*, Alfred A Knopf, 1950

Constant, L'Abbé, '*Confession de l'auteur*', in his *L'Assomption de la Femme*, Le Gallois, 1841

Constant, Alphonse Louis (*later* Éliphas Lévi), *La Mère de Dieu, épopée religieuse et humanitaire*, originally published by Charles Gosselin in 1844, republished by Elibron Classics; *Le Rosier de Mai*, Nabu Press, 2012; *La Bible de la Liberté*, originally published by Le Gallois in 1841, online at Bibliothèque National de France

Copenhaver, Brian P, *Hermetica*, Cambridge University Press, 1992

Cryer, Neville Barker, *The Royal Arch Journey*, Lewis Masonic, 2009

Darwin, Charles, 'Letter to Asa Gray, 22 May 1860', Darwin Correspondence Project, darwinproject.as.uk

Davis, Paul, *100 decisive battles: from ancient times to the present*, Oxford University Press, 2001

de Lugio, Giovanni (attrib) '*Liber de duobus principiis*', in Walter L. Wakefield and Austin P. Evans, *Heresies of the High Middle Ages*, Columbia University Press, 1991

de Voto, Bernard, *Across the wide Missouri*, Houghton Mifflin, 1947

The Year of Decision 1846, Little, Brown and Co., 1943

Descartes, René, *Discours de la méthode pour bien conduire sa raison, et chercher la vérité dans les sciences*, English translation John Vetch, Prometheus books, 1989

Donne, John, *The Poems of John Donne*, ed. Sir Herbert Grierson, Oxford University Press, 1960

Drannan, Captain William F, *Thirty-One Years on the Plains and in the Mountains*, republished by BiblioBazaar, 2006

Encyclopedaedia Ironic, online at iranicaonline.org, editor Ehsan Yarshater, Columbia University

Eusebius, *Preparation Evangelica*, trans. EH Gifford, Clarendon Press, 1903

Evelyn-White, HG (trans.), *Hesiod, the Homeric Hymns, and Homerica*, W. Heinemann, 1914

Fine, Cordelia, *A Mind of its Own*, Icon Books, 2005

Forey, Alan, 'The Military Orders 1120-1312', in Jonathan Riley-Smith (ed.) *The Oxford History of the Crusades*, Oxford University Press, 1999

Forsyth, Neil, *The Old Enemy: Satan and the combat myth*, Princeton University Press, 1987

Fowden, Garth, *Empire to Commonwealth:*

consequences of monotheism in late antiquity, Princeton University Press, 1993

The Egyptian Hermes: a historical approach to the late pagan mind, Princeton University Press, 1993

Fox, Robin Lane, *Pagans and Christians*, Harper & Row 1986

The Unauthorised Version, Viking 1991

Fraser, George MacDonald, *Flashman* (twelve titles in series) Barrie and Jernkins 1969, re-issued starting 2005, HarperCollins

Frayling, Christopher, *Strange Landscape*, BBC Books, 1995

Gee, Henry and Hardy, W.H. (eds) *Documents Illustrative of English Church History*, online at history.hanover.edu/texts

Grafton, Anthony and Weinberg, Joanna, *I have always loved the Holy Tongue*, Harvard University Press, 2010

Ha-Cohen, Rabbi Isaac ben Jacob, 'Treatise on the Emanations on the Left', discussed in *Joseph Dan*

Hafen, LeRoy R. (ed.), *The Mountain Men and the Fur Trade of the Far West*, Arthur H. Clark & Co. 1965-72. Harris is described in volume 7

Mountain Men and Fur Trappers of the Far West: eighteen biographical sketches, University of Nebraska Press, 1982

Huffier, Christopher, 'Albert Pike; asset or liability?' L.A. Pires Lecture, 1991

Halevi, Z'ev ben Shimon, *Kabbalah: tradition of hidden knowledge*, Thames and Hudson, 1979

Halliwell, James (ed.), *Regius Poem*, Kindle edition, Jazzybee Publishing, 2011

Hart, George, *A Dictionary of Egyptian Gods and Goddesses*, Routledge, 1986

Harvey, David Allen, 'Forgotten feminist: Claude Avignon (1828–1888), revolutionary and femme de lettres', *Women's History Review*, Volume 13, Issue 4, 2004

Herodotus, *Histories*, trans. G.C. Macaulay, Kindle edition

Hodapp, Christopher, *Freemasons for Dummies*, John Wiley & Sons, 2005

Horgan, Frances, *The Romance of the Rose*, Oxford World Classics, 1994

Hume, David, *Dialogues concerning natural religion*, Penguin Classics, 1990

Hurt, R. Douglas, *The Ohio Frontier*, Indiana University Press, 1996

Huxley, Julian, *Religion without Revelation*, Greenwood Press, 1979

Iamblichus, *On the Mysteries of the Egyptians, Chaldeans and Assyrians*, translated by Thomas Taylor, Bertram Dobell & Reeves and Turner, 1895, online at archive.org

Johfra (Johfra Bosschart), *Elfes, fées et gnomes*, Arista, 1989

Johnson, Humphrey J.T., *Freemasonry: a short historical sketch*, Catholic Truth Society, 1952

Josephus, *Antiquities, in The Complete Josephus Collection*, Charles River Editors, 2011; *Contra Apionem*, translated by William Whiston, John F Beardsley, 1895, online at perseus. tufts.edu

Julian the Apostate (Flavius Claudius Julianus), Contra Galileos, trans. Wilmer Cave Wright 1923, online at tertullian.org

Justin (Justin Martyr), *Apologies*, ed. Henry Chadwick, Oxford University Press, 2009

Korfmann, Manfred, 'Was there a Trojan War?', *Archaeology*, May 2004

Kreeft, Peter, *The problem of evil*, Catholic Education Resource Centre

Lawrence, Charles C., *The Key to Modern Freemasonry*, Hamilton House, 2011

Le Figaro, 2 June 1875 and 29 April 1897

Lévi-Strauss, Claude, *La Pensée Sauvage*, Librairie Plon, 1962

Lévi, Éliphas, *Dogme et Rituel de la Haute Magie*, Elibron Classics 2006, a facsimile of an edition published by Felix Alcan, Paris, 1903. The book was translated into English by A.E. Waite as *Transcendental Magic, its Doctrine and Ritual* republished by Kessinger Publishing, LLC; *La Clef Des Grands Mystères: suivant Hénoch, Abraham, Hermès Trismégiste, et Salomon*, Print on demand, Alibris *L'Histoire de la Magie*, first published 1860, online at gutenberg.org

Link, Luther, The Devil: The Archfiend in Art from the Sixth to the Sixteenth Century, Harry N. Abrams, 1996

Linnemann, Eta, 'The Lost Gospel of Q - Fact Or Fantasy?', *Trinity Journal*, Spring 1996;

Livingstone, Lucas, *Egyptian Influence on Ionic Temple Architecture*, University of Notre Dame, 2000

Lloyd, Simon, 'The Crusading Movement 1096-1274', in *The Oxford History of the Crusades*, edited by Jonathan Riley-Smith, Oxford University Press, 1999

Mack, Burton, *The Lost Gospel: The Book of Q and Christian Origins*, Harper 1994

The Christian Myth, Continuum, 2001

Mackey, Albert and Haywood, H.L., *Encyclopedia of Freemasonry*, Vol. 2, Kessinger Publishing Rare Reprints

Malcolm, Norman, *Ludwig Wittgenstein: a memoir*, Oxford University Press, 1958

Mathewes, Charles T, *Evil and the Augustinian*

Tradition, Cambridge University Press, 2001

McIntosh, Christopher, *Éliphas Lévi and the French Occult Revival*, State University of New York Press, 2011; *The Rosicrucians*, Weiser Books, 1998

McLeod, Wallace, 'The Old Charges' in *The Collected Prestonian Lectures*, Volume 3, 1975-1987, Lewis Masonic, 1988

McLynn, Frank, *Wagons West*, Pimlico, 2003

Mead, G.R.S., *Fragments of a Faith Forgotten*, Theosophical Publishing Society, 1900, reprinted by Cosimo Classics, 2007

Meyer, Marvin (ed.), *The Nag Hammadi Scriptures*, Harper Collins, 2007; 'The Gospel of Thomas with the Greek Gospel of Thomas', in Marvin Meyer (ed), *The Nag Hammadi Scriptures*, Harper Collins, 2007

Morecambe, Eric and Wise, Ernie, *The Morecambe and Wise Show*, Series 5, Episode 5, broadcast June 3, 1971

Netland, Harold A, 'Inclusivism and exclusivism', in *The Routledge Companion to Philosophy of Religion*, edited by Chad Meister and Paul Copan, Routledge, 2007

O'Shea, Stephen, *The Perfect Heresy: the life and death of the Cathars*, Profile Books, 2000

Oldridge, Darren, *The Devil*, Oxford University Press, 2012

Pagels, Elaine, *The Gnostic Gospels*, Weidenfeld & Nicholson, 1980

Paijmans, Theo, *Free energy pioneer: John Worrell Keely*, Adventures Unlimited Press, 2004

Partner, Peter, *The Knights Templar and their Myth*, Oxford University Press, 1981

Patterson, Stephen J, 'Q: The Lost Gospel', *Bible Review*, October 1993

Person, David, *Of Varieties, Richard Badger for Thomas Alchorn, 1635*, online at National Library of Australia

Peters, Tom and Waterman, Robert Jnr, *In Search of Excellence*, Harper & Row, 1982

Pike, Albert, 'Journey in the Prairie' and 'Second Journey in the Prairie', in *Prose Sketches and Poems*, Light & Horton, 1834, republished by Bibliolife; *Morals and Dogma of the Ancient and Accepted Scottish Rite of Freemasonry*, 1871, republished by Forgotten Books, 2008

Pinch, Geraldine, *Egyptian Mythology: A Guide to the Gods*, Oxford University Press, 2004

Plutarch, *Moralia*, Volume V, *The Obsolescence of Oracles*, Loeb Classical Library, 1936

Powell, Anthony, *A Dance to the Music of Time*, Heinemann, 12 volumes, 1951-1975

Pratchett, Terry, *Mort*, Victor Gollancz, 1987;

Small Gods, Victor Gollancz, 1992

Rabelais, Francois, *Gargantua and Pantagruel*, (Trans. MA Screech), Penguin Classics, 2006

Riley-Smith, Jonathan, 'Revival and Survival', in Jonathan Riley-Smith (ed.) *The Oxford History of the Crusades*, Oxford University Press, 1999

Robinson, Dr John, *Honest to God*, SCM Press, 1963

Ronson, Jon, *The Men who Stare at Goats*, Picador, 2009

Rowley, H.H., *The Servant of the Lord*, Lutterworth Press, 1952; 'The interpretation of the Song of Songs', first published in the *Journal of Theological Studies*, 1937, republished in *The Servant of the Lord above;* 'The marriage of Ruth', first published in the *Harvard Theological Review*, 1947, republished in *The Servant of the Lord above*

Russell, Jeffrey Burton, *The Devil: perceptions of evil from antiquity to primitive Christianity*, Cornell University Press, 1977

Sanders, E.P., *Paul*, Oxford University Press, 1991

Sartre, Jean-Paul, *La Nausée*, Gallimard, 1937

Schoff, Wilfred H., 'Tammuz, Pan and Christ: notes on a typical case of myth-transference and development' in *The Open Court* magazine, September 1912

Shaw, Ian, *Oxford History of Ancient Egypt*, Oxford University Press, 2003

Sibley, William Giddings, 'The Story of Freemasonry', originally published by The Lion's Paw Club, 1904; section on Taxil republished by Kessinger Legacy Reprints

Stamm, Johann Jakob and Andrew, Maurice Edward, *The Ten Commandments in Recent Research*, SCM Press, 1967

Stanford, Peter, *The Devil: a biography*, Random House, 1996

Steiner, Rudolf, *Esoteric Studies*, Vol II, Rudolf Steiner Press, 1956

Stevenson, David, *The Origins of Freemasonry: Scotland's century, 1590-1710*, Cambridge University Press, 1988

Strawson, P.F., 'Review of Philosophical Investigations', *Mind*, 1954

Taliaferro, Charles, 'Prayer', in *The Routledge Companion to the Philosophy of Religion*, edited by Chad Meister and Paul Copan, Routledge, 2007

Talmud, Babylonian, online at the Jewish Virtual Library

Taylor, A.J., *History of the King's Works*, Her Majesty's Stationery Office, 1963

Tertullian, *Ad Nationes*, online at tertullian.org

Theophilus (St Theophilus of Antioch), *Apology to Autolycus*, online at earlychristianwritings. com

Thomas, Sir Keith, *Religion and the Decline of Magic*, Weidenfeld & Nicholson, 1971

Tillich, Paul, *Shaking the Foundations*, Charles Scribner's Sons, 1948

Torrey, Charles Cutler, *The Composition and Historical value of Ezra-Nehemiah*, originally published by J. Ricker, 1896, now Nabu Books, print on demand

United Grand Lodge of England, *Constitutions*

Uzzel, Robert L, *Eliphas Levi and the Kabbalah*, Cornerstone, 2006

Vermes, Geza, *Jesus the Jew*, William Collins Sons & Co., 1973

Waite, A.E., *Devil Worship in France*, Red Wheel /Weiser reprint, 2003; *Secret Tradition in Freemasonry*, 'appendix on Pike' republished as *Albert Pike and Freemasonry*, Kessinger Legacy Reprints

Weber, David J, *The Taos Trappers: the fur trade in the Far Southwest 1540-1846*, University of Oklahoma Press, 1980

Wheatley, Dennis, *The Devil Rides Out*, Hutchinson & Co., 1934 (Film 1968)

Wilde, Oscar, *The Critic as an Artist*, Mondial Books, 2007

Willard, Charity Canon, *Christine de Pizan: her life and works*, Persea Books, 1984

Williamson, H.G.M., 'Ezra Nehemiah', Volume 16 in the series, *World Biblical Commentary*, World Books, 1985

Wilson, Ian, *Jesus: the evidence*, Weidenfeld & Nicholson, 1984

Wiredu, Kwasi, 'African Religions', in *The Routledge Companion to the Philosophy of Religion*, edited by Chad Meister and Paul Copan, Routledge, 2007

Wisdom, John, 'Gods', *Proceedings* of the Aristotlean Society, 1944, reprinted in *Philosophy and Psychoanalysis*, John Wisdom, Basil Blackwell, 1964

Wittgenstein, Ludwig, *Philosophical Investigations*, Basil Blackwell, 1958; *Tractatus Logico-Philosophicus*, trans. by D. F. Pears and B. F. McGuinness, Routledge & Kegan Paul, 1961

Yates, Frances, *Giordano Bruno and the Hermetic Tradition*, Routledge & Kegan Paul, 1964; *Occult Philosophy in the Elizabethan Age*, Routledge & Kegan Paul, 1979; *The Rosicrucian Enlightenment*, Routledge & Kegan Paul, 1972

Young, Alan, *Tudor and Jacobean Tournaments*, George Philip, 1987

Zimbardo, Philip, *The Lucifer Effect*, Rider, 2007.

Illustrations

St Laurence Lodge Golf Day, © Lawrie Morrisson

Starship Enterprise, photo of model by Yentov, courtesy of freeimages.co.uk

Le bouc de sabbat, image in public domain, coloured version supplied by Peter Currie; Éliphas Lévi, source unknown, image in public domain

Adèle Allenbach, Alphonse Louis Constant, afterwards Éliphas Lévi, image in public domain

Marie-Noémi Cadiot, Kathy Walker, commissioned by the author, © David West

Jean Dodal tarot card 15, from a set recreated by Jean-Claude Flornoy, used by permission of Letarot.com Editions and Roxanne Flornoy

Éliphas Lévi in later life, given to Wikimedia Commons by his descendent Henri Chevenier

Goose and Gridiron, image in public domain

Statue of Albert Pike, © Lawrie Morrisson

Keel boat, Jedediah Hotchkiss in 1872, courtesy of LegendsOfAmerica.com

Rivers of the Old West, Kathy Walker, commissioned by the author, © David West

Fort Laramie, Alfred Jacob Miller (1810-1874), Walters Art Museum, Baltimore under creative commons licence

The Santa Fé Trail, Kathy Walker, commissioned by the author, © David West

The Edge of the *Llano Estacado*, photo Darren Huski, used with permission

The Palisaded Plain, photo Darren Huski, used with permission

Old Bill Williams, statue in Williams, Arizona, photo Bill Petit, Wikimedia Commons

Advertisement for *Les Mystères de la franc-maçonnerie dévoilés*, courtesy of the Phoenixmasonry Masonic Museum and Library at www.phoenixmasonry.org

Bogus Masonic Ceremony, courtesy of the Phoenixmasonry Masonic Museum and Library at www.phoenixmasonry.org

Distinguished Colored Men, chromolithograph by George F Cram, published by A. Muller & Co. c.1883, courtesy Library of Congress Prints and Photographs Division

Ludwig Wittgenstein © RA/PVDE RA/ Lebrecht Music & Arts

Eric Morecambe, Glenda Jackson and Ernie Wise, publicity photograph autographed by Glenda Jackson in author's collection

Ba as human headed bird, Jeff Dahl, Wikimedia Commons

Khnum, Jeff Dahl, Wikimedia Commons

Satyr plate by Epiktetos *c*.500 BCE, Bibi Saint-Pol, Wikimedia Commons

Self Portrait as a Faun, Johfra, by kind permission of Gerrit Luidinga

Papyrus, Euclid Proposition 5, © 2011 University of Pennsylvania

Mount Sinai, Berthold Werner, Wikimedia Commons

The Achæmenid Empire, Kathy Walker, commissioned by the author, © David West

Cyrus Cylinder, Prioryman, Wikimedia Commons

Weighing of the heart © Trustees of the British Museum

Hell's Bunker, © Getty Images

Robin Lane Fox, photo Richard Woolf, © RA/PVDE RA/Lebrecht Music & Arts

Qumran, Effi Schweizer, Wikipedia Commons

Cyrus the Great, courtesy of Karen Hatzigeorgiou

Masada, Avinoam Michaeli, PikiWiki Israel free image collection

Witches' Sabbath, Goya, © RA/PVDE RA/Lebrecht Music & Arts

Elizabeth Barrett Browning, engraving by Thomas Barlow of an early photograph by Macaire Havre in public domain

Devil Chicken, © The Bodleian Libraries, University of Oxford. Shelf mark: MS. Douce 134, fol. 098r

Archangel Michael defeating Satan, Guido Reni, © RA/PVDE RA/Lebrecht Music & Arts

Elinor Glyn, © The National Portrait Gallery

Adam and Eve, Jan Gossaert, supplied by Royal Collection Trust / © HM Queen Elizabeth II 2012

Groundhog Day, publicity poster, designed by Bemis Balkind for Columbia Picture

Satyr Mason, © Trustees of the British Museum

Embraceable Ewes, Kenneth Robinson, Wikimedia Commons

Illustration for Paradise Lost, Gustave Doré, image in public domain

Le Conjurer, Heironymous Bosch, © Getty Images

Datura stramonium, Nova, Wikimedia Commons

Pentagram, Éliphas Lévi, image in public domain

Jerusalem, Dome of the Rock and the Western Wall, Berthold Werner, Wikipedia Commons

Ten-squat-a-way, George Catlin, © Smithsonian American Art Museum, gift of Mrs Joseph Harrison Jnr

Two source hypothesis, Alec Mconroy, Wikimedia Commons

Facial composite of St Paul, created by experts of the Landeskriminalamt of North Rhine-Westphalia using historical sources, proposed by Düsseldorf historian Michael Hesemann, Wikimedia Commons

Hermes Trismegistus, Joanbanjo, Wikimedia Commons

Thoth, Jeff Dahl, Wikimedia Commons

The Devil Rides Out, copy of advertising poster for the 1968 film in author's possession

Representation of religious beliefs, Kathy Walker, commissioned by the author, © David West

Double aspect picture, Kathy Walker, commissioned by the author, © David West

Templar church at Saint-Martin-des-Champs Chapelle, unattributed, Wikimedia Commons

George Washington Masonic National Memorial, © Lawrie Morrisson, used with his permission

Friday Mosque in Herat, Marius Arnesen, Wikimedia Commons

The Delta Rhythm Boys, publicity photo dating from 1951

Tree of Life, Kathy Walker, commissioned by the author, © David West

View of Heidelberg, Christian Bienia, Wikimedia Commons

The Lover and the Rose, detail from miniature 1490-1500 edition of *Le Roman de la Rose* made in Bruges, © The British Library Board

The New Master, © Lawrie Morrisson, permission of those in photograph expressly obtained.

Index

Page numbers in bold type denote the more important references; page numbers in italics denote illustrations or their captions; passim (e.g. 40-50 *passim*) conveys that the subject is referred to not continuously but in scattered passages throughout the pages; **n** refers to footnotes.